Hearts of Darkness

Hearts of Darkness

Why Kids Are Becoming Mass Murderers
and How We Can Stop It

John Liebert, MD, and
William J. Birnes, JD, PhD

Skyhorse Publishing

Skyhorse Publishing books may be purchased in bulk at special discounts for sales promotion, corporate gifts, fund-raising, or educational purposes. Special editions can also be created to specifications. For details, contact the Special Sales Department, Skyhorse Publishing, 307 West 36th Street, 11th Floor, New York, NY 10018 or info@ skyhorsepublishing.com.

Skyhorse® and Skyhorse Publishing® are registered trademarks of Skyhorse Publishing, Inc.®, a Delaware corporation.

Visit our website at www.skyhorsepublishing.com.

10 9 8 7 6 5 4 3 2 1

Library of Congress Cataloging-in-Publication Data is available on file.

ISBN: 978-1-62914-184-8

E-Book ISBN: 978-1-62914-257-9

Cover design by: Rain Saukas

Cover photo courtesy of Thinkstock.com.

Printed in the United States of America

"We live as we dream—alone."
Joseph Conrad, *Heart of Darkness*

CONTENTS

Introduction   *1*

Chapter 1: The Mass Murder/Suicide Epidemic:
     A Growing Menace   5

Chapter 2: Genes and Mental Illness   37

Chapter 3: Sandy Hook: Identifying Dangerous
     Aspects of Strange Behavior   47

Chapter 4: James Holmes: The Dark Knight Rises   69

Chapter 5: The Tucson Shootings: Who Was Jared Loughner?   107

Chapter 6: Anders Breivik and the Massacre in Norway   131

Chapter 7: Eddie Routh: The Double Murder
     at a Gun Range   143

Chapter 8: Psychiatric, Sociopsychological, and Genetic
     Backgrounds of Violence and Aggression   153

Chapter 9: Toward a New Biology: Violent Stimuli
     against the Background of Human Psychological
     Development   173

Chapter 10: Best-Practice Approaches   203

Chapter 11: Practical Guidelines for Identifying
     Signs of Potential Violence   247

Index   *259*

Introduction

An angry President Obama emerged from the White House after a minority of United States senators blocked the majority of the Senate from sending an expanded background check gun-purchase bill to the House of Representatives.[1] Flanked by Sandy Hook victims' parents, who had lobbied for the background check bill as they kept the memories of their slain children alive, the president pointed out that between 80 and 90 percent of Americans were in favor of keeping guns out of the hands of the seriously mentally ill and violent felons. He also made it clear that the bill prohibited the federal government from keeping a registry of gun owners or those who sought to purchase a gun.

Even as the president spoke about the Senate vote, bombs began to explode at the finish line of the Boston Marathon. It was a short time later that a horrified, but resolute, Governor Deval Patrick assured the residents of Boston that no matter how terrible the bombing of the marathon was, law enforcement would find the perpetrators

---

[1] Weisman, Jonathan. "Senate Blocks Drive for Gun Control." *New York Times*, April 15, 2013. http://www.nytimes.com/2013/04/18/us/politics/senate-obama-gun-control.html?_r=0 (accessed December 11, 2013).

and bring them to justice.[2] The president, too, also made that same promise. The nation's people scratched their heads about the causes of violence, even while the Tsarnaev brothers, now identified as the suspected perpetrators of the bombing, fought the police with guns and improvised grenades, killing and wounding even more victims in the process. The brothers continued their battle until twenty-six-year-old Tamerlan was shot dead and his younger brother, nineteen-year-old Dzhokhar, took refuge inside a boat in nearby Watertown and was taken into custody the following day. But as the next news cycles wash across their television screens, the public forgets about the causes of violence. America has experienced more than fifteen years of an epidemic of *mass* murders, attempted and successfully executed bombings, and deaths of innocent children by gun.

In writing this book, we sought to examine the issues of the epidemic of suicide and mass murder in America against the background of the Boston Marathon bombing and the shootings at Tucson, Aurora, and Newtown, as well as the 2007 Virginia Tech massacre. In our research, we found many paths to understanding the nature of this epidemic and the spread of mental illness, the evolution of American society and how it is affecting our children, the influence of the media—particularly, violent video games—and the nature of suicidal mental illness itself. Suicidal mental illness deserves to be studied as a separate aspect of criminal justice and of both psychiatric medicine and clinical psychology. Although the authors have proposed a number of commonsense approaches to dealing with those in America who suffer from mental illness, we also have seen a dire fate that can easily overwhelm the society we take for granted. This dire fate, because of the prevalence of firearms carried by those who should not have them, could become an epidemic of undiagnosed and untreated mental illness and the near-pathological

---

[2] "Boston Marathon Explosions: 3 Dead." ABC News, April 15 2013. http://abcnews. go.com/US/video/boston-marathon-explosions-3-dead-18964237 (accessed December 11, 2013).

adoration of suicidal mass murderers by young people who aspire to their crimes and level of nihilism. America could become "suicide central," a locus of individuals who prey upon both themselves and others and who cause waves of hopelessness and unremitting fury to crash across an entire generation.

The Boston bombings were not idiosyncratic, but rather symptomatic of our current fever of violence, broken out in an epidemic of suicidal mass murder on campuses as seemingly diverse as Virginia Tech and Sandy Hook Elementary. Make no mistake; we are the ultimate victims, unsafe on our streets, in our shopping centers, in our workplaces, and in schoolrooms and schoolyards.

Professional medical associations advise their members to be scientists who rely on data, not emotion, to assert their views. But it is hard, even for medical doctors, to stare into the face of truth while hostile advocates, like the proverbial ostriches, plunge their heads into the sands of unknowing so that they will not have to face the truth. We challenge naysayers to poll trauma surgeons at Harvard and the University of Arizona in the wake of the Boston Marathon bombing and the 2011 Tucson shooting. This is where we find ourselves today and why we have written this book.

Chapter 1

The Mass Murder/ Suicide Epidemic: A Growing Menace

From a medical perspective, we know that in epidemics, pathogens do not simply stop killing. They spread and look for new hosts in which they can survive in a symbiotic relationship. But when the host dies, they move on. These "pathogens" are moving on—not only right through our culture, but into societies from modern Western Europe and Scandinavia to the Middle East and North Africa. Governments and individuals only respond with more violence. We are consuming ourselves, and leaders of even the most civilized societies have no idea how to prevent the violence. We can only react to the violence in all-too-familiar ways, such as the literal army of police and military vehicles in Boston. Where did this army zooming past classic Copley Plaza come from? Then, from McHale Pavilion to Sandy Hook and Boston, we lament loss of life while politicians and anchormen engage in a collective head-banging about the causes and what preventive measures they can devise. But, unfortunately, the pattern of mass murder and suicide has become routine, as have the innocuous comments of the "punditistas."

We have heard this and similar stories countless times before on the news or online: A strange-looking person walks into a building filled with people. The building could be a school, a workplace, a house of worship, a shopping mall, or even a street-corner gathering. The person may be wearing a baseball cap pulled down over his eyes or turned around backwards. Maybe he wears sunglasses, a black outfit, a hoodie, a flak jacket, or even makeshift camouflage. Few notice the person at first, perhaps because he blends in with the crowd, or perhaps because he's hanging at the edge of the shadows. But suddenly, without any warning, the person brandishes a firearm—usually a semiautomatic rifle or pistol—and opens fire on people in the crowd, targeting some directly or sweeping the weapon from side to side to cut a wide swath of destruction. People cry for help and dial 911. Scores of cell phone messages light up the local first-responder dispatch boards. People begin screaming as they hit the ground. Some flee for the exits and make it out alive. Others do not. Within minutes, sirens wail. Law enforcement personnel in black uniforms and military helmets enter the building to search for the shooter. However, when they find him, more likely than not, he is already dead from a self-inflicted gunshot wound or merely standing outside in dazed silence, as if another act of murder and mayhem was happening nearby. Another act was almost part of the script in Aurora, Colorado, where a mad chase could have spread murder and mayhem through the streets of Denver but for James Holmes's quiet, almost catatonic, surrender. More lives, however, were lost in Cambridge and Watertown because the script was acted out, complete with suicide vests. In Massachusetts, an emergency room doctor, interrupted between cases, answered questions about the causes of death in the case of the older brother, Tamerlan Tsarnaev. This doctor dispassionately told reporters that the elder Tsarnaev's body was too full of bullets and shrapnel from his suicide vest to really tell anything other than that he was fatally shot by police. All in a night's shift in a US emergency room these days?

Where are we? Beirut? Damascus? Kandahar? How many times has this happened over the past five, ten, or fifteen years? Trace it back to Richard Speck's horrible mass murder of nurses in Chicago followed by the University of Texas Tower suicidal mass murder by former US Marine Charles Whitman. Those were rarities in their day, even though some will say nothing has changed. Nothing since 1966? From Virginia Tech in 2007 to Boston in 2013? A great deal has changed. Especially if you are a police chief and not a researcher in an ivory tower manipulating statistics to prove nothing has changed. The researcher may not be asking the question, but the police chief and those he protects are. How many more times will it happen? Who will be the next victims? And where? At a shopping center? In class? At church? At a sporting event?

Whether the shooter's name is Dylan Klebold, Cho Seung-Hui, James Holmes, Wade Page, William Spengler, Adam Lanza, Christopher Dorner, or the Brothers Tsarnaev, the commonalities are there and very apparent. In the aftermath of the tragedy, experts and pundits alike make the same kinds of pronouncements about loners, the unpredictability of these events, the impossibility of preventing them, and the need to have more guns and armed guards present. However, when Jeffrey Johnson shot a coworker right by the Empire State Building in midtown Manhattan in August 2012, the police officers who apprehended and shot Johnson also shot more than ten bystanders in a hail of fire, as reported by newspapers at the time and in the *Huffington Post*.[3] No matter what the various talking heads, bloggers, and self-anointed commentators say to palliate the public angst and growing fury, they seldom get us any closer to a solution.

---

[3] Eltman, Frank. "Empire State Building Shooting Lawsuit: Wounded Bystander Chenin Duclos Sues NYPD." *Huffington Post*, January 22, 2013. http://www.huffingtonpost.com/2013/01/22/empire-state-building-shooting-chenin-duclos-sues-nypd_n_2526361.html (accessed December 11, 2013).

What we now believe is that skilled clinicians can identify the behaviors of potential suicidal mass shooters and possibly prevent their crimes if they read the warning signs when legal opportunities (e.g., recurrent domestic violence, grossly psychotic communications, behavior in family or public settings) present themselves to do so. We can prevent many more of these types of crimes from happening than we currently are led to believe we can, without resorting to violation of anyone's rights under the Constitution's privacy, search and seizure, and due process clauses or the First and Second Amendments. While we cannot prevent the crimes completely, we can at least limit the number of casualties. The problem is that even the experts will not admit that the answers are already there. The many cases we examine in this book demonstrate how the behaviors of these offenders, whether in private or in front of friends and families, manifested a potential danger. The behaviors of suicidal and homicidal offenders indicated that the perpetrators were themselves victims of helplessness in their own situations and feared what would happen to them.

These psychological states of fear and helplessness that generate psychotic fury are the basis of the commonalities that stretch across all of the mass murders and suicides over the past two decades and probably well before. The fear and helplessness, when triggered by psychological traumas, tend to lead offenders to mental disorganization and threats to self and others in a person's already brittle adjustment. Some offenders, like Tamerlan Tsarnaev, may have concealed their boiling wrath at society for their perceived failure to settle into society before pulling the trigger or lighting the fuse of a pressure-cooker bomb as a final vendetta against society. The mentality of most others, however, was obviously deteriorating into fatal, psychotic, suicidal mass murder before they pulled the trigger.

When self-proclaimed experts argue that mass murder/suicide events, such as those that occurred at Sandy Hook Elementary, Tucson, or Webster, New York (the William Spengler case), are unpredictable, they are off the mark because of the clear commonalities that stretch across the landscape of suicidal offenders, and even offenders who do not commit suicide. Was James Holmes in Aurora planning to survive his shooting spree? Was his aim to spend the rest of his life behind bars while his death-penalty appeals worked their way through the courts for the ensuing decade, or did he plan to die by a police officer's bullet, thereby ending his pain in an apocalyptic moment of public self-destruction? Or was Holmes planning an escape as police and other first responders dealt with the explosive booby traps in his apartment, as they would later deal with the Tsarnaev bombs planted at MIT? In Holmes's delusion, was he the arch-villain of the world of Batman, ready to strike again?

We believe that by examining the commonalities of the mass murder events of the past decade, or by starting earlier with Dylan Klebold and Eric Harris at Columbine or with Charles Whitman, who mowed down his victims from the University of Texas's bell tower, we can understand the psychology behind these crimes, identify behavioral warning signs, and recommend preventive measures. In addition to being able to isolate the issues pertinent to suicidal mass murders and find the ways to address the common issues as warning signs, we look at ways to implement suggested preventive responses in the fields of public policy and public health policy and give advice to parents, teachers, and employers. As difficult as these tragedies are to comprehend because of their cruelty and magnitude, they are ultimately understandable as a class of crimes, even if a case such as that of Wade Page at the Sikh temple in Milwaukee differs from a case such as that of William Spengler in Webster, New York; Anders Breivik in Norway; Adam Lanza in Newtown, Connecticut; or the Brothers Tsarnaev in Boston. We also believe that the sheer number of mass murders and suicides and, more important, their frequency indicate that we are facing a growing epidemic of mass murder, with crimes feeding upon crimes as more horrendous crimes make headlines.

Is there a general wave of violent psychotic behavior spreading across the landscape? Are we looking at a new form of what traditional psychiatrists refer to as *folie à deux*, or shared psychosis, which we suspect is what Ross Ashley suffered from? In the wake of the Virginia Tech massacre, not many recall Ross Ashley, a student at Radford University, whom residents of his apartment complex long observed to be grossly psychotic; he stole a car, shot a police officer to death at nearby Virginia Tech, and then killed himself. What else was he planning? Or are we simply so inured to such seemingly senseless violence that motivations for murder and suicide do not matter anymore? If these motivations are a form of shared psychotic behavior, then the behavior might well be spread by the mass media unintentionally feeding, without malice of intent, the psychotic delusions of an offender. Thus, Cho Seung-Hui, while still a child, might have seen the news coverage of the Columbine shootings and amalgamated that into his own self-destructive, apocalyptic delusions. Therefore, it is appropriate to ask whether the news reports of horrendous crimes are reaching an at-risk population of potentially dangerous offenders, so that each crime indirectly inspires the next. If that is the case, then we may be in an area of public health where the prevention of psychotic behavior runs right up against the First, Second, Fourth, and Fifth Amendments of the US Constitution. What can be done about that, except to tell people to stay away from crowds and public places, and far away from anyone who looks just a bit out of the ordinary? Is that a solution?

Worse yet, we seek to purify society of "strange" people by criminalizing them. If someone acts out on the street by ranting about his paranoid delusions, police haul him away to jail if he is not responsive. Thus, our jails are full of the mentally ill, who cannot fend for themselves. We consider them dangerous and stigmatize them. Suicidal mass murders have broken into the public consciousness. But the mentally ill—some dangerously ill—are still out there in growing numbers while our first responders have no protocols for dealing with them humanely. The situation is worse for mentally ill combat veterans, who may have no place to go. We find crowd or people-avoidance reactions bordering on agoraphobia among combat veterans returning from war zones.

In post-deployment workups, clinicians found that veterans from both Vietnam and the Middle East had similar avoidant reactions to environments in which they might have suffered traumatic experiences. Soldiers returning from Vietnam, for example, who had suffered from invisible war wounds tended to avoid dense foliage that reminded them of the jungles where they had fought an insurgent enemy. Trees and heavy brush provided cover for that enemy; therefore, trees and dense brush were threatening to returning soldiers suffering from post-traumatic stress disorder. Similarly, veterans from Afghanistan and Iraq were reluctant to enter into ordinary civilian gatherings because an insurgent with a cell phone and improvised explosive device could wreak carnage similar to what spectators on Boylston Street witnessed in Boston. If we apply some of this residual avoidance of threatening situations to at-risk individuals whose behavior borders on dangerous, we can see how these individuals may actually be triggered into violence simply by a situational event, such as the upending of a comfort zone, as happened in the Adam Lanza case, or a perceived threat from an enemy, even if the threat is not real. A biker who just returned from Kabul may cut in front of you on the interstate at high speed and crash into the roadside because he saw a pile of dirt on the side of the road hundreds of feet ahead. Just the perception of fresh dirt is an adequate threat of an improvised explosive device, and it might be enough to trigger dangerous behavior because of loss of the sense of present time. This loss of present time takes a combat veteran back to survival instincts learned months or even years ago.

The Search for Commonalities

What are the lowest commonalities we can discern from the spate of mass murders and suicides over the past ten to fifteen years or even all the way back to Charles Whitman in Texas, whose mass shooting helped define the paradigm of mass murder/suicide? Knowing what we now know about James Charles Whitman's autopsy, for example, which he, himself, ordered in his own journal when he wrote that his mind was "going," it is clear that actual tumors on the brain can drastically affect behavior. Whitman had brain cancer, which can lurk in a silent area of the brain where it might be undetectable until either pain or extreme behavioral dysfunction requires a neurological intervention. We now believe that it was the cancer that initially set Whitman off. Whitman knew there was something wrong with him, and he was right. Thus, we now have the need to scan the brain of every first-episode psychosis sufferer, like Cho and Holmes and, likely, Lanza, too. That is actually a standard of practice over which insurance companies will usually not fight too hard and will fork over the thousand-dollar medical expense to perform, following first episode of psychosis—estimated at one hundred thousand cases per year in this country. Psychosis usually occurs in late adolescence and early adulthood—the very population concentrated on college campuses and military bases.

Undiagnosed history of mental illness, as with Jared Loughner, or underdiagnosed mental illness, as with Cho, are perhaps two of the most basic attributes we can assign to suicidal mass murderers. In any biographical sketch of the offender, we find a history of mental disturbances. These disturbances range from complete schizophrenic delusions with likely accompanying auditory hallucinations that could make a patient look selectively mute (as Cho Seung-Hui was initially diagnosed by a child psychiatrist intern)[4] to a loquatious Holmes making a classroom presentation on neurobiology.

---

[4] Liebert, John, and William J. Birnes. *Suicidal Mass Murderers: A Criminological Study of Why They Kill.* Boca Raton: CRC Press, 2011.

Loughner, and James Holmes, suffered from first-episode paranoid schizophrenia, with ominous prognostic outcomes accompanying extended duration of untreated psychosis (DUP).

In the most serious of these psychosis cases, the offender is completely cut off from reality, perhaps like Jared Loughner of Tucson, Arizona, who shot Representative Gabrielle Giffords and killed others during a "street-corner town-hall" type of event. Tragically, the offender became aware that his behavior was aberrant after he took the antipsychotic medication Risperdal for first time in prison. Loughner's psychologist testified in federal court that Loughner told her he would not have committed the Tucson shooting had he been taking this medication years before going berserk at Safeway Plaza. No one had ever offered Loughner the medication, despite his school career pattern of disruptive behavior at Pima Community College in Tucson—similar to that of Virginia Tech student Cho Seung-Hui. Why was there no official inquiry of dangerousness after these red flags? In fact, the Cho case appears to have informed Pima Community College's response. Unfortunately, the inquiry was prompted simply to get Loughner off campus and keep him off. The professionals simply dumped an emergency medical problem on his helpless parents. Is that the way they would have treated a student stumbling around with blood all over his face? Of course not. But psychiatric emergencies are different, which might be what professionals at Pima Community College and Virginia Tech obviously believed. Psychiatric emergencies are not real illnesses for which they are responsible as both clinical professionals and concerned college staff. Both colleges clearly marketed their student health and psychiatric services in promotional materials and student handbooks, leading students and parents to believe that they had the know-how and resources to take care of any student, whether on or off campus. But in the end, Pima Community College security personnel visited Loughner's home to make sure he stayed off campus.

For his part, Colorado's James Holmes, now facing the death penalty, is likely to raise the issue of insanity in his defense during his upcoming trial for the massacre he perpetrated at a movie theater in Aurora, Colorado, now referred to as the "Dark Knight Murders." What did his purchase of ammunition, explosives, and detonating material indicate even as he sought psychiatric help from university health services? And, as the authors have documented in detail in *Suicidal Mass Murderers: A Criminological Study of Why They Kill* (CRC Press, 2011), Virginia Tech shooter Cho Seung-Hui was clearly suffering from paranoid schizophrenia while on campus, although he, like Loughner, was not diagnosed with this devastating disorder while he lived on campus. Despite repeated episodes of irrational, disruptive behaviors on campus that resulted in involuntary commitment for Cho and a suspension from college for Loughner, no other official actions were taken that could have been seen as preventive for the community in general. The two psychotically behaving individuals were simply taken out of their respective communities—Cho, temporarily—even as they acquired weapons and ammunition.

Hopelessness

Psychiatrists universally agree that people who are suicidal believe they have nothing to lose. Either they are in tremendous physical or emotional pain, or they believe, realistically or not, that their lives are devoid of hope. For example, when hearing a young person tell of his devastating loss of feeling and struggle with discrimination of reality from delusions and auditory hallucinations, psychiatrists working with this seriously mentally ill population understand why the risk of suicide following discharge for first-episode psychosis in young adults is among the highest for any population, other than Huntington's chorea, which approaches 100 percent. Imagine that a young person becomes aware that she is losing her mind or that a young man is plagued by ideations of suicidal violence, but there is nothing either of them can do about it other than talk to a psychiatrist. Think of the panic, the hopelessness, then the frustration and anger. We can see these feelings in the rantings of James Holmes, the plays and writings of Cho Seung-Hui, and the ravings of manifestos written by Anders Breivik and "the Unabomber" Ted Kaczynski.

Dr. Emil Kraepelin, a German psychiatrist, gave the name dementia praecox, also called premature dementia, to the disease we now call schizophrenia. Schizophrenia is a condition that begins with a sufferer's awareness that something is very wrong with his or her ability to cope with reality. The person is aware of losing his or her grip on everyday comings and goings, and the person has strange or perhaps troubling ideations. Imagine knowing for a short while early in life that you are losing your mind. It is more than unnerving. That insight eventually goes away in form of anosognosia, or loss of awareness of sickness. Before the insight goes away, this patient, like a neurologist diagnosed with Alzheimer's disease, is one of the highest risks for suicide because for a short time he or she will know about nine years of merciless progressive dementia lie ahead. Some victims will likely take the opportunity of earliest memory loss to destroy themselves while they can.

Hopeless people rarely plan for the future. They have what is known as "foreshortened future." Therefore, in examining patients at high risk for suicide, one must patiently listen for their plans. Those planning to kill themselves really have no plans because they intend to be dead. They are not worried about Christmas shopping because they are not intending to be alive for Christmas, probably just like Adam Lanza, who possibly intended from the outset to destroy himself after the shooting at Sandy Hook. William Spengler, in his Christmas Eve ambush of first responders in Webster, New York, might have had similar intent. Perhaps James Holmes, too, had plans to destroy himself if he knew of the "success" of his booby-trapped apartment that miraculously did not level a city block.

A significant percentage of hopeless people bent on suicide are capable of violence toward others; we see this suicidal bent increasingly often in combat veterans. They will take their loved ones with them, and rarely, but increasingly, they take strangers on campus and public places, too. The courts drafted the medicolegal construct for "danger to self or danger to others" so that it met a legal rather than a purely medical standard. However, a legal standard must conform to the US Constitution—a medical standard, when not applied within a legal context, need not. Mother Nature also tends not to regard the US Constitution and usually does not discriminate between what is legal and what is not. In fact, research has shown that only a small fraction of patients who were involuntarily committed were dangerous only to others.

The cases we cite involve individuals who were dangerous to self and others. Accordingly, we believe there is rarely a more dangerous situation than intervening in, or trying to stop, an active suicide attempt by a person with a gun. We saw that public safety warning on television for days after the Boston Marathon bombing, even though the warning may have not been for suicidal mass murder, as it turned out to be. Suicide must be conceptualized within a spectrum of unremitting mental states of human destructiveness, all the way from the small percentage of suicidal mass murderers on one end of a bell-shaped curve to an elderly man who injects himself with too much insulin and is found dead in his apartment. Thinking of a suicidal person as purely dangerous only to himself is highly risky.

Ideations of Suicidal Behavior

Individuals often give off warning signs of their hopelessness, indicating by their words and actions that they have no other recourse than to destroy themselves, many times within the context of destroying others. It is an old adage that when someone tells you what he or she plans to do, especially what that person plans to do to you, you should take it seriously because it is likely that those plans will be carried out. Thus, when Dylan Klebold and Eric Harris announced their plans on the Internet to attack fellow students at Columbine High School or when Cho Seung-Hui announced in his middle school or in his short stories and plays that he planned to "do a Columbine," they should have been taken seriously. James Holmes also talked about ideations of violence and was reported to have been in touch with his psychiatrist even days before the shootings in Aurora. William Spengler wrote that he actually had a plan to trap first responders in a hail of gunfire, which he did before he died.[5] In fact, even though people who knew the shooters may indicate that the crimes simply came out of nowhere, closer examination reveals that the perpetrators of mass murder and suicides gave off clear warnings of an impending crisis as their personalities decompensated into hopelessness.

Access to Weapons

You don't need a permit in most of the United States to purchase firearms, and in many locations, background checks are rarely carried out. Criminal databases and terrorist watch lists meant to prevent felons from obtaining guns are often not checked. In almost all states—New York and Colorado might be the first exceptions— those individuals under a psychiatrist's care are guaranteed some sort of privacy, which is what Fourth Amendment advocates strongly support. You can go to a gun show in some states and purchase a firearm on the spot. The loopholes regarding gun registrations and background checks for firearms purchases allow those who are deranged, such as Spengler, to get their hands on firearms simply by "straw purchases"—acquiring by proxy. Adam Lanza used his

---

[5] Russell, Goldman. "Gunman, William Spengler, Shoots 4 Firefighters, Kills 2, in 'Trap' at Webster, NY, Blaze." ABC News, December 24, 2012. http://abcnews.go.com/US/ gunman-shoots-firefighters-kills-trap-webster-ny-blaze/story?id=18055594.

mother's guns, legally purchased and legally owned, but not legally carried by twenty-year-old Adam, to wreak violence upon the students at Sandy Hook Elementary School after he killed his mother with her own gun. James Holmes simply acquired his weapons on the Internet.

Killers Make Their Personal Statements

Mass murderers do not kill in a vacuum. As they drift closer and closer to their own violent climaxes, they project a pretext for their behavior, as irrational as that pretext might be. When Wade Page decomposed and violently struck out at worshippers at a Sikh temple in Oak Creek, Wisconsin, he had indicated his racist ideations years earlier in the military by illegally goose-stepping down the streets of Berlin and was on the watch list of the Southern Poverty Law Center.[6] He continued to express his racist ideations, also as a rock singer, even after he was chaptered out of the Army, presumably for alcohol abuse. For a suicidal mass murderer, the crime is the statement, whether it is Lanza, Cho, Klebold, or Harris seeking revenge against those they had possibly perceived to bully or ostracize them or Christopher Dorner seeking his revenge against the LAPD, which fired him, he said in his manifesto, because of racism. Because in almost all the cases, police investigators cannot fathom the rational causality of irrational behavior, the statements made by the killers are almost always relegated to a closed-case file, a kind of dustbin of history. Thus, important clues to preventing these crimes are often overlooked. Words like "sick," "demented," and "crazed," although probably valid, lay descriptors of suicidal or homicidal behavior, are too often used to dismiss the behavior of homicidal

---

[6] Goode, Erica, and Serge F. Kovaleski. "Wisconsin Killer Fed and Was Fueled by Hate-Driven Music." *New York Times*, August 6, 2012. http://www.nytimes.com/2012/08/07/us/army-veteran-identified-as-suspect-in-wisconsin-shooting.html (accessed December 11, 2013).

offenders and are unlikely to be deconstructed via suicide autopsy—a technique as necessary as the autopsy performed on Texas suicidal mass murderer Charles Whitman.

We need to know what leads up to murder and mayhem. Unfortunately, these apparently dehumanized people share most of our genome, although we cannot accept that fact and get rid of that evidence as soon as possible. We seek to execute James Holmes because he acted in what we would like to think is a social vacuum and has nothing to tell us. But despite calls for his execution, we may keep Dzhokhar Tsarnaev alive so that we can find out what he knows about a possible international conspiracy and sleeper cell at the University of Massachusetts and Dartmouth. Then we execute him, as if that execution would somehow expiate our collective sin of not discovering his plots sooner.

If we follow the breadcrumb trail of deconstructing the behavior of psychotic mass shooters and reach the end point of a brain autopsy, we will find valuable clues to explain this type of violent behavior. For example, Dr. Rey, a pathologist, was one of the few doctors who subscribed to the practice of suicide autopsy, which is a direction of investigation that medical examiners in suicidal mass murders need to push for.[7]

In cases like those of Adam Lanza, Wade Page, and Tamarlan Tsarnaev, we have great need to know what psychosocial or neurological abnormalities predated their loss of control. But among shooters who survive, like Norway's Anders Breivik and Jared Loughner, they will be sent to prison for life, probably with minimal, if any, psychiatric or psychological assessments.

Of course, one might ask what good such assessments would do for someone incarcerated for life. The research stemming from psychiatric interviews with mass murderers confined and regulated

---

[7] "Death Investigation Conference," sponsored by National Association of Medical Examiners, *The Murdering Mind: What We've Learned from Ted Bundy*, Seattle, WA, 1990.

within the prison system might go a long way toward figuring out how to identify the suicide- or homicide-inclined individuals in society and find ways to treat them to prevent violence. Pincus and Tucker did just that in prison populations and found a high incidence of head trauma, seizure disorders, and brutality within families. Their stark findings in this population of violent offenders should inform public health upstream at the mouth of the river, not downriver or at the last bridge just before bodies float out into the ocean and are lost forever to clinical research.

Maybe we are not completely certain about what James Holmes wanted to do, whether to escape or die in an explosion and take the lives of first responders along with him, but we do know that Loughner and Breivik stated flat out that they were on suicidal missions. It seems that mass shooters Major Nidal Hasan and Staff Sergeant Robert Bales, who both face Army courts-martial for their crimes, were on suicide missions as well. What if we had a legal requirement that every mass shooter who commits suicide or is shot by police must be turned over to the local medical examiner for a brain autopsy? What information would we glean from that? Similarly, what if every living mass shooter were forced to submit to a medical examination, including a battery of brain scans, psychiatric examinations, and thorough clinical psychological testing to determine their physical and mental states? We would get important information about these offenders' abilities to comport their behaviors to the requirements of the law and the social system. Pincus and Tucker have already proven that.

In the case of James Holmes, for example, what was his evasion and escape plan? If he was so well organized with intent to create disaster in Aurora, where was he going to hide for the rest of his life? Did he have a valid passport and change of clothes? How about cash in his wallet or a reserve on his credit cards? How long could he keep on driving if he had no gas money? Ross Ashley, who killed a police officer at Virginia Tech before killing himself, had a change of clothes. Why? Now, if Holmes had a passport and way to the airport with a change of clothes, one might say he was obviously not suicidal. But he stood outside the theater, just like Anders Breivik at the mass shooting scene in Norway, apparently waiting for arrest. At first, the police thought Holmes was a first responder because of his black combat outfit. In other words, had he not been detained right away, he could have slipped away to wait for the reports of the explosion in his apartment. Does that sound illogical or carefully planned? If someone is crazed or demented, logic cannot be applied to his or her behavior. Simply dismissing such behavior is a big mistake because of the clues inherent in the behavior and statements made before the acts of homicide. These clues throw light on the offender's state of mind.

Research has shown that many of the prehomicidal or presuicidal statements made by self-destructive mass murderers are very similar. The act of suicide itself, offering up the shooter as his own persecuted victim, is such a common feature that in especially severe cases, it can be seen as an offender's pretext for the crime. Klebold and Harris claimed to have been persecuted and bullied. Cho Seung-Hui claimed that the "normal" students around him victimized him. James Holmes booby-trapped his own apartment perhaps because he believed he would be able to enjoy the prospect of a second mass murder, this time of first responders, before he committed suicide, thinking he was the Joker escaping in the Batmobile through Denver streets. Perhaps once incarcerated or confined to a mental institution, Holmes will become more lucid about his motivations and demons, and he might reveal whether he had any escape plans. If he did, he had about as much intent of living to fight another day as did Dzhokhar Tsarnaev, who imagined hiding and bleeding to death in that boat, firing off his last rounds at police, most likely expecting that they would fire back and kill him. But they did not. Self-styled jihadist Dzhokhar Tsarnaev failed in his mission, and like the Fort Hood shooter Dr. Nidal Hasan, may have to exist for decades or years in a cell, unless they were killed in same fashion they doled out to others. Wisconsin has no death penalty, but Jeffrey Dahmer, while cleaning the prison shower unsupervised, was attacked by acquaintances and relatives of his victims.

Paranoid Delusions Are Commonplace among Suicidal Mass Murderers

Jared Loughner was thrown out of Pima Community College and complained in an email to his shooting victim, Representative Gabrielle Giffords, that life around him was a sham and that nobody was doing anything about it. He voiced over a loudspeaker on campus, "It's all a scam. Words have no meaning." These are obvious clinical signs that he had lost his ability to discern reality and separate it from the voices ringing inside his head. When he was arrested, he told police that life was a scam. In his delusional mind, Loughner saw himself as a victim of that scam, persecuted and shunned. However, the perceived scam was his delusion, and language was losing its meaning within his psychotic decompensation. It would not be surprising if he did project responsibility for that onto the highest authority, who, it seems, was Representative Gabby Giffords, for whom, we believe, he probably fostered erotic feelings. Psychiatrists call these delusional erotic feelings "erotomania," a delusion of passion, whose manifestations are referred to as "erotomanic delusion," "paranoia erotica," or "psychose passionelle," a form of paranoid delusion with an amorous quality. We actually saw this delusion manifested in Cho Seung-Hui when he chose fellow student Emily Hilscher as his love object. She became his first shooting victim.[8]

In psychose passionelle, the patient, often a single woman, but many times a delusional person like Cho, believes that an exalted person is in love with him or her. This condition, called

---

[8] Liebert, John, and William J. Birnes. *Suicidal Mass Murderers: A Criminological Study of Why They Kill.* Boca Raton: CRC Press, 2011.

"de Clérambault's syndrome" was originally described by Gaëtan Gatian de Clérambault as having a "phase of hope followed by a phase of resentment." John Hinckley, Jr., had a similar delusion about President Reagan being in a love triangle with him and Jody Foster.

A delusional Adam Lanza might have believed his own mother was threatening to institutionalize him, destroying the comfort zone he had built for himself inside his room, along with acute rupture of their apparent symbiotic relationship, which she probably saw no way out of by then except for confining her son to residential placement at a Washington State facility like Secret Harbor, a tiny San Juan island, which would have seemed like a prison for Adam. Nancy Lanza had visited Washington State, leaving Adam alone in the house, and she possibly investigated placing him in an institution. She even might have confronted him with that alternative if he did not voluntarily leave the house to fend for himself. Secret Harbor is a residential facility for incorrigible children on a remote, otherwise uninhabited island in the San Juan chain, not accessible by any public transport. One can reach it only by private boat. Unfortunately, Nancy Lanza might have unknowingly ruptured the symbiotic bond by going off to Mount Washington, or perhaps she was intuitive enough to know it would be her last retreat to a favorite place for New Hampshirites, as she reportedly told her friends before her death. Secret Harbor is like a humane, private Alcatraz for kids, so isolated that no one lives on the island except for the institutional staff.

Qualifying Dangerousness in the Suicidal and Homicidal Insane

Although suicidal individuals can be dangerous, none of what we suggest is to argue that anyone who believes he or she is being victimized is an imminent danger to others. Nor do we suggest that the seriously mentally ill we see talking to themselves on the streets are dangerous. Only a small percentage of those who are seriously mentally ill are dangerous, and they are mainly dangerous to others who live in subpar support systems and who are often homeless. Treatment Advocacy Center says that 10 percent of reported homicides are caused by the seriously mentally ill, but only 6 percent of this cohort of the seriously mentally ill actually carry out homicides.[9] Perhaps the fact that their victims are also seriously mentally ill and essentially abandoned by our institutions and society is the reason politicians, the press, and citizens alike ignore this astonishing homicide statistic. However, we know that people who do act aggressively in the face of a belief that they are being unfairly victimized need professional help. If these people are grossly delusional and hearing voices, particularly hallucinatory commands to harm others, they need psychiatric treatment with antipsychotic medications and close monitoring to make certain they take those medications.

Contrary to what some right-wing thinkers assert, nonadherence to antipsychotic medications—rather than taking them—is the most common cause of violence among the seriously mentally ill, especially when they complicate nonadherence to treatment with drugs and alcohol. That is why case management, all but a memory these days, along with case managers' often preferred medication, long-acting Risperdal Consta, which can be given once every two weeks and which patients generally tolerate well, is absolutely critical. Older medications had uncomfortable side effects that aggravated the problem of nonadherence. Remember, because of anosognosia, or denial of illness, the seriously mentally ill patient often does not think he needs treatment—particularly a shot every two weeks. During a grandiose delusion, whether happy ("I'm a billionaire") or dangerous, like Spengler ("kill everybody"), the delusional patient is unlikely to wish to part with the delusion for the harsh reality of

---

[9] MMWR. "Mental Health Surveillance Among Children—United States, 2005–2011." Morbidity and Mortality Weekly Report No. 2 (2013). http://www.modernhealthcare.com/assets/pdf/CH88661516.PDF (accessed December 11, 2013).

economic destitution and pain of social alienation with a cacophony of voices saying awful things.

In many cases, even the seriously mentally ill might correct their perceptions about being victimized, as did Loughner after taking medication, although, sadly, it was too late to prevent the Tucson shooting. But within the seriously mentally ill population, an extended duration of untreated psychosis, or DUP, caused both the Tucson shooting and Cho Seung-Hui's Virginia Tech massacre. Extended durations of untreated psychoses in the 1 percent of our population, the seriously mentally ill patients who will have a psychotic episode break in early adulthood, will create more victims of senseless violence and disasters from suicidal mass murders. This is the accelerating trend today in the wake of the gradual destruction of our public mental health system. Society does not have the resources to deal with a growing cohort of psychologically disturbed young people, whose mental illnesses may evolve into violent behavior toward themselves and possibly complete strangers who are misperceived as necessary targets of their delusions or the hallucinations that command them to harm others. If this seems like an implausible doomsday scenario, look at the growing numbers of suicidal individuals who launch attacks upon innocent victims, including the public safety officers who try to disarm them. On August 21, 2013, the Brothers Tsarnaev shot two Boston area police officers, one fatally, in their attempt to escape to New York. Three Arizona police officers in the Phoenix area have been shot by men who could not possibly have expected to escape alive. These suicidal offenders took their own lives in proxy events called "suicide by cop."

Incidents of "suicide by cop" are soaring in this country, and police chiefs have acknowledged the problem. "We live in a very violent society. All I can do is train my officers best I can," Sheriff Joe Arpaio, Maricopa County, told Fox News on August 8, 2013.

The Epidemic

As of December 31, 2013, there have been at least eleven major mass homicides accompanied by suicides or attempted suicides since the 2011 Tucson shooting. There have been at least three times more that were aborted and thus muted in the news. Nevertheless, they were potential mass murders by offenders with a suicidal intent. For example, a young man entered a college classroom in Casper, Wyoming, after killing his father's girlfriend.[10] He fired an arrow into the head of his father, a college instructor, who still managed to wrestle his son to the ground so that students in the classroom would have time to flee and save their own lives. Police arrested the offender while praising the father, who died to save his students' lives from his own son.

In another incident, police shot a man to death on the fifth floor of an Alabama hospital after he started firing an automatic weapon.[11] This was not officially a mass murder, because only the shooter died. He allegedly had an issue with staff members who tended to his wife in the coronary care unit, which was where he was headed before the police shot him. Hospital staff immediately announced that the gunshots heard from the coronary care unit did not affect patient recovery, which was very hard to believe, particularly in his wife's case. Tragically, in the wake of the Sandy Hook Elementary School shooting, we need to ask the question, "what happens next time?" because there appears no end to a small percentage of deranged Americans' descent into evil.

What will happen the next time a lone shooter enters a school, workplace, hospital, or shopping center? What we know is that the lone suicidal murderers learn from one another, learn from one

[10] Johnson, M. Alex. "'Bow and Arrow-Type' Attack Leaves 3 Dead in Casper, Wyo., Including 2 in College Classroom, Officials Say." NBC News, November 30, 2012. http://usnews.nbcnews.com/_news/2012/11/30/15574250-bow-and-arrow-type-attack-leaves-3-dead-in-casper-wyo-including-2-in-college-classroom-officials-say?lite (accessed December 11, 2013).

[11] Associated Press. "Alabama Hospital Shooting: St. Vincent's Gunman Wounds 3 Before Being Killed by Police." Huffington Post, December 15, 2012. http://www.huffingtonpost.com/2012/12/15/alabama-hospital-shooting-wounded-gunman-killed_n_2307505.html (accessed December 11, 2013).

others' actions and tactics, and understand, as did James Holmes in Aurora, just how to set the stage for their crimes. Even the most delusional of them are aware of headline-breaking mass murder stories. Like Cho, they may regard previous shooters as heroes and seek to emulate them. Unless we understand the nature of the epidemic, the mental health issues of those at risk, the emotional triggers that propel them into action, and the frustrations that wear down their resiliency until they resort to violence, years from now, we will still be stumbling in the dark and scratching our heads when another person perpetrates the next heinous mass murder/suicide.

The president wisely ordered the CDC to investigate the nature of the violence epidemic in America and look for causality across the entire spectrum of violent stimuli, including mental health issues. This will not be the first time such a set of recommendations was floated by the American people. We already had a governor's report on the Virginia Tech massacre.[12] Unfortunately, that Virginia report, made in the aftermath of the shootings, was written under the shadow of massive lawsuits being filed by the Virginias Tech victims' parents. Accordingly, the report had to position the state in such a way that the state had to seem blameless in its actions with respect to the security procedures on the Virginia Tech campus on the day of the shootings. The Virginia Tech panel, comprised of individuals from the academic, medical, public safety, legal, and official government communities, focused on establishing the legal difference between "imminent" and "foreseeable future" in predicting dangerous behavior, using the legal standard to determine liability. In reality, what difference will this distinction between "imminent" and "foreseeable future" make in stopping the next Adam Lanza or James Holmes? The issues go far deeper than simply demarking a timeline in which predictability becomes more accurate.

---

[12] Virginia Tech Review Panel. "Mass Shootings at Virginia Tech." August 2007. Report of the Virginia Tech Review Panel Presented to Governor Kaine. http://www.governor. virginia.gov/tempcontent/techpanelreport.cfm.

The case of the seriously mentally ill Radford University student, Ross Ashley, who arrived on the neighboring Virginia Tech campus and killed a campus police officer and then himself, tells us that little will be accomplished unless we understand that the concept of "foreseeable future" means that a dangerous person can be triggered by any stimulus, almost all of them below the radar of those of us not at risk. To this day we cannot find out how much ammunition Ross Ashley was carrying. That would tell us what his intent was before he shot himself when he allegedly saw another police officer, who apparently was unaware that his comrade had just been murdered on campus. Worse, we cannot access investigative information on Cho Seung-Hui because his case is still under investigation. Is this investigation the premise of another commission report with promises that this investigation will be different?

Even though emissaries from the White House, including the president, the first lady, and the vice president, have been dispatched to sites of four suicidal mass murders, including Tucson, the Sikh temple in Oak Creek, Newtown, and Boston, only now has the president stepped up to order CDC research on the problem of growing dangerousness as a result of mental illness in American society. We contend, however, that unless we focus on some of the suicidal shooters individually, their backgrounds, the nature of their illnesses, and their external motivations, we will learn precious little to help us stem this epidemic. James Holmes from Aurora will probably be swept away into prison, as was Loughner. Are these individuals being swept under the rug because what they might have to say is too uncomfortable for Americans to hear? That does not seem to help. Meanwhile, politicians, especially those in Congress, kick the can down the road and hope somebody else will take the political responsibility for action on the epidemic of suicidal mass murders and inner-city gang violence. Maybe, in the course of our daily lives, we care little about the seriously mentally ill locked up in prisons, the homeless on the streets, or drive-bys in bad neighborhoods because if we have the means to move out, we know where not to go. Now everything is different; that was the message from Adam Lanza at Sandy Hook Elementary.

In cities like Chicago, multiple shootings are an almost daily occurrence. In 2012, five hundred homicides were unsurprisingly concentrated in neighborhoods where gangs rule the streets in a reign of terror and outgun the average police officer on patrol.[13] What the official police reports of homicide numbers show, as reported by police superintendent Garry McCarthy and cited by the *Chicago Tribune* on December 28, 2012,[14] even as crime statistics themselves indicate a decline, is that mass murder suicides and gang violence are trending upward. An upward trend in homicides that happen, which translates to a rate of 5.3 per 100,000 persons, as reported by the CDC, as often as once or twice per week nationally "with no apparent motivation," indicates that we are in the midst of an epidemic. Although gang violence is different from suicidal mass murder because the motives are more obvious—usually involving monetary issues—inner-city young adults who have joined the military rightly feel at less risk in the "sandbox" of Iraq or Afghanistan than in their own urban neighborhoods.[15] That is sad commentary on our society.

Many commentators in response to this epidemic of what we call suicidal/homicidal violence seek one-size-fits-all solutions, as if simply putting armed security personnel in schools will eliminate the problem. That solution may be part of a deterrent, but it is not a solution to the entire problem because armed security simply would not stop a delusional, psychotic gunman. NRA executive vice

[13] Gorner, Jeremy, and Robert McCoppin. *Chicago Tribune*, January 1, 2013. http://articles.chicagotribune.com/2013-01-01/news/chi-cops-city-ends-2012-with-506-homicides-a-16-percent-increase-over-2011-20130101_1_homicide-surge-homicide-toll-chicago-homicide-victims.

[14] Gorner, Jeremy, and Peter Nickeas. *Chicago Tribute*, December 28, 2012. http://articles.chicagotribune.com/2012-12-28/news/chi-chicago-2012-homicide-toll-20121228_1_latest-homicide-500th-homicide-tragic-number

[15] Liebert, John, and William J. Birnes. *Wounded Minds: Understanding and Solving the Growing Menace of Post-Traumatic Stress Disorder*. New York: Skyhorse Publishing, 2013.

president Wayne LaPierre's recent statement after the Sandy Hook shooting that "one sure way to stop a bad guy with a gun is to have a good guy with a gun" is false on its face.[16] For example, James Holmes outgunned police entering the Aurora theater. The Jefferson County sheriff's deputies dispatched to Columbine High School had to wait outside the building until a SWAT team with heavier weapons arrived. Meanwhile, students inside the building were dying. These "good guys with guns" were outgunned by the "bad guys with guns," even in a situation involving a gun-wielding loner, who most often had a criminal record with multiple trips through the revolving doors of our judicial system or gross psychiatric impairment that had been ignored (Jared Loughner, William Spengler, and Wade Page) or undertreated (Cho Seung-Hui, Adam Lanza, and James Holmes). Even in schools with armed security on the premises, the problem is getting worse and worse each day.

An epidemic, this epidemic, at least in medical terms of a medical approach, means that there is a medical diagnostic model to ascertain the nature of the disease and the symptoms and the progression of that disease. The diligent search for causes of the disease and ways to mitigate it, as with schizophrenia, get remission, as with manic depressive disorder, or cure it if possible, as is sometimes the case with acute post-traumatic stress disorder or severe grief reactions is the core of the medical model. Looking at the epidemic of mass murder/suicide in America, we should be able to use a medical model to see whether there are scientific approaches to effect an end to the epidemic itself even if some cases of mass murder/suicide still occur. We have to reverse the trend and keep more people alive.

We have to look at causality, the nature of the offenders, the nature of the transmission of the disease, and ways to intercept the disease to control, if not to halt, its spread. In other words, we

---

[16] Ed Pilkington "NRA Chief Breaks Post-Newtown Silence to Call for Armed Guards at Schools." *The Guardian*, December 21, 2012. http://www.theguardian.com/world/2012/dec/21/nra-newtown-armed-guards-schools.

have to ask what we are dealing with and look for analytical rather than emotional solutions, although we (and even our nation's leaders) are often overwhelmed by the tragedy when we consider the innocent victims, especially at Sandy Hook.

It is not just guns and it is not just mental illness, although both are significant parts of the mix. We believe that there are larger forces at work propelling too much of society to embrace violent reactions to all forms of life's vicissitudes. Entire industries, particularly the film, television, gaming software, and music industries, make billions annually by catering to the most depraved instincts of man. Although these industries may not intentionally incite violence, many companies in these entertainment industries gratuitously promote violence to attract buyers and viewers to purchase or rent their products. Among the cohort of consumers of video and digital violence are at-risk individuals who, because of mental illness, may not have the resiliency or the emotional capacity to relegate violence to the world of guilty-pleasure entertainment. They may consider violence to be a first response, not something to be abhorred.

Dangerousness and the potential for violence can be insidiously infecting. Some people like Ted Kaczinski, the Unabomber, wait for years, fomenting waves of irrational anger deep inside their psyches and waiting to strike back at those they deem to have done them wrong. Others, victims of violence or sufferers of physical brain traumas or post-traumatic stress disorder, simply do not have the emotional resiliency to withstand difficulties that more resilient people can handle. The job of the analyst is to ask why, look at the backgrounds of the least resilient, and figure out what might have been done to turn that person off the path of violence. Doing anything less means that we are putting bags over our heads, making believe that the problem will go away if we do not look at it. That is not the way to solve the epidemic of mass murder/suicide that plagues American society today. The answer is to analyze it, determine the causes, enact remedies (both legal and political), and provide as much protection to easy targets such as schools and public facilities as we can without becoming demoralized if small steps do not solve everything. But we have to begin to understand, and analysis is the best place to start. If we look at a brief history of when mass murder/suicide broke into our collective consciousness, from Charles Whitman in the University of Texas Tower in 1966 to Christopher Dorner's final battle with law enforcement as he huddled into a wilderness-cabin-turned-arsenal in California's Big Bear Lake area, we can see the surface-level similarities between Dorner and Whitman: individuals who not only were clearly mentally ill but might have had neurological problems as well, who were decomposing and getting increasingly violent. These similarities stretch across all of the mass murder/suicides in between the two, including suicide by proxy and attempted suicides. Dorner and Whitman were both combat trained and had successful naval careers, Whitman as a Marine and Dorner as a naval reserve lieutenant. Both made their last stands as they held off police units surrounding them. So did the Brothers Tsarnaev until nineteen-year-old Dzhokhar, hiding under the deck of a tarped and shrink-wrapped boat while police surrounded him and weakened by blood loss from having been shot by police, let himself be taken into custody. Both Whitman and Dorner realized that something was mentally wrong with them, but they could not figure out what it was or how to get help. They reached out for help, especially Dorner, who broke down in tears in his patrol car while begging his LAPD training officer for help in getting into a reintegration program after return from combat deployment in Iraq. Dorner's mental state in the LAPD, like Adam Lanza's in Sandy Hook, James Holmes's in the University of Colorado's neuroscience department, and Wade Page's in Milwaukee, deteriorated until they became self-destructive and killed innocent people.

With talking heads in cable television's "punditorium" pushing grand solutions across the desks of news anchors—ban extended ammunition clips, ban assault weapons, mandate universal background checks for firearms purchases, close gun show and private sale loopholes, and create programs to help the mentally ill—we have yet to hear the most obvious approach we can take without having to negotiate with the NRA over gun control: identify the violently dangerous people so that we can head off as much homicidal and suicidal violence as possible. How do we that? First, we get our collective brains around the problem and then look at ways we can identify potentially dangerous individuals and figure out how to intervene in their lives to prevent violence. Is this asking too much? Not if we start by evaluating major mass murder/suicide perpetrators and determining how and where caregivers, loved ones, friends, or even the medical or judicial establishments could have intervened in their lives to prevent them from going over the edge.

The massacre of twenty small children at Sandy Hook Elementary School finally breached the public's consciousness to the point where President Obama publicly declared enough was enough, a commission would be established to study the epidemic of spree shootings in this country, and this commission would not merely be a political diversion to assuage public anger but a real problem-solving commission to make policy recommendations. It was not a meeting to kick the can down the road until another, even worse incident occurred. The president had already addressed the survivors and their families at McKale Center at the University of Arizona after recently suspended Pima Community College student Jared Loughner had opened fire at a Safeway parking lot in Tucson. Then, the first lady personally met with surviving victims and their families of the Sikh temple massacre in Oak Ridge, Wisconsin. The memorial for families of the deceased in Newtown, Connecticut, affected the president as personally as it would any parent of school-aged children. The memorial also provided a window of opportunity to defy the bureaucratic constituencies and Washington, DC, lobbyists resisting change to any of the putative causes of our epidemic of spree shootings and senseless mass murders, for which the Sandy

Hook massacre was the nadir in a seeming plunge of America's social descent into evil. President Obama had not recovered from the shock of Sandy Hook before he had to memorialize the dead and injured in Boston.

Was all this the result of lax gun control and easy access to assault rifles and homemade improvised explosive devices? Was it constant exposure of children and young adults to violent media from Hollywood, the television industry, or, now, the flourishing gaming industry? And even as the smoke settled after the shooting, debunkers, deniers, and right-wing fanatics were busily trying to argue that the entire Sandy Hook incident was merely staged, a false-flag operation to enable the president to confiscate weapons from gun owners so as to subvert the Second Amendment and impose a European-style socialism upon America, which Alex Jones on InfoWars has consistently argued.[17] And we wonder about the collective sanity of our population? Now Congress must ask cabinet officials and their captains and lieutenants what Tamerlan Tsarnaev was doing in this country. How did he obtain a green card, and what was learned about his past criminal record when his younger brother received a green card in 2012? Tamerlan's application for citizenship was in process, but he was denied admission to UMass/Dartmouth, where his younger brother was matriculating. Procedures for obtaining a green card on visa from Kyrgyzstan take many years. Some official must have bent the rules for the elder Tsarnaev, despite the danger he posed within immigration channels. Were the Boston police ever informed of this clear and present danger? More significantly, are we going to find another breakdown of bureaucratic and interagency communications in the event that Boston's FBI special agent was never informed of the Tsarnaev family and the agency's interview of Tamerlan Tsarnaev based on Russian intelligence tips? Questions

---

[17] "Sandy Hook Was a Total False Flag." Before It's News, March 28 2013. http://before-itsnews.com/conspiracy-theories/2013/03/sandy-hook-was-a-total-false-flag-2449694.html.

arose after the 9/11 investigation: How did the restructuring of our national security services help agents in the field connect the dots? Be assured: officials involved in the investigation of the Brothers Tsarnaev are preparing their answers for what promises to be an inquisitive and angry US Congress.

What path can we take to find a solution, even if that solution saves only a few lives? We begin by explaining why mental illness is a disease with a biological basis, just like any other illness, and how genetics interact with environment and upbringing in a society that not only misunderstands mental illness but stigmatizes it, as if the sick people are morally at fault. We must remove this stigma if we want to save lives.

Chapter 2

Genes and Mental Illness

In the wake of the horrors of Boston; Newtown, Connecticut; Aurora, Colorado; Tucson, Arizona; and Virginia Tech, people ask, "What is wrong with society?" They wonder aloud while watching a horrible event play graphically on cable news, "What is wrong with these few people who can shock the world with such cold-blooded violence against the innocent victims, whether bystanders at a sporting event, helpless first graders, fellow students, or movie-goers?" Anybody might ask whether it is in these mass killers' genes or upbringing, or whether they are simply rare mutants. The answer is all of the above.

We know that the best-informed categorization of mental illness and naming of the hundreds of apparently different disorders are based on clinical signs and a patient's history. For example, to diagnose schizophrenia, at least delusions and hallucinations or two or more other profoundly aberrant symptoms must be present for a significant portion of time during a one-month period. If the condition has been successfully in the past, the period may be shorter, and a course of such profound abnormality must continue for at least six months. These six months must include at least one month of symptoms that include most serious signs and effects, such as hallucinations and delusions, but during the period, the patient may also exhibit prodromal or residual symptoms, such as early or late social withdrawal. This is how schizophrenia is diagnosed. But what about the genetic component?

In some serious diseases of the brain, abnormal genes that predict severe neurological disease can be discovered. In Huntington's chorea, for example, genetic testing can find a gene that will predict an otherwise normal person to become seriously disabled with movement disorders similar to those associated with cerebral palsy and develop an extremely high risk of death by suicide. Is suicide the patient's response to this disease's horrible disability, or is there such a thing as a "suicide gene"?

We don't know precisely, but in the cases of mass murder, and more particularly, suicidal mass murder like that of Adam Lanza, the question of the role of genetics in causation of presumed psychotic mass homicide and suicide is far more complex and poorly understood. However, the evidence of a determinant role in causing such psychotic mass homicide and suicide or what can be called extreme "mental states of unremitting human destructiveness" is too strong to deny. Personalized medicine means identification of a patient's genetic abnormality to select effective first-line treatment. For example, advances in oncology help in predicting what chemotherapy will most likely work on a patient. For a psychotic patient meeting the criteria of schizophrenia, however, there is no such one-to-one genetic match to select the best first-line treatment.

Considering the lack of a one-to-one genetic match for serious mental illness, specifically paranoid schizophrenia, which we have shown to be the culprit in most suicidal mass murders from Cho at Virginia Tech to Lanza at Sandy Hook, personalized medicine is not yet here. However, research promises to make it available in time, perhaps decades from now. How do we know? McGiffin demonstrated successively stronger heritable influences in autism, hyperactivity, mood disorders, and schizophrenia than in personality traits or reading disability, but stronger influences do not mean causation, as they do in Huntington's chorea. Yet this research shows that most risk for psychiatric illness is inherited and genes do identify risk in individuals for psychiatric illness. But they do not correlate one-to-one with emergence of a diagnosable disorder that meets the criteria of schizophrenia as defined by the fourth edition of the *Diagnostic and Statistical Manual of Mental Disorders* (*DSM-IV*).

Genes, as National Institute of Mental Health psychiatric geneticist Dr. Daniel Weinberger states, "transcend phenomenological diagnosis," whereas genes correlate far better with microscopic examination of breast tissue, whether cancerous or not. Genes, Dr. Weinberger states, affect the mechanisms within brain cells that can identify biological pathways in the brain most sensitive to environmental stress. Thus, genes can identify people at risk for inheriting serious mental illness, like schizophrenia. Psychiatric genetics promises more valid diagnostics, when markers for certain genes associated with serious mental illness can be discovered before the disease progresses to serious disability, an irreversible chronic state, violence, or death by suicide.

Schizophrenic patients are among those with the highest risk for completed suicides when discharged after their first hospitalization. Because the first episode comes in early adulthood, often when the patient is transitioning from home to college, it is imperative we get better at identifying at-risk young people when they present to clinicians with even subtle changes in behavior or worsening interpersonal relatedness and social withdrawal, as was the case with Adam Lanza. Generally, if you look at a patient like Adam Lanza, who is clearly manifesting suicidal ideations, whether or not that person has signs meeting criteria for *DSM-IV* schizophrenia, it is possible to treat that person aggressively with modern antipsychotic medications and tell the parents that you do not want to wait to get the full criteria for a diagnosis. With a family history of serious mental illness in blood relatives—particularly one where an antipsychotic worked well—you would be practicing preventive psychiatry, practicing it for the patient, of course, but also benefitting those with whom the patient might come into contact.

Anyone might argue that there is a risk of wrongly prescribing powerful psychotropic medications in such young people, but we know that the longer the duration of untreated psychosis, the worse the prognosis. The highest-risk patients for violence are those who hear voices and have paranoid delusions of having adversaries in the world who really do not exist or at least are not a threat to them. Such young patients, although they hear voices and think hostile thoughts, in many cases will not admit this when asked. Therefore, the risk of waiting for full-blown psychosis before treating is far higher than treating and closely monitoring for side effects. It is impressive how patients who are simply becoming peculiar or irritable at home and dropping out of school can not only tolerate high doses of antipsychotic medication but get better on that medication. Unfortunately, the diagnosis is too often in the treatment.

We all know that it would be a world-changer to be able to get a swab from a patient's cheek and find a specific genetic marker for schizophrenia. But that is not going to happen today. Although there are numerous candidate genes, none has enough evidence in and of itself to proceed with treatment, which we know to have risks like any medication does. Suffice it to say, psychiatry badly needs the same personalized medicine, in the form of a genetic marker, as oncology already has for certain cancers. And when such a marker is identified, as it is in Huntington's chorea, we get to know how the brain cells of our patients are producing the wrong chemicals from inherited, schizogenic DNA.

At the very least such a genetic test would place approximately 1 percent of young adults at risk for fulminating psychosis, too often terminating in violence with imprisonment, suicide, or both murder and suicide, including mass murder. Finally, the promise of identifying the diabolical pathways in the brain, to a large part influenced by aberrant DNA producing the wrong neurotransmitting chemicals or cell receptor sites for them, can lead to discovery of better treatments, now too serendipitous. We only know in theory how DNA works for the good or the bad in brains. We need to know in fact, more than in theory, how it works to reduce such horrendously lethal outcomes as the suicidal mass murder at Sandy Hook Elementary School.

At present, what do we know? "A gene is said to be associated with a trait, i.e., blue eyes, or illness when a variant in the gene is found with increased frequency in a population with the trait or illness." So far the strength of evidence in mentally ill populations for such susceptibility genes is not robust enough for celebrating a discovery because most psychiatric disorders are polygenic, influenced by more than one gene, as in the simple one-to-one model of Huntington's chorea. In this disease, if you got the gene, you get the disease basically guaranteed full-blown, with likelihood of death by suicide. Huntington's chorea, however, is a disease for which neurologists are unlikely to miss the diagnosis when it presents. Therefore, the abnormal gene inherited through the family "encodes for the disease."

Psychiatric genetics, however, is not an easy task to practice in conditions other than Huntington's chorea. Most likely, many genes encode for cellular functions in the brain that place the person at risk for diabolical learning in his neurocircuitry. For example, how does a young man like James Holmes actually learn to be a diabolically evil person? It was as if Holmes had entered another dimension, although his actions were taking place in Aurora, Colorado. The actions were there, but his brain was not because his brain's neurocircuity was tuned for diabolically learning an entire identity that took him over. Tragically, this was a most monstrous evil identity that obliterated

41

any boundary between illusion (the Batman movie) and reality (his monstrous intrusion into the dramatic production itself).

Weinberger theorizes that multiple susceptibility sequences of genes—or alleles—inherited from biological parents, each with small effect in and of themselves, cause subtle molecular abnormalities in cells of certain regions of the brain that result in diabolical learning within an information processing system of neurotransmission. This regionalized diabolical learning within the brain's neurocircuitry then causes complex functional interactions and emergent behavioral phenomena popularly described today as that of the "pseudocommando": Cho at Virginia Tech, Holmes at Aurora, Breivik in Norway, and Lanza in Newtown. Becoming an avatar pseudocommando is as easily learned on the Internet as making a bomb from fertilizer to plant at a sporting event. This means that if the brain is genetically vulnerable to such diabolical learning of such monstrous identities as Batman or Commander of the Knights of Templar, this genetic encoding is most likely far more complex than the straight line from genotype—the patient's alleles with a sequence of DNA in the genes—to those genes' expression, for example, as a diabetes type I disease.

Penetration of the genetic matrix presumably determining risk for schizophrenia is dependent on factors other than inherited bad DNA from one or both parents. Because the cognitive capability tested by both EEGs and functional MRI imaging in the frontal lobes of random controls screened for both the disease and its inheritance, for example, is robustly silent compared with both patients with schizophrenia and their siblings without the disease, both of whom signal abnormality, even if subtle. So it is apparent that we are talking about risk with genetics in serious mental illness, rather than direct cause and effect. Most likely, environmental stress or other factors, such as substance abuse, are necessary to bring out what we diagnose from the *DSM-IV* as schizophrenia and other serious mental illnesses.

One profound example of such a genetic variant is the gene for metabolizing one specific neurotransmitter chemical in the brain, the

COMT gene. Biotechnologically engineered variations in this gene predictably weigh a mouse toward being less sensitive to stress with higher pain threshold but with poorer memory and control of attention or the very opposite on all these measurable psychological factors. A naturally occurring variant in this COMT gene results in a tenfold increase of an adolescent marijuana user becoming manifestly psychotic by age twenty-six. Here is one smoking gun—but an isolated one— evidencing inheritable risk in young adults for psychosis and, perhaps, the collapse in personal ego boundaries resulting in the rare apocalyptic suicidal violence recently seen from Tucson to Oslo to Aurora and on to Newtown. If Loughner, Breivik, Holmes, and Lanza were using significant amounts of cannabis during adolescence and had a specific variant of their COMT gene, they were more likely than not at high risk for losing their ego boundaries, knowledge of self-identity, hearing voices and experiencing delusions, whether paranoid like Breivik's or grandiose and apocalyptic like those of Holmes, Lanza, and Loughner.

Conversely, gene variants are demonstrated to alter neural structure in regions of the brain necessary for both storage of memories and experiencing emotion, but these variants can actually cancel out their destructive effects on brain function in extremely complex lineary actions and interactions. So genes affect behavior by influencing brain development and function. Genetic association at the level of behavior is context-dependent in terms of brain function. There are not natively "good" or "bad" alleles, variants of genes located along specific spots on specific chromosome that affect brain function. It is like an orchestra with different instruments playing off the same symphonic text. They either all play together in tune, mute each other to silence a bad sound, or deteriorate into dissonant noise. So it is as well with genetic interactions, whose complexities we can barely detect through the noise of serious mental illness or the healthy tuned mind as well.

As we see in the variant COMT adolescent cannabis user, environment is critically important, as is developmental chronology of age. Understanding how this symphony either harmonizes in a multitude of healthy instrumental voices or decomposes into noise and a cacophony of intolerable behavioral output is both the daunting challenges of understanding the decomposing of Adam Lanza into apocalyptic violence or of using personalized medicine for serious mental illness.

Here are some promising examples for such personalized medicine: We know that variants of the COMT gene affect both efficiency of thinking in our frontal lobes and our emotional regulation. Think how important that is for a young adult, whose neurons are still changing course in their brains while they are isolated in solitary engagement with morbid, violent video games. Parents therefore need to monitor their children's play. It was not healthy for Lanza to be alone for so long in his room with a large-screen video monitor accessing the Internet—the same with Cho, Breivik, and Holmes. They did not act out what they witnessed. They became what they witnessed. The stage became their worlds. They translated themselves into their avatars to operate in the real world—very dangerous Breivk became a lethal terrorist; Holmes a diabolical movie character; and Lanza, well-trained from playing *School Shooter*.

Where will genes take us? According to Weinberger, they promise hope for a resolution of our major deficiency in psychiatry; that is, the lack of diagnostic validity that predicts outcomes with or without certain clinical interventions. We already have a hint of what is to come: powerful antipsychotic medication, such as clozapine, which has differential effects on attention and verbal fluency in schizophrenic patients depending on the type of COMT gene they inherited.

Large and well-controlled studies demonstrate conclusively that genes do alter response, for better or worse, to psychotropic medications such as citalopam in depression, lithium in manic depressive illnesses, and clozapine. Part of the reason probably lies in the power of COMT genetic influence on the efficiency of the frontal lobe, with so central a role in thinking and comprehending signals from both the outside and inside. And, in schizophrenia, one of the major deficits in neural processing is the failure of the brain to differentiate signals coming from the inside—fantasy—and from the outside—someone walking past you and talking. Is he talking to you, or are you talking to yourself and think he's talking to you? How many innocent people get shoved into subway trains by psychotic lurkers on a platform because of this signaling chaos in the psychotic brain?

We know that genes qua genes do not cause specific *DSM-IV* mental illnesses but rather adversely affect or protect from diabolical learning in neurocircuitry. For example, we know they affect passage potassium in brain cell receptor sites, and we know that such potassium passage is necessary for normal brain cell function. But how can we use such knowledge to discover medications that alter cellular potassium passage in genetically affected people either to protect them from serious mental illness or to clear their symptoms when they fall ill? We are far from that promised land, but we see it.

Chapter 3

Sandy Hook: Identifying Dangerous Aspects of Strange Behavior

Nancy Lanza was worried about her son's increasingly strange behaviors. According to the recently released state attorney's report on the Sandy Hook shootings.[18] Adam was so closeted that he only communicated with his mother via email even though they were living in the same house. Adam had shunned social interaction, locked himself in his second-floor computer room with windows covered with black trash bags, and spent more hours than Nancy might have been willing to count immersed in violent online computer games such as *World of Warcraft* as an avatar character that might be called a "pseudo

---

[18] Sedensky, III, Stephen J. "Report of the State's Attorney for the Judicial District of Danbury on the Shootings at Sandy Hook Elementary School and 36 Yogananda Street, Newtown, Connecticut on December 14, 2012." ONLINE. 2013. Office of the State's Attorney Judicial District of Danbury. http://www.ct.gov/csao/lib/csao/Sandy_Hook_Final_Report.pdf (accessed December 11, 2013).

commando" and with an astonishing training simulator called *School Shooter*. But to the outside world, Nancy exhibited a brave face, shouldering the burden of an adult son whom his former schoolmates had referred to as "strange." Nancy herself was social, interacting with friends and neighbors and emailing old friends from New Hampshire, even while she tried to cope with the burden of a single mom caring for her strange-acting, hermit-like, noncommunicative son, even as she sought to find schools or institutions that could help him.

As worried as Nancy Lanza might have been, she didn't appear to have taken any steps to keep her personal firearms inaccessible to her son. Nancy was her son's first victim, shot multiple times with her own Savage Mark II .22 caliber rifle, a firearm that she had trained her son to use when she took him shooting on a New Hampshire farm when he was still very young. Had she acted irresponsibly in trying to bond with Adam to relieve whatever behavioral peculiarities she observed in his socially isolated life? To see what insights we can gain from Adam's behavior and what his mother tried to do to help him in her own way, we need to start with whatever anecdotal information we can glean, including conflicting reports from friends of the Lanzas that Adam had been relentlessly bullied as an elementary schooler at Sandy Hook to convincing denials by school staff committed to protecting him from bullying. Then we need to evaluate the nature of Adam's strange behavior to see what warning signs of dangerousness could have been picked up on to head off his psychotic explosion.

What we call "strange behavior" is an evidence-based clinical presentation right off the emergency room protocol rack and programmed into a checklist for noting strange behavior, verbal or nonverbal behavior, for clinicians to assess. The clinical presentation of strange behavior, which did occur with many local clinicians and at Sandy Hook: Identifying Dangerous Aspects of Strange Behavior Yale Child Development Center, particularly as it evolves into a behavioral emergency, is one of the clearest warning signs (short of perpetrating a violent act) that something psychologically dysfunctional is brewing beneath the surface tension of an individual's persona. Starting with strange behavior, we can then look for the anecdotal evidence that highlights certain aspects of a person's strange behavior to point us in a direction that a skilled clinician might take when making a preliminary diagnosis and, if necessary, triage for a patient.

In the case of Adam Lanza's strange behavior, we must assume, again anecdotally, but also based on access to high-end health-care facilities in Connecticut, that he might have had some recent clinical encounter with a professional, allegedly a psychiatrist. More probable than not, it is apparent that Adam Lanza was a very withdrawn, always socially awkward child confronted with separation and individuation challenges that he was psychologically incapable of overcoming even though, according to the state attorney's report, he was memorializing his homicidal ideations in writing. He was hermit-like when it came to human interaction because he felt safe channeling any need for communication through a digital device that empowered him through violent role-playing as if it were an objectification of his hostility and seething anger. From reports of family friends and school acquaintances, it seems that Nancy had tried over and over again to get Adam acclimated to social institutions. He attended Sandy Hook Elementary School into the fifth or sixth grade. But according to a *Salon* article,[19] Adam was bullied at school—bullying and abuse so severe that Nancy Lanza contemplated suing the school board that oversaw Sandy Hook Elementary. Adam would come home from school, an unnamed relative who spoke to the *New York Daily News* said, and sit sullenly while his mother tried to coax his problem out of him.[20] He would not respond and would withdraw further and further into himself as he waited for a

[19] McDonough, Kate. "Adam Lanza Was Bullied While He Attended Sandy Hook Elementary, Family Member Says." Salon, April 14, 2013. http://www.salon.com/2013/04/14/adam_lanza_was_bullied_while_he_attended_sandy_hook_elementary_family_member_says/.
[20] Lysiak, Matthew, and Rich Shapiro. "EXCLUSIVE: Adam Lanza's Murder Spree at Sandy Hook May Have Been 'Act of Revenge.'" *New York Daily News*, April 6, 2013. http://www.nydailynews.com/news/national/lanza-article-1.1309766.

kind of digital revenge on his targets in the world of video gaming. He must have wondered why he had to endure the abuse, likely unaware of how provocative his movement through school halls was to peers, as he clutched his computer with his back to the lockers lining the walls. Perhaps the memories of what he endured over the years stayed with him until the day he shot his mother and went on his rampage.

Abuse begets violence. We have seen that situation too many times to ignore the cause and effect. Dr. Elliot Aronson, a social psychologist, developed an exercise called "the jigsaw classroom," in which elementary students are divided into racially diverse groups to solve problems and present those solutions to the rest of the class.[21] Dr. Aronson examined the hierarchy of school and classroom cliques and the way aggression and bullying trickle down from the children at the top of the hierarchy of popularity to those in lower echelons. It is like a pyramid of cliques on a popularity scale. Dr. Aronson found that when children at the top of the pyramid make fun of children at the lower levels of the pyramid, children at the middle levels of the pyramid also make fun of those at the lowest levels because they want to identify with the children at the top. Thus, bullying, abuse, and insults tend to trickle down, sometimes having a snowball effect, so the object of scorn is picked on not just by a small clique, but by a lot of students all the way down the ladder of popularity. We believe this is what Adam Lanza experienced at Sandy Hook, and that experience lingered in his memory and stayed with him as he decomposed mentally.

After Sandy Hook, Adam attended the local middle school and even spent a year in high school. But between each school, Nancy would find she had to pull him out of classes at each school because of his fears of people. At least one of his former teachers revealed to the *Hartford Courant* that the challenge of middle school, the

---

[21] Aronson, Elliot. Jigsaw Classroom, "Jigsaw in 10 Easy Steps." http://www.jigsaw.org/steps.htm (accessed December 11, 2013).

departmentalization of classes rather than classes taught by a single teacher, was especially threatening to Adam because he shunned crowds, noise, and the press of other people.[22] What threatened Adam most in middle school probably posed an even bigger threat in high school as he, again, according to anecdotal reports from acquaintances and former teachers, seemed to shrink away from throngs of students in the corridors as classes changed, hugging the wall and hugging his computer so he would not be touched. Touching. Personal physical contact. The acceptance of a momentary trespass of personal boundaries. These are things that most people who have no boundary issues acquiesce to, even if they grudgingly endure a back slap or an arm squeeze. But not Adam.

One of the warnings that Nancy gave to friends was never to touch Adam because it unnerved him in ways that would set back any attempts she was making to integrate him into normal social relationships. Even when teachers tried to get Adam to integrate into group activities, he shied away. If they tried too hard, Adam would completely withdraw. Was this Asperger's syndrome, a high-functioning autistic behavioral issue, or was this far worse?

Nancy Lanza might have been overwhelmed by the challenge of dealing with her son as he retreated deeper and deeper into the digital cave in which he lived. Instead of following the evidence-based protocols for strange behavior, the mother, with or without professional advice, left him in the house, surrounded by a closet full of guns, while she took a vacation, possibly to find a residential facility for him. After all, Adam was an adult, although his social skills were severely impaired.

How did Nancy Lanza try to reach her son or find a way to communicate with him in a way that she thought might have been nonverbal but nevertheless successful? Perhaps she tried to reach

---

[22] Griffin, Alaine, and Josh Kovner. "Courant/FRONTLINE Investigation: Raising Adam Lanza." *Hartford Courant*, February 17, 2013. http://articles.courant.com/2013-02-17/news/hc-raising-adam-lanza-20130217_1_nancy-lanza-raising-adam-lanza-new-school.

him by exposing him to weapons, and in some misguided way, to help him mature as an individual or bond with him over her fascination with weapons. Or could it have been that she was unconsciously planning for her and Adam to die together, which they ultimately did? Was Nancy Lanza so addled that she had fallen into a state of unremitting hopelessness over her son's strange and clearly psychotic behavior for which she could see no chance of remedy? Was her only way out (again, unconsciously) to create her own suicidal assassin, a suicide by proxy to create a suicide pact?

What we do know from the attorney general's report was that Adam dictatated exactly how the house should be run, how it should be cleaned and when, how holidays should not be celebrated, and precisely how meals should be served and on what dishes. Nancy could not work because she had become a personal servant to her son's mental illness and lived to satisfy his needs. She sacrificed her own personal freedom by tending to her son and his deteriorating mental condition while he stayed locked into his computer room, where he sent his avatar into a digital world of violence, bloodshed, and gore.

One of Adam's high school teachers was perplexed by the reason why Nancy removed her son from school, because he was successfully integrating into the computer club. A photograph in the high school yearbook shows him, seemingly at ease, in the group of what might be considered the school's "geek team," a likely powerhouse of future computer engineering talent. Adam Lanza was as good with computers as anyone in the group.

Sandy Hook schools had gone to some efforts to help Adam. He had a school psychologist assigned to him to prevent bullying. The advisor who integrated him into the techie group worked hard to do so.[23] Lanza's school district was not blind to his needs and did a lot to help him adapt socially, but either Nancy had to have it her way

[23] Berger, Joseph, and Marc Santora. "Chilling Look at Newtown Killer, But No 'Why.'" *New York Times*, March 26, 2013. http://www.nytimes.com/2013/11/26/nyregion/sandy-hook-shooting-investigation-ends-with-motive-still-unknown.html?_r=0.

or no way, or the schools were in over their heads with this student from day one. We will never know because the mother and son's secrets of Sandy Hook were taken to the grave that horrific day during the 2012 Christmas holiday season.

This scenario is somewhat similar to the case of Norway's mass murderer Anders Breivik, who was all but disowned by his father for minor problems in the community that were damaging to his career. Breivik was left to an allegedly unstable mother and computer games. Both Breivik and Lanza were fascinated by the military but clearly unfit for military service. In fact, Breivik was found unfit for duty in the Norwegian military. Thus, both absorbed themselves in "aggressor" or single-shooter warrior games where they could exorcise their violent demons within a safe, framed-out digital world, a world in which the neurological pathways establishing the brain-to-muscle response of habit creation enabled them to become self-styled pseudo-commandos like Aurora, Colorado's James Holmes and embrace blood-soaked violence as their own revenge against the world.

The bare details of the Sandy Hook case are that on December 14, 2012, at about 9:30 a.m., Lanza, an awkward twenty-year-old, whose reclusive behavior was well-known among his peers and who had been reportedly diagnosed with developmental disability without serious mental illness, shot and killed his mother, Nancy Lanza, with her own gun in her bedroom. The official state attorney's report did not ascribe any motive to this shooting, leaving us to speculate what might have happened to precipitate the homicide. We know from the official report that on December 10, 2012, Nancy had told her friend, on the day she left for a three-day trip to New Hampshire, leaving her son alone in the house, that Adam had "badly" bumped his head, which bled, but he was apparently not treated medically for the injury. This raises a host of possibilities, including a concussive injury, head-banging with rage, a psychological trauma in which Adam felt that his mother had abandoned him, and the possibility that Adam's being injured was a precipitating event that set him into violent motion. Nancy Lanza was a gun enthusiast who had often taken her son to an indoor shooting range and trained him to handle weapons. This, too, is interesting because, according to the official report, Adam had told a friend that his mother was not rational and they had a "strained" relationship. After Adam shot his mother in the head four times, leaving her pajama-clad body still in bed, he drove to Sandy Hook Elementary School, and broke into the school by using his mother's Bushmaster semiautomatic rifle to shoot his way through a glass door in the front of the school. Lanza wore black camouflage-type regalia under a utility vest where he kept extra ammunition clips. He was also wearing earplugs, possibly because his mother had trained him at the indoor shooting range where earplugs were mandatory.

He made his way to a first-grade classroom. The front door had been locked for security, but the glass shattered from the impact of the bullets, and the noise alerted the school principal and members of the faculty that someone had broken in. The sound of gunshots also played over the school intercom system, which was broadcasting morning announcements.

The sound of broken glass and gunshots prompted Sandy Hook school principal Dawn Hochsprung and school psychologist Mary Sherlach to leave their meeting with other faculty members and rush toward the sound. They encountered Lanza in a corridor, confronted him, and tried to prevent him from entering any classrooms. Lanza shot and killed them both and moved into the school. By the time the gunshots that killed the school principal and school psychologist rang out in the hallway, they also played over the school intercom, which was still turned on and had an open microphone. At least one of the elementary school children heard gunshots and at least one teacher, also hearing the shots, ushered her class into a closet for refuge. As more gunshots rang out, Lanza made his way toward a first-grade classroom, where he opened fire and killed teacher Lauren Rousseau before he turned his weapon on the children.

Only one child survived the onslaught in the first-grade classroom by burying herself amidst the falling bodies and remaining motionless until Lanza left the room. Then she ran out of the building. Lanza then went to the next first-grade classroom, where teacher Victoria Soto had hid her students in a closet. When Lanza burst in, looking for potential victims, Soto told him that all her children had gone to the auditorium. Tragically, though, some of the children tried to escape and ran out of the closet, and Lanza trained his Bushmaster on them just as Soto stepped forward to protect them. Lanza shot her, shot the children, and left the room. The remaining children, who had not tried to run for safety, escaped the room and managed to find safety in a residence adjacent to the school.

Within minutes after the shooting began, teachers in other classrooms and offices began hiding their students, sending them into closets, cupboards, and storage areas as Lanza passed through the halls looking for victims. Teachers cautioned any children they could find in the hallways or in classrooms to hide, remain silent, and stay in hiding until rescuers came to lead them to safety. Some children stayed in hiding for more than an hour even though the entire rampage lasted no longer than ten minutes.

Lanza reloaded frequently, firing only half of the rounds from his thirty-round clips, which was interesting because that was how the shooters operated their weapons in the war games he was playing. He spent the most time in the two first-grade classrooms closest to the entrance of the school where he had shot through the glass doors. When two police officers found Lanza, he was already dead from a self-inflicted gunshot wound from his handgun. Ironically, under Connecticut law, twenty-year-old Lanza was old enough to keep and carry his mother's Bushmaster rifle and the shotgun police found in his car, but his possession of the handgun he used to kill himself was illegal because he was under twenty-one.

In the aftermath of the shootings, as they would do with any homicide, police investigators looked for clues to a motive for the crime: the shooter's rationale—however irrational that may be—for committing the crime. In this case, the police search of the Lanza home, where they discovered Nancy's body in the bedroom, proved to be frustrating because when they seized Adam Lanza's computer, they discovered he had purposely damaged his hard drive so that any information that might have been retrievable was lost.

Contrary to earlier reports that Lanza had no association with Sandy Hook Elementary, he had indeed been a student there before he attended Newtown's St. Rose of Lima School, and then Newtown High School. Although he was an honor student, Lanza was unhappy in the public school system, so his mother began to home-school him even while he attended Newtown High School, according to the attorney general's report. Lanza graduated from Newtown High School in 2009, and, considered to be a child prodigy, he attended college at Western Connecticut State University for about a year when he was sixteen, but he did not complete any degree. By the time he was twenty years old, he was living at home with his mother and had all but confined himself to his large, isolated basement den, locked into the digital world of games on his computer without any apparent structure or parental supervision.

Adam's reclusive attitude at home and his hermit-like behavior profoundly extended to how he behaved through his years in the public school system. As reported in the *Hartford Courant's* article,[24] Lanza family acquaintances said that Lanza was socially awkward, kept to himself, was "strange," did not want to interact with others, physically shied away from even the least physical contact, and seemed not to have any close friends. Friends of Nancy Lanza said that she told them that Adam had been diagnosed with Asperger's syndrome and that he had high-functioning autism. Although professionals may argue that neither one of these conditions should be categorized as a mental illness

---

[24] Griffin, Alaine, and Josh Kovner. "Courant/FRONTLINE Investigation: Raising Adam Lanza." *Hartford Courant*, February 17, 2013. http://articles.courant.com/2013-02-17/news/hc-raising-adam-lanza-20130217_1_nancy-lanza-raising-adam-lanza-new-school.

because they are actually brain development conditions, we can safely speculate that Adam was either decompensating within an autism spectrum disorder and moving into psychosis or unspecified illness, or we can speculate that he was emerging into full-blown schizophrenia. What is absolutely clear, both from descriptions of Lanza by his friends and from what the police have found in their ongoing investigation of the Newtown shootings, was that Lanza had hundreds, if not more than one thousand, violent video games. While hiding himself away from people and sequestering himself inside the digital world of his computer, Adam was exorcising the demons that besieged him as he practiced wielding weapons, shooting, and dispatching those who popped up to take him out of the game. How can that translate, given Adam's emotional state, into the crimes he committed at Sandy Hook Elementary?

One answer appears in the state attorney general's report, where, pursuant to a search warrant executed at the Lanza residence on Yogananda Street in Newtown, during online gamer chat sessions, an individual who logged on to the website 4Chan posted, "'I'm going to kill myself on Friday and it will make the news. be watching at 9:00 am.' When another anonymous individual asked, 'Where at?' The first individual responded, 'I live in Connecticut, that's as much as I'll say.'"[25] In addition, the report says, "On 12/14/12, a concerned individual in Texas contacted the Hartford Police Department and reported that her son was playing a video game named 'Call of Duty' approximately 20 hours ago. She continued that a gamer with the screen name [RaWr]i<3EmoGirls (hereinafter "User") stated, 'next week or very soon there maybe a shooting at my school and other schools so if i die remember me plz if I don't get on for 3-5 not

---

[25] Sedensky, III, Stephen J. "Report of the State's Attorney for the Judicial District of Danbury on the Shootings at Sandy Hook Elementary School and 36 Yogananda Street, Newtown, Connecticut on December 14, 2012." ONLINE. 2013. Office of the State's Attorney Judicial District of Danbury. http://www.ct.gov/csao/lib/csao/Sandy_Hook_Final_Report.pdf (accessed December 11, 2013).

including weeks that means i died and im being 100 percent serious.' The User then stated, 'something might go bad tomorrow this could possibly be my last moments alive.' Finally, User stated, 'as far as I know theres a list of ppl that are gunna get shot-. I hope I aint on it.'"

These are quite likely the last words of Adam Lanza as he sunk into his final delusion, amalgamating his real world, such as it was, with the world of online gaming chat.

The state attorney general's report tracked Adam's decomposing mental state from his 2002 to 2003 school years on, according to witnesses and family acquaintences:

1. In the 2002 to 2003 school year, when the shooter was in the fifth grade, he was quiet and very bright, and had good ideas regarding creative writing. He wouldn't necessarily engage in conversation, but wouldn't ignore one. There was no recollection of him being bullied or teased.

2. The fifth grade was also the year that, related to a class project, the shooter produced the *Big Book of Granny,* in which the main character has a gun in her cane and shoots people. The story includes violence against children. There is no indication this was ever handed in to the school.

3. In the fifth grade the shooter indicated that he did not like sports, did not think highly of himself, and believed that everyone else in the world deserved more than he did.

4. In intermediate school from 2002 to 2004, he was a quiet, shy boy who participated in class and listened. He did not show enthusiasm, extreme happiness, or extreme sadness. He was neutral.

5. In the fifth and sixth grades from 2003 to 2004, the shooter participated in concerts at school. He was not remembered by the teacher as having been bullied, and the shooter had at least one friend.

6. A sixth-grade teacher described the shooter as an average student with A's and B's; homework was never an issue. The shooter never made trouble or distracted others. He had friends and was friendly to others. He was a normal child with no oddities, and there were no reports of bullying or teasing.

7. In 2004, while at the intermediate school, he was described as respectful and cooperated with others.

8. One person who remembered him from the middle school never saw the shooter bullied.

9. One person who remembered him from the middle school never saw the shooter bullied.

10. In the ninth and tenth grades the shooter was reclusive, shutting himself in the bedroom and playing video games all day. In the upper classes the shooter compiled a journal instead of attending physical education.

11. In high school the shooter did not have good social skills. He did not show any signs of violence.

12. In high school the shooter would have "episodes," and his mother would be called to the school. The episodes would last about fifteen minutes each. There were no signs of violence during any of these episodes, and the shooter was more likely to be victimized than to act in violence against another.

13. In high school the shooter was not willing to talk much, was hard to communicate with, and had poor social skills. He often became withdrawn in a social environment. The shooter would have both inclusive class time and leave the class for specialized sessions.

14. At NHS the shooter was in the "Tech Club" in 2007 and 2008. He was remembered in a variety of ways, including as a quiet person who was smart. He wore the same clothing repeatedly and might not speak to you, even if you were

talking to him. He was not remembered to have been bullied or to have spoken about violence. The advisor looked out for him and tried to have him included wherever possible. He was also remembered for pulling his sleeves over his hands to touch something. He was not known to be a violent kid at all and never spoke of violence.

15. The shooter had a LAN party at his home in 2008 with Tech Club members; no firearms were seen at the shooter's home.

16. In terms of video games, the shooter liked to play *Phantasy Star Online* (a role-playing game), *Paper Mario, Luigi's Mansion,* and *Pikmin.* He also liked Japanese animated films and television, which are known to oftentimes contain sadistic eroticism.

Of specific note is Adam's project, *Big Book of Granny,* which depicts an incident of gun violence against children, an ideation of homicidal violence. This is reminiscent of Cho Seung-Hui's ideations of violence in elementary and middle school, where he wrote about violence, particularly his admiration for Columbine High School shooters Dylan Kliebold and Eric Harris.

The attorney general's report confirms that in 2005, Adam was diagnosed with ASD and presented with "significant social impairments and extreme anxiety." Nancy Lanza continually tried to help her son adjust to public school and college, but these attempts failed as he sank deeper and deeper into his reclusive state, comforted, we can only imagine, by the make-believe world of digital gaming, where he believed he could exercise more control over that created environment than he could in real life. Although mental illness can be progressive, like a form of cancer, and it can debilitate the patient's ability to separate reality from delusion and real threats from perceived threats and render a patient unable to maintain resilience in the face of life's challenges, many mentally ill individuals seek equilibrium. If they know something is dramatically wrong, they may ask or beg for help, as in the case of now-deceased ex-LAPD officer Christopher Dorner. But as long as they can avoid the stimuli that set them off, people in fragile emotional states can navigate in their own world. Adam's world involved fear of people, whom he saw as threatening, and violence inside his computer, where he destroyed those threats in a fatal fantasy. He was regularly seen at the local theater consumed and isolated in gaming, but a few months prior to the massacre, he disappeared, never to be seen in public again. Here was the opportunity; could somebody, like a well-trained security officer, ask him what he was doing in the theater while so consumed, noncommunicative, and socially isolated?

From stories about her history as reported in the *Hartford Courant,* we know that Nancy Lanza herself had emailed friends about having multiple sclerosis and was looking at a fatal disease that would compromise her ability to take care of her mentally ill son. Nancy Lanza was a New Englander, born in Salem, Massachusetts, and raised on a farm in New Hampshire, where she learned how to raise, kill, and butcher animals for food. She was more than comfortable around firearms; she would teach her son to use them. If Adam had been fearful of the outside world and retreated from it whenever his mother encouraged him to venture out beyond the confines of his room, Nancy had experienced her own issues with strangers when she, as she claimed to local police, was assaulted on the Boston Commons. At that time, she told local police that she was afraid her assailant would try to attack her at home. Perhaps that was why she owned not only a Bushmaster semiautomatic rifle, the weapon that Adam used at Sandy Hook, but also two handguns: a Glock and a SIG Sauer. We should assume, in trying to comprehend this mountain that would erupt into volcanic violence, that Nancy herself was psychologically impaired from post-rape syndrome and post-traumatic stress disorder. Nancy ventured out, but nobody was allowed into the neat New England home to experience its likely emotional emptiness—and, particularly, her son's den of iniquity.

Adam might also have been frightened about what was happening to his mother, who frequently left Adam alone in the home, and, most important, left him alone and out of contact with her for three days immediately preceding the Sandy Hook shooting. She was possibly preparing him for their ensuing separation, getting him accustomed to her periodic absence in his life. This separation broke a bond nobody was allowed to witness—a distant one of only emailing, but, nevertheless, one that was as if they were psychological Siamese twins who could not be separated without both dying in the process. Did she know that? We will never know, as the answer was deleted with her murder and the destruction of his hard drive. Allegedly a frequent traveler, Nancy went to the famed Mt. Washington Resort in Bretton Woods, New Hampshire, to seek pre-Christmas rest and relaxation from her lonely, burdened life. In her absence, home alone, Adam's fears played heavily on his progressively deranged mind. The complete disruption of his comfort zone, his having to face strangers, and his having to focus on integrating socially with people he feared might have burdened him psychologically. Nancy had not spoken to Adam during the three days she was at the resort. Thus, Adam had ample time to break into her locked gun cabinet, stir his emotional cauldron of hate and anger, and face the fear of going somewhere other than his basement den, where he had holed himself up for his short lifetime. If, as one of his acquaintances surmised, Adam was a devil worshipper, which we cannot confirm at this point, we can speculate that he was indeed a sick individual.[26]

Others said that Adam Lanza was almost ghostly in his withdrawal from other people, which his mother, reportedly, agonized over.[27] He

[26] Griffin, Alaine, and Josh Kovner. "Courant/FRONTLINE Investigation: Raising Adam Lanza." *Hartford Courant,* February 17, 2013. http://articles.courant.com/2013-02-17/news/hc-raising-adam-lanza-20130217_1_nancy-lanza-raising-adam-lanza-new-school.
[27] Ibid.

was assessed and treated by a professor of child psychiatry at Yale University Child Development Center a few years before his rampage murder, but a nurse practitioner stated that he was nonadherent with his prescribed medication. It is not clear what medication he was prescribed, or why it was prescribed, as there is no psychotropic medication for Asperger's. This same nurse stated that Nancy was resistant to supporting adherence with the medication, so it is unlikely that Adam Lanza ever took psychotropic medication in any meaningful way that could inform us of his apparently unmedicated descent into psychosis. Rumors say that Nancy even brought Adam to a psychiatrist as his behavior worsened, but investigative records to date have not revealed the scope of his clinical encounters. The facts of those encounters are known but are yet to be revealed to the public. For his part, Adam most likely did not understand why his mother was pushing him to go out into the world. A family friend told the newspapers that Nancy simply could not understand why Adam was so resistant to her attempts to get him to engage with others so that he would be a functioning adult instead of a hermit. Nancy did not understand the depths of her son's mental illness, which, by all accounts, was certainly beyond Asperger's syndrome. But in the days before Nancy left for New Hampshire, she did notice that her son's condition was deteriorating rapidly. A friend, reporting to the newspapers on what Nancy Lanza had revealed, said that Adam would not emerge from his room for hours at a time, completely absorbed in his fantasy world, as his mother looked for every opportunity to push him into the real world so that he would adapt the social skills that would enable him to survive outside of the home. When Nancy continued to express the need for her and Adam to move away from Newtown so that he could push out on his own, he was beyond resistant. Nancy complained that Adam did not understand why she wanted him to go out into the world. Nancy also tried to get Adam to accompany her on a vacation to the southern states, but he refused. He did not want to leave the home, go to college, or move into his own residence. His response to everything Nancy suggested was hostility, only worsened by Nancy's three-day absence. That might have been the fatal breach in their solitary, symbiotic relationship. Adam had cut all ties with his father, brother, and uncle years before.

Adam did have episodes that frightened his friends and his mother, even though there was never any direct threat of violence. A friend told the newspapers that Adam would start yelling at the world, as if he were a six-year-old having a tantrum, but the problem was that Adam was nineteen at the time. Though not violent, he would get mad and be unable to control his impulses. Any psychiatrist working with seriously mentally ill patients would know that this, more likely than not, meant that Adam was talking to the voices of auditory hallucinations.

There is conjecture over whether Nancy had set a deadline for Adam to leave the house. Maybe, she thought, pushing him out by a certain date would force him to confront reality, but it did not work. Adam, according to Nancy's friends, became even more distant from his mother. Conjecture that Nancy had planned to commit Adam to a psychiatric facility could not be confirmed, either; nor could the realities of her either knowing or being able to do so with Connecticut's involuntary commitment law. She was becoming desperate in her desire to find a way for Adam to provide for himself because she was committed to his well-being, even though, in our opinion, she did not know how to manifest that commitment. Another friend surmised that Nancy would have never sent her son to a psychiatric facility because she felt that she was the best provider for him; our understanding of the circumstantial evidence to date supports that speculation more than any other, unless she had given up, knowing that she could not, with her progressive neurological disease, care for him. Thus, they would die together, as they did.

As the police investigation into the Sandy Hook shootings continued throughout December 2012, Adam's father, Peter Lanza, retrieved the body of his son for interment. We have no results of any autopsy, nor do we know whether any autopsy was performed on Adam. However, from stories of prior diagnoses of Adam's physical condition, a theory emerged, stating that part of the reason for Adam's clinically established "strange behavior" was an extremely rare sensory input dysfunction, a failure to filter sensory information. In that case, Adam must have always felt overloaded by external stimuli. This dysfunction might have also been an early onset stage of childhood schizophrenia, which is a progressive disease. In this condition, Adam had to be in complete control of his environment in order to filter mental and physical sensory information in ways that allowed his brain to organize it. Thus, Adam shrank away from any interactions with others, was called "awkward" by acquaintances, and refused to leave the safety of his room and the world inside his computer, where he could deal with the bullying and abuse in the only way he could: through violence. Therefore, we believe, the threat that his mother was about to upset his entire world by moving him out of the house was so threatening to him that that, absent any remediating clinical intervention, he felt hopeless and desperate.

Another theory about Adam Lanza involves the possibility that he was so connected to his mother that he had no male identity. Both his father, Peter Lanza, and his older brother Ryan, whose ID Adam had been carrying when he committed the shooting at Sandy Hook Elementary, had not been in contact with him for more than a year, according to reports.[28] While lack of male identity is not a precipitating cause for violence in itself, it might help explain Adam's search for any form of identity in his life and what he might have found in war-themed video games such as *Call of Duty*, which was reportedly the game of choice for Norwegian mass killer Anders Breivik as well. Here, the story becomes particularly frightening, if reports about what Lanza thought about Breivik are true.

---

[28] Ibid.

In war games such as *Call of Duty*, which, according to an article in *Forbes Magazine*,[29] Breivik used to train himself for the carnage, players have said that one of the avatars in the game is called a "templar," a powerful figure that exacts revenge on all those he deems enemies. We know that Anders Breivik, whom Adam Lanza supposedly admired, boasted about being a templar and exacting revenge. This theory might help explain why Adam deteriorated into violence: he was emulating Anders Breivik and his mass murder in Norway. Breivik had his own history, as we shall see. He was a follower of Unabomber Ted Kaczynski and read parts of Kaczynski's manifesto, which Breivik tailored to his own writing.[30] Kaczynski, now in federal prison in Colorado, had written in his manifesto about how his goal was to destroy a human society that had been compromised by science. He intended to destroy, by computer technology, which had come to dominate the very civilization that invented it.

Kaczynski's nihilist dystopian views, which first appeared in 1997, seemed to have influenced successive people who believed that society had become the enemy. In an incisive June 2000 article in *The Atlantic Monthly*, Professor Alston Chase, who attended Harvard at the same time Kaczynski did, wrote about an experiment that social psychologist Henry Murray conducted at Harvard. This experiment mostly likely crushed the already at-risk Kaczynski emotionally because the purpose of the experiment was to see how much emotional abuse a subject could withstand. The experiment, which was a continuation of an experiment Murray had conducted for the Office of Strategic Services and the Navy during World

---

[29] Gaudiosi, John. "Norway Suspect Used *Call of Duty* to Train for Massacre." *Forbes Magazine*, August 24, 2011. http://www.forbes.com/sites/johngaudiosi/2011/07/24/norway-suspect-used-activisions-call-of-duty-to-train-for-massacre/.

[30] Hough, Andrew. "Norway Shooting: Anders Behring Breivik Plagiarised 'Unabomber,' the Telegraph." July 24, 2011. http://www.telegraph.co.uk/news/worldnews/europe/norway/8658269/Norway-shooting-Anders-Behring-Breivik-plagiarised-Unabomber.html.

War II, was likely sponsored by the CIA by 1958. Following a speculative line of logic, if Kaczynski's hopelessness about the fate of human society and his rage at what he saw for the future inspired his bombing attacks against those he saw as the "techies" who were responsible, and if Anders Breivik, similarly under the delusion of his dystopian vision, copycatted Kaczynski in committing his mass murders, the same murders that influenced Adam Lanza, we can see how pathogenic ideations can be transmitted from person to person. Worse, if the CIA was behind Murray's experiments at Harvard and if those experiments ultimately caused such emotional trauma in Kaczynski that, years later, while he seethed over what he saw as the collapse of humanity because of what technology had wrought, can we speculate that we are still in the throes of an intelligence operation that has been running for almost sixty years and that the children of Sandy Hook became the innocent victims? If this theory is true, it is frightening, especially in light of the history of D. Ewean Cameron's bizarre therapeutic experiments on private patients at the Allan Memorial Institute in Montreal during the 1960s. Cameron's experiments were possibly sponsored by the CIA's Project MKULTRA Program. This hypothesis is for the government that sponsored MKULTRA to disprove. It is unlikely, however, that the papers of those responsible for these brainwashing experiments of the Cold War, experiments that amounted to emotional and physical torture and were likely based on data that came out of Dr. Josef Mengele's torture of prisoners at Auschwitz, will ever be released to the public.[31]

While everyone can agree that the Sandy Hook shooting was heinous beyond any rationale, it might even be more frightening if Adam, comparing himself to Anders Brevik, had decided to compete with the insane mass killer whom Norwegian prosecutors fought

---

[31] Ruffner, Kevin C. "CIA's Support to the Nazi War Criminal Investigations." CSI Publications, April 2007. https://www.cia.gov/library/center-for-the-study-of-intelligence/csi-publications/csi-studies/studies/97unclass/naziwar.html.

hard to declare insane. They lost to Breivik, who fought for the Norwegian court to find his manifesto, which rambles incoherently through a world of paranoia beyond the imagination of European intelligence agencies, to be a product of a sane mind.

For example, from what Cho Seung-Hui had told classmates, that he was competing with Eric Harris and Dylan Klebold, the mass shooters at Columbine, we know that Cho emulated what he saw as their "sacrifice" to demonstrate that students who ostracized them would pay the ultimate penalty. Did Adam Lanza see himself in a contest with Anders Breivik, who was also so attached to his single mother that he was rumored to have been found unfit for military duty because of her, rather than himself?[32] It was also said, as in Lanza's case, that Breivik had no male identity figure. It is possible that Lanza might indeed have seen himself in a contest with Breivik because, according to police investigators, who are still compiling their final report on the case, Lanza was obsessed with Breivik's crime and specifically chose Sandy Hook Elementary School as a target because there he would find the largest numbers of helpless victims.

[32] Landsend, Merete (27 July 2011). "Skrøt av egen briljans, utsende, kjærester og penger". Dagbladet (in Norwegian) (Oslo). Retrieved 2 August 2011.

Chapter 4

James Holmes: The Dark Knight Rises

Kaitlyn Fonzi, a graduate student at University of Colorado Hospital, may never forget what happened at midnight on July 20, 2012, when the simple twist of a doorknob she knew was unlocked would have blown her to pieces and leveled her apartment building. She had gone upstairs to ask her neighbor, former graduate student James Holmes, to turn down the deep bass of his reverberating techno music. She did not really know Holmes and had vaguely recalled seeing him only a couple of times. She stopped with her hand poised above the doorknob. Her instincts saved her. She would not turn the knob because she thought the occupant was not home, even though the door was unlocked. Something seemed amiss. In case Holmes was inside, she yelled out that she was calling the cops because the driving beat was vibrating through the walls.

Fonzi called the police nonemergency number when she heard that the police were responding to a shooting in the area. They could not handle a noise complaint at the moment. She later realized the music was on a timer because it shut off at 1:00 a.m. As we now know, all hell had broken loose at the Century 16 multiplex at Town Center shopping mall in Aurora, Colorado, just moments before her phone call. But Kaitlyn Fonzi would not know that until after she dozed off when the music quieted down. Then a SWAT team appeared at her door prepared for battle.

Fonzi's elusive and unknown neighbor in that apartment, James Eagan Holmes, had just slipped out of theater 9 at the multiplex to reenter the side door of the theater showing *The Dark Knight Rises*, the newest Batman movie. He was there not to watch the movie, but to fill the role of the Joker. Screenwriter Christopher Nolan had left the Joker out of the last of the Dark Knight trilogy after the death of actor Heath Ledger, who had posthumously won an Oscar for his performance as the Joker in the 2008 production of *The Dark Knight*. The Joker role was made famous in the Batman comics, on television by Cesar Romero, and by Jack Nicholson in the first Batman feature film. Devout Batman fans had wondered whether the Joker's absence in this last part of Nolan's trilogy was out of respect for Ledger's performance. Or was the Joker's absence from this opening meant to imply his death, imprisonment in, or possible escape from the fictional Arkham Asylum, where the worst of the worst had been sent? Thus, some fans insist, despite the Joker's absence from the opening of the last of Nolan's trilogy on July 20, 2012, that the villain is still out there, lurking and planning. What is clear, however, is that James Holmes, in and out of psychiatric care even as he pursued a graduate career in neuroscience, was also an obsessed fan of the Joker character.

The shooting reported to James Holmes's neighbor Kaitlyn Fonzi was likely the answer to the question regarding the Joker's fate, as conceived by Holmes out of his paranoid delusion. About thirty minutes into watching *The Dark Knight Rises*, police say, around 1:00 a.m., Holmes reentered the theater through the exit door.[33]

---

[33] Cable News Network. "Timeline: Colorado Theater Shooting." CNN.com. http://www.cnn.com/interactive/2012/07/us/aurora.shooting/index.html (accessed December 11, 2013).

According to the *Denver Post*,[34] which has become the standard description and the timeline of the event, Holmes was dressed in black and wore a gas mask, a load-bearing vest that was not bulletproof, a ballistic helmet, bullet-resistant leggings, a throat protector, a groin protector, and tactical gloves. For an instant, the audience believed him to be the fictitious Joker and did not consider the masked figure a threat. When questioned, those fortunate to have escaped told the police they thought it was a prank by another fan. Others thought that the figure barging through the exit door was special effects for promotion of the long-awaited opening of the last of the Dark Knight trilogy. After all, Holmes's sudden appearance beside the movie screen seemed non-threateningly fan-like because he was wearing a costume, as were other audience members who had dressed up for the movie screening.

However, that was not the case. The moment suddenly became a horrific scenario after the intruder threw a smoke-emitting canister. When the audience could not see and felt their throats and skin itch and their eyes burn, they hardly had an instant for reality check. This was not theater. It was reality. The intruder in the SWAT costume began firing a twelve-gauge Express Tactical shotgun, first at the ceiling and then at the audience. The intruder followed this with rapid rounds from a Smith & Wesson M&P15 semiautomatic rifle equipped with a one-hundred-round drum magazine. The gun jammed and fired fewer than thirty rounds. The gunman's last fusillade came from a Glock 22 handgun.

During a preliminary hearing laying out the prosecution's case, spectators said they heard thirty shots in twenty-seven seconds along with the terrified shrieks of the screaming movie-goers.[35] A 911 call was placed eighteen minutes into the movie. Nick Allen of

---

[34] Minshew, Charles, and Daniel J. Schneider. "Interactive Timeline: Shooting at Aurora Theater." *The Denver Post,* July 20, 2012. http://www.denverpost.com/ci_21119904/interactive-timeline-shooting-at-aurora-theater?IADID=Search-www.denverpost.com-www.denverpost.com.

[35] *People v. Holmes,* 12 CR 1522 (2012).

The Telegraph described the chaotic 911 calls: "The calls included a harrowing four-minute plea for help from a thirteen-year-old girl, Kaylan Bailey, who told an emergency responder that two of her cousins were shot and bleeding on the cinema floor and that 'one of them is not breathing.' With screaming in the background, the hysterical teenager repeatedly said, 'I can't hear you' as the operator tried to instruct her on chest compressions." Kaylan's two cousins were hit, one of whom was Veronica Moser-Sullivan, a six-year-old, the youngest victim. Veronica's mother, Ashley Moser, was also hit and remained paralyzed. Audience members made forty-one 911 calls during the shooting. Many movie-goers could not hear the dispatcher because of the sounds of rapid-fire gunshots.

Holmes shot first toward the back of the room, probably looking to cut off escape routes with a hail of bullets. Then he aimed toward people in the aisles. This situation was murder and mayhem, with bullets passing through the wall and hitting unsuspecting people in adjacent theater 8, where *The Dark Knight Rises* also was playing. The fire alarm system blasted as managers tried to evacuate theater 8, even though some movie-goers were afraid to leave because someone had yelled that there was a gunman shooting up the lobby. Holmes, within less than a minute, had manifested the core relationship between his lifetime neuroscience studies of external reality and his internal perception. The two realities, separated in the minds of those not mentally ill, had become one. In Holmes's mind, there was no difference. Truth, objectified in a brief but constant barrage of bullets, had become stranger than fiction. No novel had to be written to fill in the absence of the Joker from this finale to the Dark Knight trilogy. The Joker was part of the movie experience after all, only not making his own chaos among the coup of fictional Gotham. One of Holmes's jailers would later comment, "He thinks he's in a movie."[36]

---

[36] Lysiak, Matthew, James Arkin, and Larry McShane. "Aurora Shooting Suspect James Holmes Jailed in Solitary: 'All the Inmates Were Talking about Killing Him.'" *New York Daily News*, July 21, 2012. http://www.nydailynews.com/news/national/aurora-shooting-suspect-james-holmes-jailed-solitary-inmates-talking-killing-article-1.1119173 (accessed December 12, 2013).

Holmes certainly seemed to believe he was. Now incarcerated, facing the death penalty, and awaiting trial after a judge entered a "not guilty" verdict on his behalf, Holmes heard the 911 tapes.

"Gunshots!" Manager Quinonez can be heard saying. The dispatcher pleaded with Quinonez to give the theater address, but the sounds of gunshots and chaos drowned him out.

"Say it loud," the dispatcher pleaded before the line went dead.

In a second 911 call, young Kaylan Bailey called to say that her two cousins had been shot. Kaylan said one cousin was breathing, but the other was not. "Are there officers near you?" the dispatcher asked. Then the dispatcher pleaded with Kaylan to start CPR on her six-year-old cousin, who had stopped breathing and would soon die. Aurora police detective Randy Hansen testified that the first 911 call was made that morning at 12:38 a.m. This call was the first of forty-one calls that came in within ten minutes. Those calls prevented the police from responding to Kaitlyn Fonzi. Victims and families listening to the calls in the courtroom wept openly and held hands. One woman buried her face in her hands, while, shockingly, the Joker, Holmes, showed no emotion.

The 911 calls amid the sounds of gunfire and screams from victims in the audience attested to the frenzy of mayhem Kaitlyn Fonzi had nearly set off as prelude to the grand finale of her neighbor's insertion of himself into *The Dark Knight Rises* before the police told her that there was a shooting. Fonzi was fortunate that she did not turn the knob of the door she believed to be unlocked, because the apartment was booby-trapped for even more murder and mayhem. So was Holmes's getaway car.

Holmes appeared in an almost catatonic emotional state when the first officer approached him in the parking lot. Holmes was going nowhere, his avatar-like fury now expended as he stood in place like a robot without a set of instructions. The wild and certainly suicidal chase through the streets of Denver amid the sounds of sirens responding to the explosions at his apartment complex would not be the final act for the Joker. Holmes still exhibited this catatonic emotional state when he heard the 911 calls in his first court appearance months later. The Joker has no heart. Victims witnessing his indifference were outraged. One of them yelled out, "Holmes, rot in hell."[37] (The character of the Joker not only is impervious to such condemnation but feeds on it.)

Videos of Holmes's behavior and demeanor in court during that hearing six months after his shooting rampage showed a person who in no way resembled the person who had shown videos of his science presentation six years before on the brain's functional dynamics for differentiating internal perception from external reality. The image of James Holmes's indifference to the judge's orders that next day was like a nightmare come true. He was the living example of a man whose brain had totally lost differentiation between internal perception and external reality. Was his persona totally captured by that of the Joker through solitary immersion in the movie director Nolan's exclusion of that character? Had he internalized this character to exclude external reality? It is just a movie, but not for Holmes, who fashioned himself the Joker after an escape from Arkham Asylum. That belief would be his only defense, the insanity he may have already feared long before becoming one of six selected by the National Institutes of Health for a special scholarship in neuroscience.

Because Holmes has entered a plea of not guilty by reason of insanity and now faces the death penalty, the prosecution may argue that his outlandish costume and courtroom demeanor were all an act over which he obviously had control from the very beginning of such intricate, diabolical planning. The defense should argue that it was not an act and that Holmes had likely internalized the

---

[37] Taibbi, Mike, and Tracy Connor. "'Rot in Hell, Holmes!': Anger after Judge Postpones Aurora Suspect's Arraignment." NBC News, January 11, 2013. http://usnews.nbcnews.com/_news/2013/01/11/16451776-rot-in-hell-holmes-anger-after-judge-postpones-aurora-suspects-arraignment?lite (accessed December 11, 2013).

Joker from the Internet and had lost all ability to differentiate this internal perceptual reality from a screenplay and one of the most evil and violent movie characters. Even if he knew that his acts were wrongful, the defense can argue under Colorado law that, because he was suffering from a mental illness, Holmes could not comport his acts to the law, and therefore he was legally insane at the time he committed the crime and should be found not guilty by reason of insanity. In many states, the defense must prove to a jury that this is the case in a plea of not guilty by reason of insanity. In short, the burden of proof in insanity pleas in many states is shifted from the prosecution to the defense because the defense has admitted the crime. That is why it is a difficult defense under the criminal statutes of most states, as we saw in the Milwaukee trial of serial killer Jeffrey Dahmer. But Colorado is different. Under Colorado law, the state must prove beyond reasonable doubt that Holmes was acting out his crime with full knowledge of his diabolical behavior. In other words, the burden is on the prosecution, not on the defense, to prove that the defendant is not insane and that the defendant knew what he was doing, knew right from wrong, and intentionally comported his actions to be contrary to law. This may be tough to prove for the prosecution, which is why they are seeking access to Holmes's medical records. There could very well be no trial at all, and Holmes could be sentenced to spend an indefinite amount of time in an institution for the criminally insane. As federal legislators did in the wake of the Hinckley verdict of insanity after his assassination attempt on President Ronald Reagan, the Colorado legislators may seek to change the insanity defense in that state as a result of the Holmes case.

The mass murder Holmes had perpetrated inside the theater was shortly discovered to be far more widespread and lethal than imaginable, at least to anyone except a person in the protracted mind-set of a mad genius like James Holmes. When the police confronted him in the parking lot of the theater, he reportedly raised his arms dramatically and seemed surprised. His nearby car was filled with lethal tools for a high-speed and terror-stricken chase through the streets of Denver. Police found Road Stars, which are used for immediate roadblocks both to block police pursuit and stop a vehicle from escaping. Holmes also had tire-puncturing devices, a canister of tear gas, a 40-caliber handgun, plenty more ammunition, backpacks, and his smartphone. This arsenal perhaps ultimately revealed his mental state. He was the Joker, who prepared for a car chase that would have had the whole world watching. This car chase would certainly be one likely to kill him, along with, he probably intended, many more people.

Holmes's intention after his crimes inside theater 9 is subject to speculation, and prosecutors have not drawn conclusions about his escape and evasion plans. Even details of his arrest are still in some doubt because he gave up without a fight mere minutes after his massacre inside the theater. An officer, however, said Holmes was in his gun-sight when Holmes raised his hands to surrender "without any significant incident."[38] The police thought he looked surprised. They would later say that Holmes had prepared as if to hold off the cavalry and infantry by throwing lethal devices out the window of his car to immobilize pursuing vehicles in a mad pursuit. Even former FBI profiler Mary Ellen O'Toole said that the getaway stash found in Holmes's car could be more help to the defense than prosecution, as it was so over-the-top and might sound "crazy" to a layperson.[39] If Holmes had planned a mad dash through the streets of Aurora and Denver, dropping gas canisters and tack strips along the way to foil police units chasing him, he might imagine, in his delusional state, a

---

[38] Minshew, Charles, and Daniel J. Schneider. Interactive Timeline: Shooting at Aurora Theater. *The Denver Post,* July 20, 2012. http://www.denverpost.com/ci_21119904/inter-active-timeline-shooting-at-aurora-theater?IADID=Search-www.denverpost.com-www.denverpost.com.

[39] Sickles, Jason. Evidence Suggests Suspected Killer James Holmes Had a Getaway Plan. *The Lookout,* January 10, 2013. http://news.yahoo.com/blogs/lookout/evidence-points-suspected-killer-james-holmes-possible-getaway-200829868.html.

flight from the Batmobile. Holmes might have provided himself with a number of options to process as he fled. For him, the world had become a stage for the return, grand revenge, and flight of the Joker.

Kaitlyn Fonzi's discomfiture at the strange music coming out of the apartment next to her would be aroused again when the police banged on her door and ordered her to evacuate her unit. Holmes had booby-trapped his apartment so that first responders would twist the doorknob and set off the explosives, creating a diversion that would allow Holmes to escape after terrorizing more victims. But upon being taken into custody at the multiplex, Holmes tipped the police off so that they could understand what he had planned for them if they entered the apartment hot. Was that another act in his final screenplay?

It was almost two in the morning when Kaitlyn Fonzi was startled by a loud crash that sounded like an air conditioner falling to the ground. She was going to call the police again until she looked out her window and saw the police already outside. Soon someone knocked on her door, and police SWAT personnel armed with assault rifles confronted her. They took her and all the residents of the complex outside for their safety and for questioning. The fire chief was surveying the scene, believing from Holmes's tip that unlocking Holmes's door could have blown up the whole apartment building and adjacent structures. Police evacuated neighboring buildings, and the once-quiet community of health-care students from the University of Colorado now milled about in the street in confusion. The Joker, who wanted more terror-driven mayhem, had likely staged all of the confusion. The obvious theory police developed was that first responders would set off an explosion because of the music complaints, diverting attention away from Holmes's murder at the theater and enabling his escape. The Joker had created three separate crime scenes for them, all extremely lethal and confounding.

Once taken into custody and remanded to the local lockup, Holmes began behaving childishly in jail, acting out as if he were in another reality. He acted as a puppeteer with bags on his hands, and he tried to insert metal into a live wall socket. Meanwhile, Holmes's booby-trapped apartment presented a challenge to the police. He told an FBI agent that he had rigged his apartment to divert the police from his murder scene at theater 9. He had soaked his carpet with gasoline and computer-timed his radio to disturb the neighbors so that they would call the police, which they did. He told the FBI agent he expected the police to open his apartment door and set off the explosion, thus destroying them and every other resident, giving Holmes the opportunity to escape.

The apartment's front door was rigged with a tripwire connected to a mixture of chemicals. Upon ignition, this mix would spark nothing less than a fireworks display, thus setting the gasoline-soaked carpet afire. Holmes had placed rows of white ammonium chloride on the floor; this chemical would have created a cloud of smoke to terrify any first responder. Fonzi's intuition was correct. Something was not right inside that apartment, and she was not going to turn that unlocked doorknob. The timing of the loud music also worried her. Holmes had set his computer for twenty-five minutes of silence followed by loud techno rock to startle neighbors into doing exactly what Fonzi did: call the police. The Joker's ambush also included a rigged fuse between three jars containing a lethal chemical mix. When the mixture exploded and burned, this special homemade concoction could not be extinguished with water. Holmes had set yet another deadly trap outside the building by rigging triggering devices known as "pyro trip boxes." These boxes had a remote control next to a remotely controlled car. Holmes had placed this triggering device on top of a white trash bag near the building. Inside the bag was a portable stereo programmed to play forty minutes of silence, after which the techno rock would blast on. Holmes expected a resident to hear the music and get suckered into picking up the remote control. Picking up the remote to start the car would have also triggered the building—and all the residents within—to explode. This plot was indeed the kind that the Joker would have dreamed up to cause absolute mayhem in Gotham City.

James Holmes was always known as a genius. What nobody knew is that he was a mad genius. He was also a sick genius whose internal perceptions had wiped out reality. *The Dark Knight Rises,* whether intended or not, would last all night with murder and chaos never imagined except in Batman comics or movies. As Holmes saw it, the world would learn that the Joker had escaped the asylum. The world would soon know the Joker's final act and ironically see him back in the asylum. But this time, it would not be the fictional Arkham Asylum, from which Holmes may have tried to prove he had escaped. This time, Holmes would likely remain at the Colorado Mental Health Institute at Pueblo until his death, which inmates at the jail have said could not come too soon. In March 2012, Holmes told a fellow student that he wanted to kill people "when his life was over."[40] On July 20, 2012, and likely long before, James Holmes's life as he knew it was over.

"You kind of got that feeling that he was a loner," an employee of Nick's Liquors in Aurora told Matt Nager of the *New York Times.*[41] In his article, Nager accurately juxtaposed Holmes's public image of someone who navigated quietly through the world to the psychosis that had taken him over. Seemingly invisible to the outside world, except for those who could recognize the emerging signs of danger, Holmes was animated by the personality of a pseudocommando killer lurking and festering within the slender, almost hermit-like graduate student. It is clear that the magnitude of the attack was partly the result of the nature of the weapons used, the capacity of the ammunition clip, the use of gas to mask the gunman's setup,

---

[40] Goode, Erica, Serge Kovaleski, Jack Healy, and Dan Frosch. "Before Gunfire, Hints of Bad News." *New York Times,* August 27, 2012. http://www.nytimes.com/2012/08/27/us/before-gunfire-in-colorado-theater-hints-of-bad-news-about-james-holmes.html?pagewanted=all.
[41] Ibid.

and the enclosure of the movie theater itself. All of these elements combined resulted in an appalling number of gunshot casualties.

Maybe we can understand the ominous sharing of his apocalyptic perception of death within the context of his life and the sudden postponement of a pre-trial hearing in November because of Holmes's emergency hospitalization for attempting suicide in jail. Holmes was hospitalized after repeated attempts to injure his brain by ramming his head into the wall. Although skeptics quickly asserted that this was just one more example of Holmes trying to deceive and escape responsibility for his murders, Holmes, despite gag orders for critical information from University of Colorado and the police, showed clear evidence of significant behavioral change in the months leading up to the massacre in Aurora.

The defense is threatening a suit against Fox News, whose reporter Jane Winter was threatened with jail for refusing to disclose her source after being ordered to do so by the Colorado court, which obtained information about a package sent to the psychiatrist alleged to be responsible for Holmes's treatment while he was enrolled at the University of Colorado, Dr. Lynne Fenton.[42] This package was opened a few days after his rampage and contained writings predictive of what he was planning. In a way, it was reminiscent of what Cho Seung-Hui did when he sent a video to NBC News.[43] We do not know how much contact the psychiatrist had with Holmes, because she appears to have worked in an administrative and consulting role, likely assessing students judged to be in need of psychotropic medications. Three visits to this clinic have been reported, but this psychiatrist was known to have reported Holmes's fantasies of violence to the university's threat-assessment team. Campus police

---

[42] Fox News. "Free Press Fight: How Fox News Reporter Wound Up Facing Jail for Doing Job." FoxNews.com, April 5, 2013. http://www.foxnews.com/us/2013/04/05/free-press-fight-how-fox-news-reporter-wound-up-facing-jail-for-doing-job/ (accessed December 11, 2013).

[43] Liebert, John, and William J. Birnes. *Suicidal Mass Murderers: A Criminological Study of Why They Kill*. Boca Raton: CRC Press, 2011.

reportedly offered to take Holmes to the hospital for seventy-two-hour detention and examination, but Dr. Fenton apparently decided not to pursue that route for concerns that Holmes would not meet the criteria for admission after finding he had no history of violence or criminal behavior. Strictest interpretation of the Colorado law for involuntary commitment requires probable cause to expect imminent violence from a person, but past acts of violence are the best predictors of future acts of violence.

Significantly, James Holmes had no prior history of violence or criminal behavior. The police found medication in his apartment, but the type of medication is unknown, as are toxicology studies to determine whether Holmes was taking any prescription or nonprescription drugs. According to an article in the *New York Times* by Erica Goode, Serge E. Kovaleski, Jack Healy, and Dan Frosch, Holmes told a stranger at a Los Angeles nightclub in 2011 that he "enjoyed taking LSD and other hallucinogens."[44] We do not know whether misusing or abusing drugs or not adhering to prescribed medication were factors in his dramatic personality change months preceding his rampage, but one has to wonder whether he had been preoccupied by hallucinations that kept him isolated and locked in a private world. Once the gag order is lifted, now that Holmes has entered a plea of not guilty by reason of insanity, it may allow us to know what, if anything, Holmes was prescribed or previously abusing. Until then, there can only be informed speculation from apparently reliable witnesses acquainted with him.

Drug and alcohol abuse is a major factor in aggravating psychotic patients to commit violent acts, but these acts are more impulsive. We doubt Holmes could have sustained his attention and thinking for such a complex and meticulously planned scenario with three

---

[44] Goode, Erica, Serge Kovaleski, Jack Healy, and Dan Frosch. "Before Gunfire, Hints of Bad News." *New York Times*, August 27, 2012. http://www.nytimes.com/2012/08/27/us/before-gunfire-in-colorado-theater-hints-of-bad-news-about-james-holmes.html?pagewanted=all.

crime scenes spread across Denver if he were intoxicated on drugs or alcohol. We know he drank. He had possibly been prescribed psychotropic medication. But other than the recollection of a stranger at a bar in Los Angeles, there is no evidence that Holmes abused illegal drugs.

No one who knew Holmes and was willing to talk to reporters described him as being a normal kid or young adult, although he functioned at a very high level until 2012. Holmes was born on December 13, 1987, in San Diego, California, to parents who were professionals in their fields. His mother is a registered nurse and his father is a mathematician and scientist with degrees from Stanford; the University of California, Los Angeles; and the University of California, Berkeley. Holmes has one sister. He was raised in Castroville, California, where he attended elementary school, and San Diego, where he attended high school. A pastor stated that Holmes attended a local Lutheran church with his family, but Holmes now reports himself as agnostic.

As a student at Westview High School in San Diego, Holmes achieved a reputation as both a standout soccer defender and a performer with improvisational talents that could make people laugh. In a video from a school production of *A Farewell to Arms,* he was remembered for playing the bartender's goofiness to the peak, ad-libbing the role as if he really were the character. This dramatic talent, hidden beneath an otherwise fading figure around the University of Colorado campus, would soon morph into one of the darkest and most tragic figures in the history of comic book lore: the Joker.

According to Hugo Gye, Meghan Keneally, and Daniel Bates in the *Daily Mail,*[45] Holmes was reported to be obsessed with role-playing video games like *World of Warcraft,* graduating in 2009 to games

---

[45] Gye, Hugo, Meghan Keneally, and Daniel Bates. "Dark Knight Gunman Faced Eviction and 'Broke Up with Girlfriend' Just Before Killing Spree." *The Daily Mail*, July 22, 2012. http://www.dailymail.co.uk/news/article-2177294/James-Holmes-broke-girlfriend-just-Dark-Knight-Rises-shooting-spree-Colorado.html.

like *Neverwinter Nights 2*. Just as he did before his attack, Holmes took photos with his smartphone that showed his high school propensity to make funny faces. By 2012, however, his contorted self-portraits on his phone were almost like Bosch paintings of people trapped within their own seven deadly sins and displaying extremely dramatic morbid expressions. Holmes was observed to laugh when he saw those paintings in court, but nobody else in the courtroom found them funny. They were grotesque. They might possibly have been photos of Holmes's emerged identity, the Joker who was taking him over, not the actor playing the role of the Joker and aware of the difference between reality and art or even the role of the goofy bartender from the Hemingway play in high school.

Holmes's personality in high school was mercurial in that he seldom made eye contact but then could clown for high school videos. Goofy facial expressions seemed to have been his delight, particularly when caught on camera. Classmates recall his playing Irish folk tunes on the piano, but when he realized he was noticed, Holmes suddenly stopped playing. He was so socially awkward that some described him as all but mute, without any eye contact. But then there would be bursts of excitement out of nowhere, like those later described in the hospital cafeteria line when Holmes overheard somebody talking about professional football.

Graduating from Westview High School in the upscale Torrey Highlands community of San Diego in 2006, Holmes attended the University of California, Riverside, and he received his undergraduate degree in neuroscience with the highest honors in 2010. He was a member of several honor societies, including Phi Beta Kappa and Golden Key. Holmes graduated in the top 1 percent of his class, with a 3.949 GPA. Holmes was an effective leader and a person who evidenced a great amount of emotional maturity in class. In 2008, Holmes worked in Glendale, California, as a counselor at a residential summer camp that catered to needy children from seven to fourteen years old. At the camp, he was responsible for ten children and, again, most significantly, he had no disciplinary problems. Nobody doubted his intelligence or abilities as a leader. In fact, he was considered brilliant, a sometimes comical geek, but those who worked with him increasingly described him as shy and hard to get to know. He probably could have fit the profile of a socially awkward adolescent or someone with Asperger's syndrome, both of which are highly controversial diagnoses because there is dispute over whether Asperger's is a behavioral issue or a mental health issue.

In 2006, Holmes worked as an intern at the Salk Institute for Biological Studies, where he wrote computer code for an experiment. Holmes, whose supervisor described him as stubborn, uncommunicative, and socially inept, presented his project to the other interns at the end of the internship but never actually completed it. He did not tell the whole truth in his next application for a professional position. Writing of his experiences at the Salk Institute, he revealed his own recognition of what later would become the neural networking mysteries into which he would plunge. Using high-powered computers, Holmes likely already knew that software developers with backgrounds similar to his had already mapped the ebb and flow of serious mental health issues in somewhat primitive form. As reported by Reuters,[46] Holmes wrote, "I had little experience in computer programming and the work was challenging to say the least. Nonetheless, I taught myself how to program in Flash and then construct a cross-temporal calibration model. . . . Completing the project and presenting my model at the end of the internship was exhilarating." He apparently had not finished the model, but his pursuit of neuroscience was almost prophetic when he interned at the Salk Institute. In retrospect, he was already changing for the worse, becoming increasingly isolated and unpredictable in his responses, as he was likely searching for

[46] Slosson, Mary. "Accused Colorado Gunman Applied to Illinois School with Stellar Grades, References." Reuters, August 11, 2012. http://www.reuters.com/article/2012/08/11/us-usa-shooting-denver-idUSBRE87A02620120811.

the inner sense of his own brain wiring that was already starting to tangle and misfire.

His advisor, John Jacobson, recalls having to ask simple questions to get him to answer, for example, "Yes, James?" or "No, James?"[47] This same advisor was also seeing the ultimate deterioration of a promising science career of brilliance. Holmes probably had the brilliance of his own father, but he never completed any of the assignments. Again, his interests were prophetic, in that they were about, as he described in his application essay on programming, developing visual illusions in the laboratory and putting them on the Internet. This advisor might not have been quite so shocked with the enigma presented by *New York Times* reporter Matt Nager because Holmes found out Jacobson spoke Mandarin. Soon the advisor started receiving more and more emails from Holmes, one that started with "Ni hao John,"[48] which means "Hello," or "How are you?"

Holmes was already starting to withdraw socially, isolating himself from other interns, eating by himself at his workstation, and avoiding the program's tradition of afternoon tea. He would arrive for his internship duties, even though he rarely performed them. Then, his lone, gangling figure would simply drift away without any socially appropriate acknowledgment of departing from a room. He would just walk off. That may have been the clinical sign of "social blunting" seen in serious mental illness. To punctuate this impairment in its relation to Holmes's situation, Jacobson was particularly struck by the fact that this was the only intern who never contacted him again after finishing the program at the Salk Institute. Jacobson's experiences with Holmes certainly did not deter his advancement toward Holmes's search for the inner workings of

---

[47] Goode, Erica. Serge Kovaleski, Jack Healy, and Dan Frosch. "Before Gunfire, Hints of Bad News." *New York Times,* August 27, 2012. http://www.nytimes.com/2012/08/27/us/before-gunfire-in-colorado-theater-hints-of-bad-news-about-james-holmes.html?pagewanted=all.
[48] Ibid.

the brain, particularly and most likely his own, which he must have already felt to be breaking.

In June 2011, Holmes enrolled as a PhD student in neuroscience at the University of Colorado, which accepts only one in ten applicants for its program. He received a $21,600 federal grant from the National Institutes of Health and a $5,000 stipend from the university. This young man had potential stars on his shoulder had it not been for his progressively deteriorating mental condition. Holmes had rejected the University of Illinois, where he was offered a $22,600 stipend and free tuition. Typical of his peculiarity and inappropriateness, Holmes submitted a picture of himself with a llama on his University of Illinois application. Yet, surprisingly, the school accepted him with extreme generosity in grants.[49]

The neuroscience program at the health sciences campus of Denver's University of Colorado is a new and powerful interdisciplinary program designed to merge the talents of University of Colorado neuroscience researchers with clinical researchers. On the University of Colorado's Anschutz Medical Campus, 150 high-powered scientists operate under one roof to unlock the secrets of a wide spectrum of the brain's highly complex functions, such as neurobiology of perception, as well as diseases ranging from strokes to spinal cord lesions and the more challenging mysteries of impaired brain function in Alzheimer's disease and schizophrenia. The center is known to facilitate socialization among scientists and students, and normally everyone is known to bond well in the environment. Such bonding could have been predicted to be all but impossible for Holmes, based on his experience at the Salk Institute.

He concentrated his studies in the perceptual process of hearing: synaptic signaling between neurons and regions of the brain and messenger chemicals in the brain. He also studied stem cell

---

[49] Slosson, Mary. "Accused Colorado Gunman Applied to Illinois School with Stellar Grades, References." *Reuters*, August 11, 2012. http://www.reuters.com/article/2012/08/11/us-usa-shooting-denver-idUSBRE87A02620120811.

transplants in patients with Parkinson's disease. Ironically, these are all critical areas of research for psychiatrist Emil Kraepelin's modern construct of the brain's disintegration in dementia praecox (now known as schizophrenia) in the late nineteenth century. The core disease process is believed to be increasingly chaotic signaling between neurons and regions of the brain, causing misinterpretation of external reality and internal fantasies, dreams, and emotions.

In our normal state, we wake up from a complex dream—even a nightmare—and soon realize, much to our relief, that it is not real and a new day has begun. Before our first cup of coffee, we usually cannot even remember the dream. But in psychosis, disrupted signaling from neurons makes the dream become reality and reality the dream. The untreated psychotic patient never awakens to reality, as was the case with Tucson shooter Jared Loughner, who wounded Representative Gabrielle Giffords. The neurotransmitter considered the major culprit in psychosis, dopamine, is the same chemical that reduces the physical impairment of Parkinson's disease. Holmes would therefore learn a lot about the abnormalities of dopamine and signaling in schizophrenia.

Psychosis is accompanied by hearing voices. Thus, auditory perception is a critical area of study for understanding how the psychotic patient hallucinates and hears voices of authority commanding him to commit heinous crimes, among other severely distracting extrasensory perceptions. Holmes, whether consciously or unconsciously, had entered one of the best laboratories staffed with the best of experts to understand what was already most likely happening in his own brain and probably already scaring him. It is during the process of the first psychotic break, which affects one out of one hundred adults over the age of eighteen, that insight is present enough to know that Holmes knew of Kraepelin's findings. Holmes was certainly smart enough to find a way to diagnose the increasing noise and scrambled messaging in his own brain, which probably caused his increasing isolation, social withdrawal, social blunting of relationships with others, and increasing mutism. The last item was particularly bothersome to his advisor at the Salk Institute, who could get him to respond only to concrete yes or no questions.

At this point, Holmes was not the team leader he had been known to be. He was not the highly respected soccer defenseman. Holmes needed serious help, but he searched for it until it was too late, in the laboratory rather than in a doctor's office. He would even present a paper on dopamine transmission, known, when out of control, to cause amphetamine psychosis, one model for researching schizophrenia. He would lecture, even before attending the University of Colorado, on the differentiation of internal and external perception and the core impairment of psychosis, when disrupted signaling among neurons involving impaired dopamine transmission in the brain surge, almost always between mid-adolescence and mid-twenties, into first-episode psychosis in schizophrenia.

As reporter Matt Nager of the *New York Times* discovered in his interviews with sources willing to speak of Holmes, even for a graduate student immersed in research, Holmes was particularly a loner, revealing very little about himself to others and not even making any small talk with fellow students.[50] Another student commented that Holmes didn't even seem to be on this planet.[51] He was a world unto himself. Could it have been that Holmes was already preoccupied with the very phenomenon he was supposed to be studying? We observed the same disintegrating process with Cho Seung-Hui at Virginia Tech, Jared Loughner at Pima Communiy College, and Adam Lanza at Western Connecticut State University.

In Aurora, Holmes would take up residence on Paris Street in a one-bedroom apartment in a building with other students involved

---

[50] Goode, Erica, Serge Kovaleski, Jack Healy, and Dan Frosch. "Before Gunfire, Hints of Bad News." *New York Times,* August 27, 2012. http://www.nytimes.com/2012/08/27/us/before-gunfire-in-colorado-theater-hints-of-bad-news-about-james-holmes.html?pagewanted=all.

[51] Ibid.

JAMES HOLMES: THE DARK KNIGHT RISES

in health studies, the same building that he nearly demolished a year later. He described himself as "quiet and easygoing" in his rental application. That was somewhat true, at least superficially, but hardly fully descriptive of his identity. The police investigation has revealed that he left some digital footprints, like a dating profile on Match.com and a profile on Adult FriendFinder.[52] Acquaintances also reported Holmes to have hired prostitutes. Holmes was also said to leave reviews of them on an online message board.[53]

The distinctive contrast of a smile with an air of one who walked a solitary path attracted attention of shopkeepers in the low-rent housing near Anschutz Medical Campus in Aurora. Holmes was remembered for cruising home slowly on his BMX bicycle toward the red-brick apartment building where he lived on the third floor, a gangly figure almost clownishly too big for the small bike. Neighbors also saw a Subway sandwich bag characteristically swung from the handlebars. The crux of the matter is that James Holmes was considered a "weirdo" by anyone who regularly saw him—obviously, residents of his apartment rarely did. That is probably because he was immersed in his private world, likely driven to merge it with characters in Internet games. We know that Anders Breivik immersed himself in gaming on an average of sixteen hours per day. Adam Lanza competed with Breivik and likely exceeded his record. We may also find out that Holmes was a gaming addict.

The local pawn broker knew who Holmes was because Holmes spent time looking over the electronics on display. Now we know

---

[52] Ferner, Mark. "James Holmes' Dating Profiles Asked to Be Thrown Out by Defense." *Huffington Post*, October 7, 2013. http://www.huffingtonpost.com/2013/10/07/james-holmes-dating-profile_n_4057957.html.

[53] Graham, Caroline, and Ian Gallagher. "Gunman Who Massacred 12 at Movie Premiere Used Same Drugs That Killed Batman Star Heath Ledger and Messaged Web Lovers to Ask . . . Will You Visit Me in Prison?" *Daily Mail,* July 30, 2012. http://www.dailymail.co.uk/news/article-2176377/James-Holmes-Colorado-shooting-Gunman-used-drugs-killed-Heath-Ledger.html.

why he was looking at those electronics: he was concocting his booby traps to blow up his apartment building and make his getaway chase through Denver. All this may make sense to them now, but how could police investigators looking for clues to his behavior have ever known that this "weirdo" was becoming the worst of the worst, merging with his avatar, the Joker? He would sit at the bar of Shepes's Rincon, a Hispanic club, and drink a few beers, but he never spoke to anyone. He could not speak Spanish, which may have been a social milieu that made him less anxious. He was rarely seen with anyone else, and nobody could tell reporters if he ever dated. He must have bought alcohol, because a clerk at the neighborhood liquor store remembered him and said he was a loner. "Sometimes," she said, "I would get a smile out of him."[54]

Holmes's public appearances at the University of Colorado became obviously more troubled and often were interrupted, as they were back in his high school impromptu videos and when he was clowning, with jokes. The potential for violence was the last thing that came to mind when a graduate student at the university met Mr. Holmes at a recruitment weekend for the neuroscience program in February 2011. She remembered Holmes as nonchalant and relaxed. His exaggerated tranquility was very apparent and seemingly inappropriate for the occasion.[55] Others noticed that he was disengaged from everyone around him. And, true to form—but progressively more noticeable—he made jokes when people introduced themselves to him. These jokes were grossly inappropriate, out-of-nowhere; maybe not obscene, but simply out of context. For James Holmes, however, the context was not in that

---

[54] Goode, Erica, Serge Kovaleski, Jack Healy, and Dan Frosch. "Before Gunfire, Hints of Bad News." *New York Times,* August 27, 2012. http://www.nytimes.com/2012/08/27/us/before-gunfire-in-colorado-theater-hints-of-bad-news-about-james-holmes.html?pagewanted=all.

[55] Ibid.

social reality where he hid in a Spanish-speaking nightclub sipping brews to manipulate his nervous system.

This profile of James Holmes is consistent and reliably portrays the outward manifestations of an inner soul descending into the terror of premature dementia, as described by Emil Kraeplin, or schizophrenia. No other source of information exists because of the gag order imposed by the judge and the University of Colorado's refusal to provide any information, including the names of his professors, to the press. But it is safe to say that few who encountered James Holmes on a regular basis in the academic setting would remember this apparently quixotic person if it had not been for the murders on July 20, 2012. That was probably his social impact, just like the experience of his advisor at the Salk Institute recalled: a total absence of relatedness he had never experienced with an intern before. James Holmes dropped off the map then, and he had possibly already dropped off the map again. When Holmes reappeared at the University of Colorado, no evidence pointed to any semblance of the healthier person he had been in high school. It was as if James Holmes had disappeared.

As fall term approached, Holmes was notably anxious. He presented as more mercurial. Once, he inappropriately pointed his laser at a slide in an exaggerated laid-back posture, one hand in his pocket. He gave a loud "Oooooooooooh," which likely shocked his audience, who knew him only as reclusive. His remoteness would suddenly be broken with a smile from nowhere, and his disarming casualness would be broken by the habitual joking he brought from high school. Presenting technical details of enzymatic biochemistry of neurons, he would stick in an inappropriate, off-the-wall comment, such as "Take that to the bank."[56] However, concern about him increased. Acquaintances spoke of his floating apart from them, as was also observed in his internship. Holmes seemed to be

---

[56] Ibid.

absorbed in an impenetrable inner world. This absorption was the scrambled thinking and perception of a slow descent into mental disintegration. James Holmes was rotting inside and about to implode, only to explode later.

"James is really smart," one graduate student whispered to another after a first semester class. Classmates would share opinions of him as being awkward, yet they would express surprise at the quality of his critical comments shared on their papers. When professors tried to bring Holmes out in class, he took a long time to tune in, often appearing not to be there.[57] Frequently, the professor would apparently catch him in a his dream state, and Holmes would delay response with a long, "Uhhhhhhhhhh."

Everyone had to take notes in class, but Holmes reportedly never did. Nobody doubted his intelligence. Ironically, just a few months before his attack in Aurora, a professor assessed his midterm essay as "spectacular," and beautifully written. The professor expressed surprise that Holmes was a student and not an experienced researcher. However, Holmes's detachment from the world around him was highly visible. He always pushed himself in front of the class to grab the best seat in the lecture hall and clumsily perched there. He wore adolescent-style T-shirts.[58] At best, everyone would agree that he was very different. At worse, he was rapidly descending into a state of inner chaos and ultimately a state of unremitting human destructiveness.

Holmes's personality noticeably changed in spring 2012. Typical smiles disappeared during his classroom presentations, and he no longer made jokes. This change in outer appearances likely ran concurrently with his inner morphing into the Joker, because at the same time, he was buying weapons and paraphernalia online. Packages started arriving at his apartment. At this time, Holmes showed his

---

[57] Ibid.
[58] Ibid.

hand, casually telling a classmate that he wanted to kill people when his life was over.[59] Holmes even showed a semiautomatic Glock to a classmate later in the spring of 2012. If statements or actions like those did not trigger his entry into psychiatric treatment at the University of Colorado Counseling Center, it certainly should have. But we know that at some point, for whatever reason, whether voluntarily or under administrative pressure, he began seeing a therapist in the counseling center where Dr. Lynne Fenton consulted. On May 17, Holmes gave his final laboratory presentation on dopamine precursors. The presentations typically ran fifteen minutes or so, but this time, he spoke for only half that time. In earlier presentations, he had made an attempt to entertain, but this time, he spoke flatly, as if he wanted only to get the presentation over with. This behavior was way out of character for him, but his inner persona was distracting him. He had already been stockpiling six thousand rounds of ammunition he had purchased online. He had bought firearms, a shotgun, a semiautomatic rifle, two Glock handguns, and body armor. He was likely already planting deadly booby traps in his apartment. We do know that on May 22, 2012, Holmes purchased a Glock 22 pistol at a Gander Mountain store in Aurora. Six days later, he bought a Remington Model 870 shotgun at Bass Pro Shops in Denver. In the four months before the shooting, Holmes also bought, via the Internet, three thousand rounds of ammunition for the pistols, three thousand rounds for the M&P15, and 350 shells for the shotgun. Holmes's neighbors did not seem to notice. Narender Dudee, who lived in an apartment next to Holmes's, did not even hear the loud techno music that blared from his rooms on the night of the shooting. As in the cases of Adam Lanza and Anders Breivik, nobody noticed or was willing to comment or act on anything peculiar that they witnessed.

Local television news reported that Holmes met with at least three mental health professionals at the University of Colorado

---

[59] Ibid.

before the massacre. The extent of his treatment at the University of Colorado Counseling Center is unknown, but Dr. Fenton, whom he had been seeing, possibly prescribed him medication. Ordinarily in clinics such as college counseling centers, students are not evaluated by psychiatrists unless they are deemed to require medication. Again, there is a gag order on Holmes's therapy, although Dr. Fenton and the University of Colorado have already been sued for inadequate clinical management of his serious mental illness.

According to Dan Elliott and Nicholas Riccardi in the *Huffington Post*'s Denver edition, Dr. Fenton reportedly did ask the police to find out if Holmes had a criminal record,[60] but she did not push the matter to potentially involuntary commitment, out of concern that Holmes would not meet the criteria of imminent dangerousness required for seventy-two-hour detention. However, Holmes had reported a violent fantasy to somebody in the clinic, a fantasy of which Dr. Fenton had knowledge. It is not known whether Holmes told her directly or even how much direct contact he had with her. Dr. Fenton had to consider the equal possibility that this was a savvy young man, perhaps deeply troubled but not imminently dangerous, able to assert his right to due process were he to be remanded for involuntary commitment. Given the current laws regarding involuntary commitment of the mentally ill, institutions and their mental health professionals have to be very careful about the decisions they make. One day, we might know what Dr. Fenton really thought and how much she knew or suspected about James Holmes, but that will have to wait until the criminal trial is completed and all civil litigation is settled or adjudicated.

---

[60] Elliot, Dan, and Nicholas Riccardi. "Dr. Lynne Fenton, James Holmes' Psychiatrist, Warned Campus Police of Threat a Month before Theater Shooting." *Huffington Post*, April 4, 2013. http://www.huffingtonpost.com/2013/04/04/district-judge-carlos-samour-james-holmes-arrest-documents-released-unsealed_n_3017933.html (accessed December 11, 2013).

Ultimately, even Holmes's perception of his behavior, as in the case of Loughner, may change, particularly his differentiation between inner experience—like a fantasy—and reality, when he is treated with an antipsychotic. Holmes could possibly say what Loughner said: "Had I taken this medication years ago, I wouldn't have done this." Interestingly, Holmes, unlike Loughner, would know that antipsychotics now inhibit the action of psychotogenic dopamine in the emotional centers of the brain that cause the limbic music of violence and psychosis. But dopamine, unlike the older class of antipsychotics such as Thorazine, can actually enhance dopamine in the frontal lobes, which is necessary for higher functions such as comprehension of consequences of a specific action. This means that with the proper medication to adjust his dopamine uptake, Holmes might have realized in a moment of rationality that his plans were indeed insane. However, it was too late for aggressive clinical intervention.

In what may have been his last formal presentation at the University of Colorado, he came across as emotionally flat with an abbreviated delivery, communicating total disinterest in subject matter that should have been of great interest: enzymatic processes in the neurons that are essentially the drivers of brain function. At about the time of Holmes's last presentation, a student with whom he had clumsily flirted received a text message after a class. She read, "Why are you distracting me with those shorts?"[61] Their electronic exchanges started in February or March, but she got two uniquely strange messages in June and July, when she was out with the flu. . . . "You still sick, girl?" Holmes texted.[62]

Somewhat startled, she immediately responded, "Who is this?"

Right away, he replied, "Jimmy James from neuroscience."

Presumably from reports, this is the same woman whom he had asked to go hiking, but Holmes was more and more preoccupied

---

[61] Goode, Erica, Serge Kovaleski, Jack Healy, and Dan Frosch. "Before Gunfire, Hints of Bad News." *New York Times,* August 27, 2012. http://www.nytimes.com/2012/08/27/us/before-gunfire-in-colorado-theater-hints-of-bad-news-about-james-holmes.html?pagewanted=all.
[62] Ibid.

those days and would walk by her on campus without any sign of recognition. As final oral exams approached, he signaled to her what would become the end, or at least his final message, when he wrote, "I will study everything or maybe I will study nothing at all."[63]

Holmes did not study, and his academic performance declined. He received poor grades on the comprehensive exam in spring 2012. As the graduate students reached the end of their second semester, wrapping up coursework, finishing lab rotations, and looking toward the oral exam that would cap their first year, some noticed a change in Holmes. If possible, he seemed more isolated and alone. His smile and silly jokes were gone. The companions he had sometimes been seen with earlier in the year had disappeared. The goal of the one-hour exam, said Dr. Angie Ribera, the neuroscience program director, was to ascertain and assess how the graduate students amalgamated their coursework and lab rotations into their ability to orally communicate their findings to their classmates. How were they able to communicate on their feet? This was not, as in reality television contests, a "who's in and who's out" moment but simply a way to grade a student's presentation and integration skills. However, James Holmes was in no shape for any of this. His self-identity was disintegrating, likely transforming into a more well-delineated character, caused by an isolated immersion on the Internet. His identity was morphing into Batman's nefarious antagonist, the Joker.

Holmes became preoccupied with the details of constructing a final scene of chaotic terror at the opening of *The Dark Knight Rises*, a scene with shocking mass murder and destruction that the whole world would never forget. He was deluded into acting omnipotent, but he was likely losing any self-critical ego functions to detect his own change into a delusional state. He made it to his

---

[63] Ibid.

final oral exam on June 7, 2012, and, not surprisingly, he failed the exam so badly that the professors who questioned him told him to find another career.[64] In another exchange of texts, a classmate asked him how it went. He responded, "Not well, and I am going to quit."[65]

"Are you kidding me?" the classmate asked.

His reply, peculiar as it seemed, had a seed of meaning: "No, I am just being James." James would be dead soon, to be replaced by the Joker. He had already communicated that in public.

Near the end of June, the program administrator, Dr. Ribera, explained Holmes's absence at the Cedar Creek Pub, where graduate students celebrated completion of their first year. Her serious tone put a damper on the students as they reminisced and decompressed with their favorite brews, as if having completed their first marathon.

"I want to let you guys know that James has quit the program. He wrote us an email. He didn't say why. That's all I can really say," said Dr. Ribera.

One member of the group was less circumspect, noting that Holmes seemed articulate but nervous and on the meek side. And prescient in his recent observation, the student added, "He was obviously interested in the body count."[66]

The body count was indeed the truth about Holmes's distraction. On June 7, just hours after failing his oral exam at the university, he purchased a Smith & Wesson M&P15 semiautomatic rifle at the same time the threat assessment team was reviewing Dr. Fenton's reports of Holmes's potential dangerousness. Holmes had told the administration that he was dropping out. He never followed up with formal written notification because, we believe, he was busy with his planning.

---

[64] Ibid.
[65] Ibid.
[66] Ibid.

On July 2, he placed an order at an online retailer for an urban assault vest, two magazine holders, and a knife. On July 6, he purchased a second Glock 22 pistol. He was already off campus in early June, either forcibly (like Loughner) or voluntarily. The factual timeline of these events is still under investigation. Court documents, which are indexed online at Colorado State Judicial Branch 2012,[67] contain official statements asserting that Holmes was revoked access to the University of Colorado campus because he threatened a professor. But the University of Colorado administration denies this allegation and says that Holmes was denied access to nonpublic parts of the campus because he had withdrawn from the university. His key card was routinely deactivated on June 10 as part of the standard procedure for withdrawal.

Holmes appeared to have dropped off the radar screen of any threat assessment team at the University of Colorado or any responsible law enforcement agencies of the jurisdiction where he resided. He also apparently dropped off the radar of university psychiatric case management, although Holmes did not think he had been officially discharged, when in fact, he had been. Holmes thought he and Dr. Fenton had a therapeutic relationship, substantiated when he sent her the information about the full details of his violent fantasies and perhaps even his plan for murder at the midnight opening of *The Dark Knight Rises* at theater 9 of the Aurora Century multiplex on July 20.

Fox News published an article by Jana Winter that cited two unnamed law enforcement officials who said that the notebook contained "full details about how he was going to kill people" and "drawings and illustrations of the massacre." Dr. Fenton never received the notebook. When the article was published, a gag order on the case was in effect, and Holmes's attorneys have been trying

---

[67] Colorado State Judicial Branch. "12CR1522 *The People of the State of Colorado v. James Holmes*—Documents from 07/20/2012 to 09/27/2012," 18th Judicial District. http://www.courts.state.co.us/Courts/District/Case_Details.cfm?Case_ID=152.

to determine who leaked the information to Fox News. At a hearing in December, several law enforcement officers testified that they were not the source of the leak, and Jana Winters, according to the *Huffington Post*'s Denver edition,[68] made clear that she was not backing down and revealing her sources. Sometimes legal arguments over journalistic source disclosure can become a distracting courtroom side show, obscuring the real questions about Holmes's diagnosis and treatment at the University of Colorado.

In retrospect, we believe that involuntary commitment might have prevented this disaster, or Holmes would possibly have been released back to the counseling center's care, as Cho was. Of importance in this context is the concept of "acting out in therapy." This concept involves a psychotic's acting-out process in his therapeutic relationship with his therapist. Acting out is different from acting "bad" or "strange," both of which Holmes also did. The clinical concept of "acting out" is a patient's resistance to verbalizing fantasies, even fantasies about the therapist. Instead, the therapist may learn later in the course of the patient's treatment that her patient just started visiting prostitutes. Any psychotherapist trained and experienced in psychoanalytic processes of transference and countertransference would interpret this sign as possible erotic fantasies about the therapist that the patient could not verbalize. Hence, the fantasies are "acted out" outside the therapeutic frame of a face-to-face session that requires their verbalization. Perhaps there will be another explanation of this final message of death, if the contents of the box Holmes sent to Dr. Fenton are ever released for the public record, which they may well be if Holmes's not guilty by reason of insanity plea proceeds to trial, opening the door to the workings of his mind and his penultimate actions.

---

[68] Tsai, Catherine. "Jana Winter, Fox News Reporter, Ordered to Testify about Who Leaked James Holmes' Notebook." *Huffington Post*, January 18, 2013. http://www. huffingtonpost.com/2013/01/18/jana-winter-fox-news-repo_n_2508208.html (accessed December 11, 2013).

We do not know what, if any, contact university administration, professors, security, or therapists attempted to make with Holmes after he left campus. No one saw Holmes much after he left school in June. Once, a classmate spotted him walking past the Subway sandwich shop near campus, his backpack in tow. A neighbor saw him in mid-July, when his hair was still its normal brown. At the time of his arrest, he gave his occupation as "laborer."[69] On June 25, less than a month before the shooting, Holmes emailed an application to join a gun club in Byers, Colorado. According to Fox News, the owner, Glenn Rotkovich, called him several times over the following days to invite him to a mandatory orientation but could only reach his answering machine. Because of the nature of Holmes's voice mail, which he described as "bizarre, freaky," guttural, spoken with a deep voice, incoherent and rambling," he told staff to keep him informed about Holmes.[70] Rotkovich was obviously concerned, and he was right to be; nobody else was. Rotkovich was reported as having said, "In hindsight, looking back—and if I'd seen the movies—maybe I'd say it was like the Joker—I would have gotten the Joker out of it . . . it was like somebody was trying to be as weird as possible."

He never heard back from Holmes, who never showed up at the range. In early July, the college student who conducted the text exchange with Holmes sent him a message to ask if he had left town yet. "No," he wrote back; he still had two months remaining on his lease.[71]

[69] Goode, Erica, Serge Kovaleski, Jack Healy, and Dan Frosch. "Before Gunfire, Hints of Bad News." *New York Times,* August 27, 2012. http://www.nytimes.com/2012/08/27/us/before-gunfire-in-colorado-theater-hints-of-bad-news-about-james-holmes.html?pagewanted=all.
[70] Winter, Jana. "Exclusive: Massacre Suspect James Holmes' Gun-Range Application Drew Red Flag." Fox News, July 22, 2012. http://www.foxnews.com/us/2012/07/22/massacre-suspect-james-holmes-gun-range-application-drew-red-flag-for-owner/ (accessed December 11, 2013).
[71] Goode, Erica, Serge Kovaleski, Jack Healy, and Dan Frosch. "Before Gunfire, Hints of Bad News." *New York Times,* August 27, 2012. http://www.nytimes.com/2012/08/27/us/before-gunfire-in-colorado-theater-hints-of-bad-news-about-james-holmes.html?pagewanted=all.

Then, just two weeks before the shooting, he sent a text message asking her if she had heard of dysphoric mania and warning her to stay away from him. He never replied to the fellow student's last text message, which asked if he wanted to talk about dysphoric mania. Whether Holmes or a mental health professional had made the diagnosis is unclear. His parents have an attorney who has blocked all communications regarding whether Holmes had a history of mental illness.

Dysphoric mania is also known as a mixed state of bipolar mood disorder. In this disorder, psychic energy is hyped, and the patient can go days without sleeping. However, instead of experiencing the euphoria and grandiosity that are considered the signature symptoms of mania, the patient feels depressed. Such patients can also develop paranoia with delusions—which likely occurred with Holmes. In such a state, patients can incorporate images and characteristics from video games or movies into their delusions. The press has expressed concerns that Holmes may have been mistakenly prescribed antidepressants in this state, which can hype the patient to the point of psychotic thinking and extreme agitation or even impulsive violence. Holmes never displayed the signs of such a mood-swing disorder. Instead, he showed the social withdrawal and progressive deterioration with inappropriate behavior that is more typical of schizophrenia. This behavior can erupt suddenly in young adults, but it usually presents as increasingly peculiar behavior, preoccupation with internal experience to the exclusion of reality, and, in rare cases, delusional identity that can be violent. Holmes likely fits that profile.

Regardless of diagnosis, on July 19, Holmes prepared for his attack. He gathered all his bullets and shotgun shells, the gas mask, an urban assault vest, a ballistic helmet, and a groin protector. He photographed his delusional identity on his smartphone, left the phone behind for police to find in his getaway car, and mailed a notebook to Dr. Fenton that arrived on July 23. In many ways, this was a replay of Cho Seung-Hui's actions at Virginia Tech years earlier. At about midnight, Holmes bought a ticket for the late-night premiere of *The Dark Knight Rises* with his phone and finally entered the theater as inconspicuously as other patrons. He did not stay in a seat. He soon left through the exit to arm himself for attack. About that same time, Kaitlyn Fonzi was climbing the stairs in the apartment building on Paris Street because the noise of her neighbor's techno music was keeping her awake. Many other neighbors were also calling the police because of the disturbance. Miraculously, nobody opened the door or touched the booby-trapped garbage bag outside. Dispatchers told Fonzi that it would be some time for nonemergency response; the police were responding to a shooting. Fonzi probably thought it was the ordinary violence of her run-down neighborhood. She noticed that the music stopped, as if timed. About an hour later, she heard a crash and a disturbance outside. She stopped dialing 911 when she noticed that the police created the disturbance. The fire chief was trying to figure out how to get into Holmes's apartment as the SWAT team rushed through the building to evacuate residents before the preset explosive devices demolished it and blew them to pieces. The SWAT team, dressed for war, knocked on her door without much formal introduction and ordered people out. Fonzi might have begun to think that this was no ordinary neighborhood shooting. Holmes had merged with the identity he had been imagining, and now the Joker had struck the city of Denver. Dozens were injured and twelve were dead, including six-year-old Veronica Moser Sullivan.

In the aftermath of the shooting, Holmes was taken into custody, charged with murder, and set up for arraignment. These events happened relatively quickly even as prosecution and defense skirmished over what records the prosecution could inspect. Although the defense, under American law, has an almost absolute right to be given complete access to the prosecution's case, the prosecution, depending upon the criminal procedure statutes of a given jurisdiction, does not enjoy that right in most cases because of the Fifth Amendment protection against self-incrimination, hence the pretrial maneuvering regarding what records the prosecution could see. At issue are Holmes's medical records and private communications—privileged communications— he might have had with his doctors. The prosecution also wants to inspect records of the meticulous, month-long plan of his attacks, which is evidence they will use to argue that he was beyond reasonable doubt not innocent by reason of insanity.

The insanity defense means that, in Holmes's case, such a seriously mentally ill person cannot form the necessary intent to commit the crime by reason of a mental illness, which renders the defendant unable to distinguish right from wrong or, in Colorado, to comport his actions to the law even though the defendant can distinguish right from wrong. However, the prosecution, upon whom, under Colorado law, the burden of proof rests, will assert that Holmes executed his crimes with such complex technology and consistent method that he perfectly understood what he was doing. Of course, all psychiatrists working over long periods of time with patients with schizophrenia, particularly the paranoid type, know that these patients can indeed plan and execute as long as their actions are executed within the confines of a tight paranoid delusional system.

For example, Norwegian prosecutors knew that Anders Breivik was delusional and fought for the court to declare him insane. He committed a highly complex bombing attack in Oslo and the massacre of scores of young people gathered at Utøya (an island near Oslo) for a political event. Any suicidal autopsy of Cho Seung-Hui would definitely come to the conclusion that he was deteriorating from schizophrenia at Virginia Tech just like Holmes was at the University of Colorado. Jared Loughner was diagnosed as having had schizophrenia after the 2011 Tucson massacre. Of course, Loughner's attack was not as meticulously planned as Holmes's or Cho's massacre; nonetheless, he killed a lot of people and disabled one of Arizona's most effective representatives with a bullet aimed point blank at her head. Representative Giffords has since recovered considerable function in extensive rehabilitation—enough to be in the public political spotlight once again and skydive on her birthday. Unabomber Ted Kaczynski carried out his highly sophisticated murders by mail from a remote cabin in Montana, riding his bike to the post office and avoiding detection from authorities. He was reliably diagnosed with paranoid schizophrenia, although he has refuted this diagnosis and claims he was and is completely sane.

The news media will follow the trial to see whether the state of Colorado will have a particularly hard time proving beyond reasonable doubt that Holmes was not committing this murder as a direct product of insanity. He was clearly insane for a long time, more likely than not on that horrific night of July 20. One might speculate whether he played *Batman: Arkham Asylum*, a video game set in the fantasy world of Batman lore. In the game, the Joker would have been either the lone inhabitant of the asylum or an escapee on the loose. If his life as James Holmes is ever distinguished from his death and reincarnation as the Joker, he very likely will spend that life in an asylum for the criminally insane, although he will not be the sole inhabitant. He is also more likely to be killed in any institution than he is to escape.

Politically, the state of Colorado has to go after Holmes with a vengeance because there is little understanding and almost no sympathy for the insanity defense in America. According to the *Denver Post*, although silent on the matter of Holmes's mental state, the state has consequently charged him with 166 counts of first-degree murder, attempted murder, possession of explosive devices, and other crimes, including inciting violence.[72] For each person killed in the shooting, Holmes is charged with one count of murder with

[72] Ingold, John. "James Holmes Trial: Prosecutors Seek Death Penalty in Aurora Theater Shooting." *Denver Post*, April 1, 2013. http://www.denverpost.com/breakingnews/ci_22915093/prosecutors-will-seek-death-against-james-holmes-aurora (accessed December 11, 2013).

deliberation and one count of murder with extreme indifference. The state added ten new charges against Holmes and asked to amend seventeen others, bringing the total counts against Holmes to 152. That would certainly be leverage for any competent man to consider a plea agreement, rather than going to trial, which is what Holmes's lawyers have offered and the prosecution has rejected. We do not yet know whether Holmes is mentally competent enough to stand trial without the administration of antipsychotic medication. Over the next eighteen months, we will see how this will play out. The American public may be facing another legal circus, which was almost the situation in the 2011 Tucson shooting before Loughner's plea bargain, this year or next as the prosecution and defense argue over the state of Holmes's mind.

The public will ask questions: What went wrong at the Salk Institute and the University of Colorado? James Holmes was not at a community college like Loughner was. He was not studying under the tutelage of engineering professors like Adam Lanza at the University of Western Connecticut. Nor was he studying English, allowing a certain expansion of the boundaries for imagination, as in the case of Cho at Virginia Tech. James Holmes was studying under the tutelage of some of the top neuroscientists in the world, including leading experts in schizophrenia. He is known to have been evaluated and treated by a University of Colorado psychiatrist. This case, therefore, raises even more serious issues than the horrid tragedies of Virginia Tech, Sandy Hook, and Tucson. The University of Colorado has documented much information about James Holmes, but the answer to the question is less certain. Will we ever be able to read the question, as we were able to in the Virginia Commonwealth Commission report on Cho, and likely will in the final investigative reports on the Sandy Hook and Tucson massacres?

Plea bargains to avoid a trial requiring the State of Colorado to prove all of Holmes's crimes to be the products of a sane mind, while also possibly defending civil lawsuits for failing to manage his serious mental illness, will make for a tough balancing act for state attorneys now that they have decided to pursue the death penalty. There is also a possibility, if no one goes to trial and all critical information is sealed, that we may be left with what we have now: reliable witnesses to the progressive sickness rotting the mind and soul of James Holmes and the logical clinical impressions based on those witness statements.

As a judge caught Loughner at a moment of mental competency to plead guilty, the political and economic risks of trying James Holmes and finding out the facts may get him a life sentence in the penitentiary, where he will certainly be considered a "special offender" rather than a madman. That is what Norwegians wanted with Breivik, despite their prosecutors' judgments to the contrary. That is also what Americans wanted with Loughner. So the book can be closed, and, like the Unabomber, these dangerous psychotics can be buried away in secure prisons. We will get on with our lives. Will there be a next massacre? Inevitably. Will we learn from Virginia Tech, Tucson, Aurora, Newtown, or the Boston Marathon? Perhaps a little. We hope that information will be forthcoming, because there is a lot to explain about James Eagan Holmes, with plenty of experts to do the explaining.

Chapter 5

The Tucson Shootings: Who Was Jared Loughner?

Jared Lee Loughner was a portrait of isolation, a nobody, a "nowhere man." Only his parents and a small circle of old friends ever knew him. Then, on the otherwise unremarkable day of January 8, 2011, he strode into a crowd with a semiautomatic pistol in his hand. That day became a headline. Loughner was there to kill Representative Gabrielle Giffords, who he believed had disregarded his pleas for help against a world he called a "sham."[73] When Loughner approached Giffords at point-blank range, he fired and put a round through her brain. He continued firing, killing a young girl and a federal judge, among others. By then, his gun ran out of bullets and he was assured of exploding into the public's consciousness. Yet little is known about Loughner's activities in the

[73] Becker, Jo, Serge F. Lovaleski, Michael Luo, and Dan Barry. "Looking Behind the Mug Shot Grin." *New York Times*, January 16, 2011. www.nytimes.com/2011/01/16/us/16loughner.html.

three months between his ouster from Pima Community College to his visits to stores and a motel starting late on January 7. He had purchased a gun and got two tattoos of bullets in November 2010.[74] Otherwise, investigative records show that he rarely ventured far outside his ZIP code. He was repeatedly kicked out of his home and from school for disruptive behavior. In response to his difficulties, Loughner posted on the Internet, "My sleeping bag is an interstate wash from Tucson to Phoenix." His Internet posts revealed more of his consuming thoughts. "His videos and online rants, plus new scraps of investigative evidence, portrays a young man at the end of a road, in his childhood room, tapping out messages to an indifferent world." One of these postings foretold the inevitable: "I'll see you on national TV. Why doesn't anyone want to talk to me? You're going to regret not talking to me."

And indeed we did. In fact, on Christmas Eve before the mass murder in Tucson, Loughner was hardly imbued with holiday spirit. Instead, he was busy posting a picture of the extended magazine for a 9mm Glock pistol on MySpace. Loughner, as if he were the Antichrist, titled his picture "My Countdown." Then he posted the portrait of insanity to MySpace for the whole world to see, along with the words, "Wow! With every day on torture, the hours are painful isolation: these dreams, which are realistic, vehemence feeling of greatness— ñ finally! Dear reader, I'm searching. With every concern, my shot is now ready for aim. The hunt, a mighty thought of mine."[75]

Like many mass murderers, Loughner had a target in mind, and it was Representative Giffords from the Congressional district encompassing Tucson. Loughner might have had a passing fancy for

---

[74] Ibid.

[75] Pitkin, James. "Local Blogger Posts Arizona Shooter Jared Loughner's MySpace Rants." *Willamette Week*, January 10, 2011. http://www.wweek.com/portland/blog-25438-local_blogger_posts_arizona_shooter_jared_loughners_myspace_rants.html (accessed December 11, 2013).

the pretty representative, and like many deeply psychotic individuals, he might have felt burned that Giffords had not responded personally or empathically to one of his fantasy complaints. He had actually communicated with her during a personal encounter in 2007. But the impersonal response he received from her office turned his anger to a low boil. She had rebuffed his attempt at a dialogue.

Loughner had prepared himself in response to what he perceived to be Giffords's impersonal reply. The brief public encounter at that 2007 town hall meeting became intractably entangled in the scrambled web of neurocircuitry that was Jared Loughner's deteriorating mind. Representative Giffords certainly would not have remembered that encounter because his question to her was an expression from the interior of psychic chaos, not the language of a sane man.

"What's government if words don't have meaning?" he had asked her in that 2007 townhouse meeting.[76] The question seemed reasonable to him. Reportedly, she appeared caught off balance and had no facile reply—at least not to Loughner's need for an answer—to a question from a mind that was losing all sense of meaning. His question was one for which there was no answer from any sane person not engaging in a philosophical debate. These tilting-at-windmills encounters and nonsensical talk in public were nothing new; his high school career had just ended early, as did his attempted soapbox career in politics.

At Pima Community College, Loughner's behavior, like Cho Seung-Hui's on the Virginia Tech campus, was becoming increasingly bizarre. This behavior could no longer be ignored or denied in its potential dangerousness for college authorities. At night, Loughner would carry a video camera around the college campus, railing

---

[76] Berzon, Alexandra, and Charles Forelle. "Suspect Showed Signs of Imbalance/" *Wall Street Journal*, January 10, 2011. http://online.wsj.com/news/articles/SB10001424052748703667904576073002519837620.

about the "genocide school" he was attending and about which he said, "It's a terrible place" because "it's a genocide school" and one of the biggest scams in America."[77] Genocide. What could he possibly have meant by that? The voices of auditory hallucinations most likely had captured his mental life to the exclusion of reality: the signature trait of insanity. "We're examining the torture of students," he exclaimed to students and faculty, who assumed he either was a madman or on drugs. Arizona Republic reporter Sean Holstege described Loughner's facial expression as "deadpan."[78] What Holstege thought was "deadpan" was really the flat emotional expression of the devastating schizophrenia enveloping Loughner's persona.

Loughner was not just being glib in his postings and videos. For whatever reason, however, experienced counseling and clinical staff did not take him for treatment, as would be expected at a large academic institution, especially one that constructively acted *in loco parentis*. Instead, Loughner was suspended from the college. Two months later, he would make the final YouTube video that shocked the world that frightful day at the Tucson Safeway. He would soon go berserk, killing six and wounding twelve, including Giffords, who is recovering remarkably well from Loughner's gunshot wound to her brain.

Jared Loughner's State of Mind as a Student

Most of us dream and wake up wondering if those familiar people from our past and current lives, along with some unfamiliar ones, are really entangled with us in those bizarre plots. We wake up fast and realize it was just a dream. But why the plot? Why the sensation

---

[77] *Wall Street Journal.* "Jared Loughner Gives Tour of 'Genocide School.'" *Wall Street Journal,* January 15, 2011. http://live.wsj.com/video/jared-loughner-gives-tour-of-genocide-school/BA7DA718-99CF-4A65-8422-C73A230C21E5.html.

[78] Holstege, Sean. "Jared Loughner's Lonely World before Attack." *The Arizona Republic,* January 5, 2012. www.azcentral.com/arizona republic/news/articles/2011/12/2320111223jared-loughner.

of present and past? Sometimes the dream is so real that it is scary or maybe joyful. But it does not make any sense. "I knew those people, but they have no connections in my life to be entangled in such a complex plot," we might say to ourselves while groping to shut off the alarm clock. Then we go about our day and may continue to think about an especially powerful dream. Then we forget the dream. We forget dreams unless we can afford to spend thousands of dollars every week for a psychoanalyst who awaits the "aha" moment of his interpretation as he makes us remember through free association. Of course, as Freud said, dreams are meaningful.[79] In psychoanalytic terms, they are known as "primary process thinking." That is, dreams both emotionally drive and determine drama that defies the organizing cognitive abilities of our brains to suppress powerful emotions and adapt to the realities of our daily lives. Imagine if you could not suppress such primary process thinking and your entire waking life is that dream. No other reality exists. Consciously, you are awake, but you cannot shut the dream off. Then, imagine yourself also trying to get through the day with two people with different stories talking into your ears. If you can imagine yourself in such a state of mind for even an hour of your normal day, then you get a sense of what it is like to be in that state of mind for the rest of your life: the fate of untreated schizophrenia. This was the fate of Jared Loughner at Pima Community College, Adam Lanza at Newtown, and James Holmes at the University of Colorado. It was also the fate of Ross Ashley at Radford University, who had tried and failed to get into Virginia Tech and murdered a police officer there before committing suicide on campus as Cho Seung-Hui did. We still do not know how much ammunition was found at the site of his suicide, a fact withheld by the police that have informed us of Ashley's motivation. Was this a revenge murder—could suicide or suicidal mass murder have been aborted by campus police?

---

[79] Freud, Sigmund. *Interpretation of Dreams*. 1899. Reprint, New York: Basic Books, 2010.

Loughner's psychologist and attending psychiatrist at the US Medical Center for Federal Prisoners in Springfield, Missouri, have both testified in preliminary competency hearings that their patient manifested early signs and symptoms of serious psychiatric illness as far back as 2006 and that he was blatantly schizophrenic by 2008. They said in their repeated examinations that he could not distinguish reality from hallucinations. In other words, his daily life was like that imagined hour you spent with two people talking simultaneously in each of your ears, while you could not suppress the last dream of your night's sleep. How could you focus on your environment to make sense of it or know reality from what you were constantly being told? Then consider being unable to stop those two people from talking into your ears. That is the state of mind dominated by auditory hallucinations: totally out of conscious control, in a dream state, and under the control of others who talk to you in alien voices. That is what it is like to be in Loughner's confused state of mind—the psychosis of schizophrenia.

Loughner said that he could manipulate his own dreams. He referred to the concept known as "lucid dreaming." If you are constantly in a dream state, that might be your last sense of control over a world of perceived utter confusion. Loughner was correct, although just for himself and not everyone else, when he said, "The line between the inner self and the outer universe is meaningless."[80] It was so for untreated schizophrenic patients such as Loughner, Lanza, and Holmes.

Speaking of his mangled version of conscious or lucid dreaming, Loughner wrote that "conscious dreaming" was his favorite pastime. Only the naïve would believe that. It was no pastime. It was what Steven Stahl describes as the diabolical learning of the brain's

---

[80] Wright, David. "U.S. Did Alleged Arizona Shooter Jared Loughner Think He Was Dreaming During Attack?" ABC News, January 11, 2011. http://abcnews.go.com/US/jared-lee-loughner-lucid-dreams-alleged-arizona-shooter/story?id=12585475 (accessed December 11, 2013).

neurocircuitry, preventing the schizophrenic patient from waking up and turning off his primary process dream state.[81] Loughner could not turn it off, so he may have thought it a pastime. "What is the universe?" he asked the paranormal conspiracy website forum, Above Top Secret. He communicated on the Internet, drew a diagram of the universe with him leaving it, pondered alternate universes, and challenged that day's date and asserting that the year could be infinite.

Reality for the schizophrenic can be completely illusory. For example, when you analyze your dream after waking up, it might seem as if your deceased mother is in your living room, vividly talking with a friend you met recently but she had never known. It seemed so real. You may ruminate over it for a while just to try to fathom the connections that do not really exist. Then you forget it. In Loughner's schizophrenic mind, however, such disconnections of chronological events and dramatic interactions cannot be dismissed and forgotten. They dominate the schizophrenic mind, as they dominated Loughner's mind for years and made him question the very nature of reality.

Language is distorted beyond comprehension in schizophrenia to the point of "verbigeration," the compulsion or inability to stop repeating meaningless words or sounds in clanging or echoic associations: "blue, due, you, Lou." Would it be surprising if such forced repetition of words related only by sound suddenly took on meaning: "Lou who is blue and due"? Loughner wrote that he could create new words, numbers, and symbols. He did not actually have that special power. He was describing the verbigeration of schizophrenia forced upon him by diabolical rewiring of his brain's neurocircuitry. Like Anders Breivik, who spoke in terms only meaningful to him, called "neologisms" by state examining psychiatrists in Norway, Loughner seemed to have his own internal

---

[81] Balt, MD, Steve. Thought Broadcast, "The Carlat Psychiatry Blog." Last modified October 2, 2011. http://thoughtbroadcast.com/tag/stephen-stahl/(accessed December 11, 2013).

semantic connections. Imagine the World War II Japanese radiomen trying to comprehend our Navajo Code Talkers and talking like them without any understanding of what they were saying. They could say the words in Navajo sequence, but their language was meaningless, at least to them. Their neurocircuitry was scrambled by excessive concentration on words and syntax for which they had no template established in the centers of language in their brains. There were no linguistic deep structures for the Navajo language among the Japanese radio operators. Thus they could become victims of diabolical learning in their own brains. No doubt, this happened to a few of them who were prepsychotic themselves. So it is with the diabolical learning of neurocircuitry for language in schizophrenia—a symptom that Loughner manifested.

Logic and language are impaired for schizophrenics. Schizophrenic neurocircuitry causes thought blocking and disruptions in the train of thought and resulting communication. Loughner's tangled rant, the product of one Internet session, was documented. He wrote about mainline freight trains passing his home and used more expletives than we can print in this book. Sure, some of the anger was frustration with his inability to filter out extraneous noise, whether real or hallucinatory, from reality. But most of it was the emotional dyscontrol of schizophrenia—the splitting between what he was thinking—exciting thoughts—and what he was feeling— dying. The split, or schism, in schizophrenia is not, however, of multiple personalities, as commonly misinterpreted.

Multiple personality disorder is a split between separate person- alities that do not know of each other's existence. The split in schizo- phrenia is between thinking and emotion. Such a split is most often seen in this disease, which was Loughner's crazed portrait of enigmatic emotion. We look at his smiling, almost frightening mug shot. What was he thinking? What he may have been thinking in that photograph shown around the world could have been far different from what the viewer interpreted as threat. He was smiling. He may have been

THE TUCSON SHOOTINGS: WHO WAS JARED LOUGHNER?

thinking of going to bed early because he felt tired, but expressed the emotion of a madman through his smile. Perhaps he really was a madman. It was enigmatic, indeed, only because others could interpret that smile differently. Loughner was certainly unable to express how he felt; his emotional control was completely split from his thoughts.

He constantly displayed such splitting in public, showing the core defect long known in schizophrenia. Those who knew him from school or from the world of online gaming commented on Loughner's casual demeanor during his online campus rant about genocide, a complete disconnect from reality. People posting online were right about Loughner, but they did not know why. Tragically, nor did counselors, nurses, security, parents, teachers, or administration during Loughner's psychotic break while his schizophrenia was still responsive to early intervention and prevention of the malignancy of duration of untreated psychosis, the condition apparent in Cho Seung-Hui. The condition went untreated by professionals both in court and on campus who should have known how to identify such a diseased mind and take responsibility for its treatment. Would they similarly avoid doing something for a man with labored breathing, nausea, and chest pain? Of course not, because that is real disease: a likely heart attack. Loughner, like Holmes, Lanza, and Cho, was just a "weirdo," as far as most staff saw him. Had these young men been diagnosed as seriously ill—as with a heart attack—someone would have taken responsibility for getting them treatment. In the case of Loughner, what a difference that could have made! Loughner even said so himself.[82] But Loughner's condition went undiagnosed and untreated. After presumably being tranquilized with an antipsychotic, possibly Risperdal, Loughner told his therapist that he would not have perpetrated the Tucson shooting—he referred to it as "all of this"—

---

[82] Kiefer, Michael, Michelle Lee, and Joe Dana. "Psychologist: Loughner Competent, Feels Badly about Shooting." *AZ Central*, August 7, 2012. http://www.azcentral.com/news/20120806arizona-shootings-change-plea-hearing-set-loughner.html (accessed December 11, 2013).

had he been given the same medication years before. That would have been 2006, which his federal prison treatment team establishes as the beginning of his unremitting progression into schizophrenia and inevitable march toward madness that culminated in the horrors and national tragedy of January 8, 2011.

In *Clan of the Cave Bear*, we can see the ingenious use of weeds, probably heavy in plant sterols, selected by cavemen for treatment of congestive heart failure. But that was thousands of years ago, before written language. Loughner grew up in Tucson, Arizona, a highly educated and progressive city, the seat of the state's first university and college of medicine. Tucson was the home of one of the largest community colleges in the nation, where Loughner was a student. Tucson was also a modern city with superior health facilities. But Loughner might have been living in a cave in northern Europe hundreds of thousands of years ago for all the good that modern society did for him.

The Pima Community College administration, possibly informed by the Virginia Tech massacre, was simply intent on getting a troubled and confrontational Jared Loughner off campus and keeping him off. The shock of the Cho Seung-Hui murders and the lawsuit making its way through the court were clear warnings to college administrators everywhere. That is probably why lawyers in Virginia decided to attack college security in their lawsuits, rather than failures of Cho's psychiatric treatment. Thus, because it was security first, the Pima Community College campus police came to Loughner's home to make certain he was gone. Did nobody know that his family had failed to pick up on his psychosis long before he had shown up at Pima Community College? That the family would likely miss it again? The college security personnel certainly did not miss Loughner's insane comment about the situation: "Now, I realize this has all been a scam," he said. A "scam," he told them! Campus police certainly thought that verbal response to a traumatic suspension was very strange. Such inappropriate emotional response is another hallmark of schizophrenia.

Security personnel were face-to-face with the pathological splitting between emotion and reality that defines schizophrenia. Where was Loughner's rational reaction to the reality confronting him? He had no rational reaction because he was wallowing, totally distracted from chaotic signals of his decompensating brain, in his own delusion.

Normally, a forced suspension from college is certainly traumatic for a young student, but Loughner simply uttered the word "scam." He had used the term before. What did he mean by it, if anything? Perhaps all life seemed a scam to him by now because reality was rapidly disappearing from his internal world. Or he may have been too far gone in the disease process to attach any cognitive comprehension to the word. He had posted his intent to "commit "suicide again" on MySpace, emphasizing it with his further admonition, "notice the again." Just before the shooting, his final words to those on the Internet who were still tuned in to him were, "Goodbye Friends." Recall James Holmes's peculiar statement that proved so prescient: "After I die, I want to kill a lot of people." Are these not signs of impending failure of college students' minds, rather than academic failure or disciplinary matters? Holmes, Loughner, and Cho were dumped on the streets by their colleges, presumably expected to fend for themselves and stay away, which Cho did not. What did the Virginia Tech massacre and the Commonwealth of Virginia's multimillion dollar investigative report inform university and college administrators and trustees of? Tragically, in the wake of so many tragic suicidal catastrophes either brewing or exploding on campuses nationwide, the answer to date may well be a frantic "call the attorneys," "say nothing to the press," and "hunker down" to let lawyers solve the problem, even when hundreds are dead and thousands of lives are ruined. Did anyone think to ask what was going on with Tamerlan Tsarnaev, who had been a part-time accounting student at Bunker Hill Community College before he dropped out? He was studying to become an engineer and had been there for three semesters and had dropped out three times without any explanation.

There is no record of Loughner's clinical encounters at Pima College, and it appears, from the behavior of the campus police who visited his home, that he was administratively sequestered into a security-only protocol. The public still does not know the details of Loughner's aborted college career. Loughner had been expelled from Pima Community College, and campus security had left its own jurisdiction on campus to deliver Loughner the message that not only was he off campus but he had better stay away. Was this the method by which Pima had promised the public that it was committed to public safety: keeping problem students off campus? As set forth in the catalog statement to prospective students and their families, Pima's administrators wrote:

> Families of Students: Families play an important role in the academic success of our students. See why Pima is the right place for your student and learn how you can help them succeed. Why Pima Services for your Student Health & Safety? We understand the importance of knowing that your student will be safe and secure at Pima. With thousands of students spread out across multiple campuses, we take our health and safety responsibilities seriously. Pima Community College's Department of Public Safety serves each of our six campuses 24 hours a day, seven days a week. Pima Community College Police is a full-time, fully certified law enforcement agency. Counselors to provide referrals to community agencies Community Health Clinics at two campuses.

Technically this very large college of more than fifty thousand students entered the commercial market in delivering clinical services. The question then arises: Why was such an obviously psychotic student not referred to the "community agencies" advertised to parents and prospective attendees?

One such agency every counselor certainly knew in the Tucson community is the Kino campus of the University of Arizona Hospital.

It has ease of access for psychiatric care, whether voluntary or involuntary, second to no other facility in the nation that we know of. It should be favorably compared to similar public psychiatric hospitals in California, Wisconsin, Maine, New Hampshire, Massachusetts, and Washington state. California public psychiatric hospitals, for example, are defensively administered, attuned more to be responsive to the implied rights of the seriously mentally ill and due process rights that protect people from being involuntarily committed to psychiatric treatment facilities. In Tucson, Arizona, Loughner could have easily been held involuntarily and admitted for treatment. Involuntary commitment in Arizona, although monitored by the courts, is not the adversarial training ground for young trial attorneys that it is in California, Washington state, and Wisconsin. Arizona is far from ideal and does not have assisted treatment requiring committed patients to take prescribed medications, but it works relatively well. It also has acute and persistent disability as grounds for long-term involuntary commitment with case management. That is based on relapses of psychosis, not dangerousness nor suicidality. Pima Community College advertises its knowledge of such resources in its Tucson neighborhood. Did no one—and there were plenty of professionals and clinicians involved with Loughner—know what could be done with Loughner besides forcing him off campus? What they did in forcing him off campus flies in the face of their own testimonials of health and counseling services with adequate community resources for care of psychotic students, likely 1 percent of 55,000 students, equaling hundreds on their campuses. Had no one heard of the Kino campus, one of the largest and most accessible acute care psychiatric hospitals in the nation?

Months and years too late, after having finally been medicated on an emergency basis at the United States Medical Center for Federal Prisoners in the wake of his shooting rampage, Loughner was reported by an attending psychologist at a formal court hearing to have told her, "Had I taken this medication years ago, I would not have done this." By then, of course, it was too late. He had committed his crimes and effectively forced Giffords out of Congress, disabled, possibly in some capacity for life. The left and the right pounced on the political winds blowing in Arizona. Tucson liberals were quick to blame the strident "self-reliant" rhetoric of new Arizona resident Sarah Palin, who had screamed, "Don't retreat; reload;" for the massacre, while the right-wing gun lobby circled its wagons. Right-wing commentators, sensitive to near-incitement speech by Tea Party politicians, were mounting their counter-offensive. Who was left to answer for the victims? Certainly not Loughner, who was awash in delusion.

In March 2012, a Virginia jury returned a verdict in favor of two plaintiff victims' families, who had opted out of the original settlement in the case, and awarded each family $4 million, an award reduced to $100,000 for each family and which is now under appeal to the state's supreme court, which must decide whether the commonwealth had a duty to protect students from third parties.[83] In the wake of that verdict and looking at what lawyers do in wrongful death cases, we must become curious about what Pima Community College knew about Loughner, why they decided to merely suspend such an obviously deranged individual, and what actions they took in response to his recurrently bizarre and threatening behaviors on campus. By then, of course, Pima Community College Chancellor Roy Flores knew from the Virginia Tech debacle the dire consequences of allowing such a potentially dangerous mentally ill patient to remain on campus without any clinical intervention. What he did not know at that time, however, was the latest jury verdict in the case of Cho's ultimate suicidal mass murder on campus. This verdict sent a strong statement to the public and university administrators

[83] Vieth, Peter. "State Gets Appeal in Va. Tech Lawsuit, Plaintiffs Shut Out." *Virginia Lawyers Weekly*, February 26, 2013. http://valawyersweekly.com/2013/02/26/state-gets-appeal-in-va-tech-lawsuit-plaintiffs-shut-out/ (accessed December 11, 2013).

that the presence of students on campus was greatly different from shoppers at malls.

It is unlikely that two surviving victims and loved ones of the nine killed by suicidal mass murderer Robert Hawkins at the Westroads Mall in Omaha would claim to hold the owners and management responsible and liable for the rampage. The success of any such claim would rest on how the court interpreted the mall's duty of care to its patrons. Not so with a college or university. The Virginia jury, finding that the university had a duty to protect its students, recently decided in favor of the two plaintiff families of the students that Cho killed. Trustees and administration of Virginia Tech were held to a higher standard of responsibility for the health and safety of their students than visitors at a commercial shopping mall because, under the doctrine of *in loco parentis*, college and university campuses had a special duty of care. And, as in Pima Community College's catalog, such special protection is promised as a benefit of choosing this college. Hence, the college placed itself into the market of providing special care, under which students are not merely consumers of courses on campus as if they were shoppers in a mall, but residents entitled to a higher standard of protection against violence perpetrated on campus. Reading the Pima Community College catalog statement, families of students and students alike could be led to believe that they should feel safer with ease of access to health-care facilities in the event of illness, whether a physical (medical/surgical) or psychiatric illness. Of course, that was not the case in the Virginia Tech massacre.

Chancellor Flores made a special effort to keep Loughner, who was recognized as being seriously mentally ill and called out for behaving strangely by members of the Pima College faculty in whose classes he acted out, off campus by suspending him and presumably making efforts to keep him from returning until it was safe for him to be on campus. We have no knowledge, however, whether any efforts like those advertised in the college catalog were made to refer him for diagnosis and treatment, despite what might be constructively implied as knowledge that he was suffering from serious mental illness. In the authors' opinion, Pima administration had to know, or should have known, that the Kino campus of the University of Arizona Hospital had ease of access for the most seriously mentally ill patient. Students and faculty of this school had to have been rotating through this hospital for their training. It was no remote "loony bin" in the Sonoran Desert but a significant Pima County health-care institution that recently completed a high-profile transformation from a county hospital to an integral teaching hospital for the University of Arizona College of Medicine in Tucson.

As Linda Valdez succinctly said,

A young man's strange behavior raises concerns on his college campus, but he does not get needed mental-health care. Later, he goes on a deadly shooting rampage in Tucson. It's not Jared Loughner. This isn't last year's shooting. The young man in this story was 41-year-old nursing student, Robert S. Flores, who killed three University of Arizona professors before killing himself—in 2002. Then, as now, Arizona failed to have the very uncomfortable conversation about the consequences of untreated mental illness. Then, as now, Arizona missed an important opportunity. Advocates for the mentally ill have tried for years to end the stigma associated with diseases of the mind [brain]. Linking the massacres in Tucson to mental illness assumes that mental illness caused the traged(ies). It furthers one of the ugliest stereotypes about people with mental illness. Nobody wants Jared Loughner for a poster boy. But we need to talk about this. Last year's shooting near Tucson led to a great deal of discussion about civility.

It also led to a thinly disguised, politicized memorial uncomfortably led by President Obama, as if Loughner were a Lee Harvey Oswald hatched by Arizona's right-wing extremists with a political agenda that pandered to the gun manufacturing lobby. When Sarah Palin screeches into a microphone, "Don't retreat; reload," what about that should an at-risk, potentially violent individual not understand? However, it was not a politically motivated murder. It was a public suicide attempt. As Ed Montini put it, "But while memorials help us remember those who die, they don't help us understand the reason for a tragedy. We remember the 'who' but rarely the 'why.' And in this case the 'why' is muddled." This horrific event at the Tucson Safeway will remain muddled as it snakes through a maze of legal proceedings from Phoenix and Tucson to California—then to the United States Medical Center for Federal Prisoners in Missouri and back for years to come. Will Loughner's moments of lucidity that allowed the presiding federal judge to determine him competent to cop a plea in exchange for life in prison be the end? It is doubtful that this high-profile case will go quietly into the night, as politicians on both sides would prefer. After all, conspiracies fuel politics during these polarized times. But once the word "schizophrenia" came out of the mouths of a federal prison psychiatrist and a psychologist, it is almost like politicians do not know where to turn to exploit this tragedy for their own careers.

The destruction of public psychiatric services and disabling of involuntary commitment in the name of protecting innocent eccentrics from the hands of psychiatrists hungry for control and treatment fees is hardly the stuff of headlines. Most Arizonans—most Americans—do not believe in this anyway. Thus, the deal is made. The ceremonies are over. The politicians had their day. That is the intention of life sentence without parole. It closes the case without further investigation instead of examining a crisis about which politicians know little or nothing. Nor do they appear to care to know, as long as it goes away. There is no political hay to be made off Loughner. In fact, there is nothing but liability all around, from Phoenix to Tucson.

Occasionally, the proceedings have given interested clinicians and the public a glimpse of what really happened that horrific day at the Tucson Safeway. But for the most part, the sporadic hearings led by the US attorney general and federal judiciary are deliberately obfuscated by advocacy processes designed to punish the bad while protecting their rights in our society. Such proceedings are not meant to exorcise emotions over events as apocalyptic as the Tucson shooting, in which the public only gets glimpses of adversarial hearings with agendas that dissect events and strip them of the palpable human flesh of blood, horror, and lost or shattered lives. Legal proceedings are methodical and just that: a process. They have little meaning to anyone other than law practitioners and professors-in-the-making who will build their law notes and sometimes entire courses around the proceedings and outcome that nobody but they can begin to comprehend.

If we thought, however, that everyone would have simply forgotten what really happened at the Safeway on January 8, 2011, because of the Aurora or Newtown shootings, we would have been wrong. Even the churning of the news cycle, which has brought us more horrible atrocities, did numb us to the immediacy of mass murder in our shopping malls, our movie theaters, our elementary schools, or even at the finish line of a marathon. We now know that the justice department has brought legal closure to the Tucson shootings.

We now know that Jared Loughner was no simple case of attempted political assassination, despite the bombastic efforts on all sides of the media to make it so. No, Jared Loughner was not Arizona's resident surrogate political assassin. Nor was the gunman even mentally fit enough to comprehend the nuances of right-wing political rhetoric in Arizona. Nor was he mentally competent enough to have purchased a gun legally, which is at issue not only in Congress as it wrestles with new gun legislation, but in the individual states, where measures to require background checks for mental illness and criminal convictions are making their way through legislatures. From the Loughner case, specifically, Gabrielle Giffords, now in rehabilitation therapy and now gaining back her mobility and ability to speak in public, has become an advocate for gun control measures that would keep firearms out of the hands of mentally ill individuals like Jared Loughner.

Issues still swirl around the Loughner case even years later, however. After the shootings occurred, the Pima County sheriff attributed the crime to rancorous political debate. Seemingly incognizant of the role of undiagnosed and untreated serious mental illness as a major factor in the massacre, the sheriff was in part responsible for managing and investigating it. But could it have been both? Loughner had passed through his court on misdemeanors but was never given consideration for a psychiatric examination. Are at-risk, potentially violent individuals particularly prone not only to the blood and gore of video gaming but to political incitement speech as well? Have our own First and Second Amendment guarantees become fuzzy in the face of new technology and new understandings about the neurological intricacies of the human brain? In the instance of someone acting strangely, especially on a college or school campus, is there a point when the court should have the authority to allow police to monitor the person's social networking sites? The vast majority of gamers and social media posters are not known to the police and courts for disruptive behaviors or behavioral emergencies. However, in cases like those of Jared Loughner, Adam Lanza, James Holmes, and the Brothers Tsarnaev, where parents, teachers, or authorities notice extremely strange behavior, should not a warrant arise, upon reasonable cause, that a student's privacy be trumped by public safety concerns and concerns for that student's own health?

In August 2012, Jared Loughner was judged competent to stand trial. His forensic psychologist, Dr. Christina Pietz, testified that her patient had been medicated with antipsychotics for a year and that he recognized what he had done, felt remorse over his murders and the injuries he caused, and was competent to stand trial. Loughner pleaded guilty to nineteen murders and was sentenced to life in prison without the possibility of parole, a sentence mandated by law.

Loughner's victims, including Gabrielle Giffords, approved of the guilty plea and plea bargain that spared Loughner from the death penalty. While the guilty plea and sentence might have brought an end to the Loughner case, questions still lingered. These questions can be applied to Holmes, Lanza, Eddie Ray Routh, ex-LAPD officer Christopher Dorner, and Tamerlan Tsarnaev, along with scores of other mass murder suicides or attempted suicides. Were Jared Loughner's warning signs red-flagged at Pima Community College to the point where when the shooting occurred, anyone believed it might have been Loughner pulling the trigger? Loughner's parents certainly noticed the warning signs. His mother had said that she could hear Jared having a conversation with himself in his room and knew something was dramatically wrong, and Loughner's father, Randy, even took away his shotgun and disabled his car so that he couldn't drive away.[84] The Pima Community College nurse seemed to believe that Loughner might have been responsible for the shooting when she publicly voiced concern hoping that the perpetrator was not Loughner. Others in the college community might have thought the same thing even though they did not express it publicly.

After the sounds of gunfire had stopped at the Tucson Safeway while Loughner reached for his next ammunition clip and was held by intervening witness Patricia Maisch, first responders rushed in to care for the wounded. Nobody questions their effectiveness and that of the University of Arizona Medical School Trauma Center. But how did they know for sure that there was only one shooter? How well did the Pima County Sheriff's Department know Loughner, and what was their anticipation of what he would ultimately do? Tucson is not a small town, but it is not that large, either, particularly for the ratio of police officers per citizen and its close proximity to the

---

[84] Wagner, Dennis. "Tucson Shooting Records Shed Light on January 2011 Rampage." *AZ Central*, March 27, 2013. http://www.azcentral.com/news/articles/20130327loughner-records-release.html?nclick_check=1 (accessed December 11, 2013).

Mexican border. Like Anders Breivik in Oslo, Loughner was known by authorities in Tucson—or he certainly should have been.

Veteran Phoenix police officer Nick Margiotta provided some background for the question of whether Loughner was known to authorities. Describing his years dealing with psychiatric patients on the streets, he estimated that at least half of his calls were "psych." Maricopa county attorney Bill Montgomery, who supported Margiotta, asserted with respect to the Newtown massacre, "Currently, and even for us in Arizona, the criminal justice system becomes the default mental health provider."[85] Our justice system was never intended to be a mental health system, at which it functions badly and at an extraordinary cost to the taxpayer. In fact, it costs twice as much per capita to incarcerate a mentally ill person than to treat that person medically as a matter of public health. Incarceration neither protects the private citizen from the delusional and suicidal crimes of the mentally ill nor does it protect the mentally ill from themselves. It fails on every level, which is ironic in the city of Tucson, where access to care for the seriously mentally ill is among the easiest in the nation.

In Loughner's case, a seriously mentally ill man with multiple encounters with law enforcement and the Tucson criminal justice system was always repeatedly released into diversionary programs without any consideration of motivations for the disruptive behaviors that signaled fulminating and progressive schizophrenia. He, like Anders Breivik, was also rejected for military service, but we don't know why. Tragically, his disease was belatedly diagnosed in federal prison after too many lives of consequence were extinguished and many more damaged forever. In fact, Loughner posted his opinion about his target victim on MySpace just days before his suicidal mass murder: "I can't stand to look at a [f'n] pig without thinking

---

[85] Gratehouse, Donna. "You Are Not the Boss of Me, Bill Montgomery." *Arizona Politics*, December 15, 2012. azcvoices.com/politics/2012/12/15/you-are-not-the-boss-of-me-bill-montgomery/.

about murdering that [f'n #%&##])f***!"[86] He would continue to post increasingly violent wrath toward the police, including specific threats to kill police officers. Nobody noticed? Or maybe Pima County law enforcement was simply waiting for the inevitable chance for a felony arrest, which is perhaps why they suspected the Safeway Plaza shooting was the work of a lone gunman whose identity was not a mystery.

In Arizona, had Loughner been a couple of shades darker, he might have been detained for a minor crime and asked, "Papers, please." But he managed to get out of any real societal intervention with his own mental state time and again until he created his own ultimate confrontation, leaving it to opposing counsels to argue over whether he could even be brought into a courtroom to answer for what he did.

Loughner may have had erotomania for Representative Giffords, as John Hinckley had for Jodie Foster. The attractive image of female power provided some cohesiveness to otherwise volcanic mix of erotic and violent forces inside Loughner. With grandiose beliefs, he saw himself as not only in control of evil, but able to destroy it wherever he perceived it, such as in political campaigning.

His political tirades had no theme, merely fragmented targets of his omnipotent powers as a god cemented together only with hatred and aggression, not logical political belief. His parents described him as getting "weirder and weirder" over time.[87] They would find him facing a wall inside the home and talking to it. He was arguing with threatening voices of auditory hallucinations, which had completely taken him over. Not only was Loughner incapable of comporting himself to the logic of social reality, he was almost a robot, a zombie provocateur preconditioned to respond to any stimulus that created a delusional reality for him. He had become suspended in time, waiting

---

[86] Berzon, Alexandra, John R. Emshwiller, and Robert A. Guth. "Postings of a Troubled Mind." *Wall Street Journal*, January 12, 2011. online.wsj.com/news/articles/SB100014240 52748703791904576075851892478.

[87] Wagner, Dennis. "Tucson Shooting Records Shed Light on January 2011 Rampage." *AZ Central*, March 27, 2013. http://www.azcentral.com/news/articles/20130327loughner-records-release.html?nclick_check=1 (accessed December 11, 2013).

for his stimulus. That stimulus came in the form of a line of assembler code to a microprocessor sitting on a circuit board embedded within a remote computer somewhere miles away on a server farm that fired up an autodial program at 3:40 p.m. on January 7, 2011. This program transmitted the announcement of Giffords's "Congress on Your Corner" event to Loughner's home phone the next morning. It was literally the switch that set him into motion.

Loughner would soon become one of America's most notorious assassins, one from the Internet Age that provided him a worldwide audience for his hypergrandiose paranoid aggression that targeted the very human heart of American politics and its up close and personal encounters between representatives and their constituencies. American politics would change dramatically for the worse that day. In Newtown, Connecticut, less than two years later, and in Boston less than six months after that, it would change again.

Chapter 6

Anders Breivik and the Massacre in Norway

The first indication that Norway was under siege took place on July 22, 2011, when Anders Breivik, who had described himself as a "commando wreaking revenge on a too-liberal and complacent Norwegian society," bombed key government buildings in Oslo, killing eight people.[88] In a matter of hours after the bombing, having donned a police uniform, he traveled to a Labor Party youth camp on the island of Utøya where he systematically gunned down sixty-nine teenage campers. It was a horrifying rampage that shocked all of Norway and most of Europe.

Days before the Oslo bombing, Breivik released a fifteen-thousand-plus-page manifesto, emailing it to more than one thousand

---

[88] Public Intelligence. "Anders Behring Breivik's Complete Manifesto '2083–A European Declaration of Independence.'" Last modified July 28, 2011. http://publicintelligence.net/anders-behring-breiviks-complete-manifesto-2083-a-european-declaration-of-independence/ (accessed December 11, 2013).

recipients, documenting the preparations he made for his attacks, and setting forth his political manifesto in which he said he was providing a justification for his actions. The manifesto reveals how meticulous Breivik was in planning the attacks and assembling not only the weapons and explosives, but also the logistics for the attack. He acquired a Volkswagen van small enough to avoid requiring a commercial truck registration or license, the requisite amount of weapons and ammunition for his attacks, and enough explosives to set off multiple bombs at the government buildings in Oslo. In a striking section of his manifesto, Breivik copies directly from Ted Kaczynski's Unabomber manifesto, a rant, albeit sophisticated and internally logical, that decried the ultimate collapse of human society because the machines and the "techies" who built them were the enemies of human civilization. Although we now believe that Kaczynski's visceral hatred for modern machine-driven society might have been instilled in him thirty years earlier at Harvard, it was not until the 1970s that he began his rampage as the Unabomber, operating under the radar and eluding federal law enforcement for over a decade until he disclosed his intentions in his manifesto and ultimately disclosed his identity to those who knew him the best: his mother and his brother.

Kaczynski was methodical as he chose his targets, built his homemade explosive devices, rode them to the local post office on his bike, and then returned to his isolated Montana cabin to contemplate his next attack. It was not until thirteen years after he began his rampage that he finally published his manifesto, giving copies to newspapers such as *The New York Times*, and the document caught the attention of his brother and mother, who ultimately turned him to federal authorities. Kaczynski had successfully eluded the FBI while carrying out bomb attacks against those in society he saw as his enemies, all the while staying to any agency that could identify him. Breivik tellingly changed Kaczynski's references from "techies" to liberals and added racial slurs about black people and Muslims.

It was therefore clear that Breivik admired and even copied the Unabomber as he planned his attacks.

In Breivik's convoluted writings, unintelligible to all except a psychiatrist practicing in an institution for the insane, he set forth his political declaration of war on Europe. Writing from his delusion of self-bestowed omnipotence, Breivik justified his own war as Hitler did in *Mein Kampf*. After reading his manifesto and discussing it with him, Norway's leading criminal attorney, Geir Lippestad, went public with a statement: under no circumstances would he represent Breivik unless he agreed to plead insane. Lippestad said that Breivik did not think like any of us, presumably referring to people who know the difference between reality and illusion. Because he found the manifesto and Breivik's YouTube video shortly before the bombing, clear and convincing evidence of insanity, Lippestad could not defend him as a rational person. Lippestad could not refer to Breivik's political pleadings for a final solution to Islamization of Europe—what in Breivik's mind was simply no less than a second crusade waged in Europe to eradicate all Muslims from Europe and especially from Norway—as any measure of sanity. Although many Europeans might share Breivik's belief in ridding Europe of multiculturalism and the values of population diversity, Breivik's declaration of war replete with unlimited bloodshed is nothing less than a hate crime and act of terrorism on a horrific scale that Norwegians had not experienced since World War II.

As an attorney, Lippestad's reaction to Breivik's ravings had to be his concern over the disparate philosophical bases of this manifesto that ran the gamut from Norwegian folklore, including poetry in Old Norse, to neighboring President Vladimir Putin, who referred to Breivik's citation of admiration for him as "the delirium of a madman." Of all summary judgments of Breivik's manifesto, Putin's came closest to reality for anyone needing to follow logic to survive in this world. Breivik also asserted that feminism has eroded the fabric of European society as well. It has weakened men, he claimed, turned them into followers instead of leaders, and threatened to destroy the very society that he believed was responsible for modern civilization,[89] hereinafter referred to as "manifesto." His response was mass murder.

Of utmost significance in assessing Breivik's mental state is his grandiose delusion of being the sole member of a cell emerging in Europe for the Knights Templar, an organization that Norwegian authorities unambiguously deny exists. Breivik had tailored a uniform complete with epaulets and claimed he was the Norse epic hero Sigurd and that his mentor was Richard the Lionheart, King Sigurd Jorsalfar of Norway, or Sigurd the Crusader. Breivik even tried to tease the court into revealing the mysteries of his Knights of Templar network throughout Europe, describing its formation by an antijihad crusader organization whose mission is to fight against Islamic suppression. Formed in April 2002, according to Breivik, in England the Templars are nine men: two Englishmen, a Frenchman, a German, a Dutchman, a Greek, a Russian, a Norwegian, presumably Breivik himself, and a Serb. The Serb might have been one of his self-images as a heroic crusader against Islam in the 1990s war in Kosovo when NATO intervened to protect the Muslim population from what the Serbian leadership under President Milosevic referred to as "ethnic cleansing."[90] Breivik put himself on the side of the Serbs.

The prosecution and the court rejected Breivik's offer to explain the nature of his incarnation of the modern Knights Templar. Breivik's pseudoavatar, as a Templar knight or a crusader guarding European battlements against the tide of Islam, was his projection of a pseudocommando. The pseudocommando is on a mission of vengeance. He is a warrior whose mission, though unspeakably cruel, is one of purification. He eliminates the threat to whatever society

---

[89] Ibid.
[90] Gardner, Frank. "How Do Terrorists Communicate?" BBC News World, November 2, 2013. http://www.bbc.co.uk/news/world-24784756.

or group in whose defense he believes he is fighting. Breivik donned the trappings of the Templar, and it became his delusional avatar of an avenger, remorseless in his attempt to remake society into his own image and calling it "purification." In doing so, he convinced himself that the only way to galvanize like-minded thinkers about the dangers of multiculturalism and the threat to Europe posed by Middle Eastern and North African Muslim fundamentalism was to attack the very centers of multicultural acceptance. Hence his targets were Labor Party symbols—government buildings—and the inheritors of Labor Party politics, the teenage children of party leaders.

The bottom line, however, is that Breivik, partly as a result of his upbringing, his failure to socialize with his peers, his inability to relate to a male authority figure during his formative years, and his addiction to violent video games, fell into a world of mental illness where his role as the single shooter became his ongoing delusion. It is as if he never awoke from a dream in which he was the avatar in his game. If there is a danger posed by violent video games to at-risk psyches, Anders Breivik is a poster boy of this form of psychosis. But, for the three psychiatrists brought in under public pressure following the findings of insanity by state prosecutors, Breivik's omnipotent delusions of grandeur were found real because the psychiatrists were taken in by the methodical nature of Brevik's fabrication. All this magical thinking passed the reality test of the last three psychiatrists and relieved him of his fears of being held hostage to the system like a Soviet dissident. How these three connected the dots in Breivik's chaotic conspiracy thesis is unknown, and assuming they actually tried to explore it with him, it would have been a most astonishing work of forensic psychiatry.

Unfortunately, fiery public reaction to the state's ruling that Breivik was insane played more in these psychiatrists' diagnosis than pure medicine. Breivik had to be found sane because a guilty verdict at trial satisfied the Norwegian public, who were both shocked and outraged by such carnage in their model of civilized life. As in Colorado right now, psychiatric diagnostics mean nothing to a crowd with pitchforks and torches. Ironically, unlike many failed not guilty by reason of insanity cases, it satisfied even Breivik, who felt that if judged insane he would spend the rest of his life as a crackpot dissident rather than a political prisoner. In his persona of Sigurd the Crusader, he is a political prisoner of war who might one day see freedom. Americans, whose familiarity with the insanity defense comes from the famous "Twinkie defense," likely believe that Breivik rightly lost his case and did not get off on an insanity. But attorney Lippestad changed his original opinion about defending Breivik and won the case by getting a judgment of sanity for his client.

Politics were at play in the prosecution team as well because they had fought to have Breivik declared insane, despite the public reaction and Breivik's own wishes. To have him declared sane meant that his political ravings would resonate as reality among extremist groups all across Europe. Breivik would become the political prisoner that he saw himself to be. It would be better for him to be judged insane, his version of reality dismissed as the manic ravings of a lunatic, and that he be shut away in an institution indefinitely. The prosecutors were correct in their insistence of an insanity ruling because Breivik's manifesto spewed forth with the disruption of thought connectivity best understood in the psychoanalytic interpretations of schizophrenic patients at Chestnut Lodge sanatorium, before the advent of safe and effective antipsychotic medications to clear thinking disorders.

Two state-appointed psychiatrists who listened to Breivik's neologisms and convoluted train of thought agreed with the prosecution. Breivik was indeed floridly psychotic and insane. Few have had the patience to sit for hours trying to make sense of schizophrenic thought disorder and interpret disparate fragments to the patient so that he could see his illogic and start thinking straight. No psychiatrist today would consider doing this again, but the Norwegian court heard neologisms and twisted logic, quite appropriately embodied in Putin's words: "the delirium of a madman." Probably at the instruction of his client, Lippestad defended the sanity as that of an inchoate defiance of reality. After all, had the court not investigated Breivik's claims of the commanders of the Knights Templar and the organization itself and found them to be a complete fabrication? Even the attempt to track down evidence of a training camp for right-wing militia in Bulgaria, where Breivik said he visited, turned out to be false. An ex-Serbian general had such a camp, but Breivik was never there. He only visited Bulgaria to track down a girlfriend.

As any criminal defense attorney will tell you, the rules of ethics demand that you follow your client's wishes. If those wishes are so to the client's detriment that the attorney can no longer mount a satisfactory defense, the attorney's duty is to resign. This rule should explain Lippestad's willingness to plead his client sane even though the evidence might really be that his client was insane. The judge, however, was not so convinced of even the slightest possibility of Breivik's sanity and sent the psychiatrists Lippestad hired to go back to reexamine Breivik, believing they had been superficial in their examination and Breivik might have deceived them. Something had to be wrong because all European intelligence services certainly could not find any evidence of the existence of these right-wing military groups or the reality of his claims of secret cells. Lippestad's two psychiatrists, however, came back with the same clinical opinion, totally opposite from that of the two-state appointed psychiatrists who found Breivik's ramblings totally incomprehensible: they again insisted that the defendant was sane. Had Breivik been allowed to stand up without his handcuffs, he would have saluted his attorney's psychiatrists with a powerful right fist that had to have resonated with perturbing memories of Nazi occupation of Norway for those in the courthouse old enough to remember the terror of Nazi occupation.

Breivik displays all of the characteristics of a paranoid schizophrenic. We know from working with paranoid and paranoid schizophrenic patients that they can plan and execute in detail as long as their plans and execution are encapsulated within their delusional system. They are never social at this time. Thus, being a loner like Adam Lanza or James Holmes does not mean that one's mind is inactive. Just the contrary; they see themselves as invisible in the darkness of their delusions. Their sick and decomposing minds can be active with voracious appetites for destruction. The psychotic mind is fully engaged in constructing its fantasy, out of which a methodical action plan may or may not come. At Breivik's pretrial hearings, a professor of psychiatry would be brought in to break the impossible tie between the opposite views of the previous two psychiatrists. Although such examinations with diagnostic conclusions are not rocket science, the court brought in a professor of psychiatry to review all four reports. He never examined Breivik, but with the skills of an academic politician, he carefully appeased the court and assuaged the opposing pairs of forensic psychiatrists, essentially saying nothing in the most ambiguous technical language. Thus, the final stamp of approval for a wild miscarriage of justice and humiliation of the profession of psychiatry was allowed a peaceful exit from that mess under the guise of legal and medical professionalism. Spectators, lawyers, and families of victims could shake their heads in utter confusion with this circus of forensic psychiatry and finally put this bloody and horrific disaster to rest—or maybe not because an act so insane to be beyond human comprehension was judged to be the product of a sane political assassin.

The Norwegian public, as they clamored for the sanity ruling, might have been shocked to learn that as a sane guilty man, Breivik would serve a maximum of twenty-two years in prison for all the deaths and damage to life and Norwegian society he had caused. Despite the findings of his defense-appointed psychiatrists, who claim he was sane throughout preparation for and execution of the attacks on the heart of this small nation, Norwegian authorities know better and prepared a prison cell for him with access to psychiatric treatment—namely antipsychotic medications to manage his grandiosity, social blunting, delusions, and hallucinatory voices. Breivik therefore has special guards who are prepared to take care of a grossly psychotic prisoner for many decades and protect him from other inmates and outsiders who will want him executed.

His moment of reality when hearing the insanity read from his own manifesto, like that of the shattering of grandiosity and omnipotence Don Quixote experienced when he awakened from a dream, was brief. A cameraman in court had caught him at a rare moment when Breivik, again like Don Quixote, had seen himself in the new magical invention called a mirror. Though he saw reality in a flash and was photographed in tears, the delusion soon kicked back in as if he was Don Alonso becoming Don Quixote of La Mancha again. So, though his sanity was declared in public, Breivik would soon rise again in court to deny its authority over him: the martyred knight, defender of Aryan Europe, Sigurd who angrily saluted with his right arm raised Nazi-style, emotionally unaffected by it all, his right fist tightly clenched in defiant but delusional omnipotence. His future—in fact, his very pulse—would depend on guards protecting him as if he were a dependent baby. All of this was a deadly and contagious delusion that infected Adam Lanza as he followed Breivik's every move in the news. And, like Lanza and most suicidal mass murderers, Breivik was not as invisible to authorities as the Norwegian director of security asserted. Not even the STASSI, Communist East Germany's dreaded intelligence arm of the KGB (the Soviet Union's Committee for State Security), could have detected the menace of Anders Breivik.

State security personnel had no explanation when they were confronted with security video films of Breivik walking past the Norwegian equivalent of the White House in a SWAT uniform and armed with assault weapons, only to find out later that he was on the security watch list for importing explosive chemicals from Poland. Wishing she had never spoken so carelessly without knowing the facts—or, perhaps in a state of shock—the state security director quietly resigned. The police commissioner who could not even muster a helicopter to get police to Utøya resigned as well. Impatient with the police response time, Breivik called the police and asked what was taking them so long. He made a feeble attempt to swim away amidst the hemorrhaging bodies he ruthlessly destroyed. But he had no escape and evasion plans and returned to shore, quietly surrendering to the police.

Breivik later said that he had not given himself more than a 10 percent chance of surviving his preemptive strike on Islamo-Europe. He overestimated his enemy, Norwegian security, which was as inexcusably unprepared for Breivik as was the FBI for the Brothers Tsarnaev. Norwegians have to be frightened by the complacency and incompetence of their security services that claimed Breivik came out of nowhere, because, as in all the cases we present, he did not. He was in their faces from the very beginning, but they chose not to look at him even while he strode within their highest security zone fully attired and armed in a combat camouflage uniform and armaments. Security guards must have been dozing as they monitored the cameras.[91]

Security films depict Breivik walking away from his car, which was timed to explode and rip Norwegian state headquarters to smithereens. He sauntered undetected to the dock to catch the ferry to Utøya and introduced himself as a policeman. Upon his arrival on the island, he opened fire on everything that moved, and, like Lanza, set his sights on helpless children. Had personnel monitoring Norwegian headquarters security been awake, they would have recognized a dangerous man within the highest security zone of Norway, interdicted him, and maybe prevented the lethal explosions just in time. Then, through interrogation, they would have matched

---

[91] Reuters. "Anders Behring Breivik Captured on CCTV During Oslo Bomb Attack." *The Telegraph*, September 15, 2011. http://i.telegraph.co.uk/multimedia/archive/01999/ br_1999357c.jpg.

his name to their security watch list for importing explosives from Poland. It could have been a shootout, as was the case of Watertown, Massachusetts, in the wake of the Boston Marathon bombing, but that is security's job: to watch for suspicious behavior in high-security zones and confront such suspicious people as their images showed onscreen.[92]

By coincidence, the prime minister of Norway was neither in his office nor on the island with his youth movement for the Labor Party as Breivik might have expected him to be if he was one of Breivik's targets. Idyllic Norway would never be the same. Anders Breivik will enjoy a short life in his grandiose delusion, although that delusion lived on in the minds of Adam Lanza and perhaps Dzhokhar Tsarnaev.

---

[92] Reuters. "Anders Breivik, Making a Salute as He Appeared in Court." *The Telegraph*, April 16, 2011. http://i.telegraph.co.uk/multimedia/archive/02194/breivik_2194965b.jpg.

Chapter 7

Eddie Routh: The Double Murder at a Gun Range

Former Navy SEAL Christopher Kyle had a plan. The heavily decorated sniper, whose bestselling book *American Sniper* described his experiences as the sniper with the most kills in the military, believed that by helping veterans with post-traumatic stress disorder (PTSD) work through their issues by relating to other veterans in a familiar surrounding, he could effect some form of remedy. At least, he believed he could provide therapy to relieve their immediate anxiety. However, when Kyle and his buddy Chad Littlefield took combat veteran and PTSD sufferer Eddie Ray Routh to a gun range at the upscale Rough Creek Lodge in Glen Rose, Texas, on February 2, 2013, things went horribly wrong. Both Kyle and Littlefield were killed when Routh, seemingly without provocation, turned his weapon on them and left them for dead, lying in pools of blood, then took their pickup and tried to escape. Why would Routh, now in police custody, turn a weapon on brother veterans trying to help him?

As with most cases of psychotic murderers with apparent suicidal intent, the absence of any records of their case management leaves few facts, numerous clues for speculation, and a plethora of questions in the wake of their crimes. As is typical in these cases, salient background facts are initially kept from the public while police assemble evidence during the investigation. These background facts may or may not make it to the surface once the flood of civil litigation from responsible parties begins, especially those who demand answers to what the nature of the psychotic killer's case management revealed, particularly with respect to a psychologist's or psychiatrist's duty to warn and protect, which is the legal standard in California and many other states.

The Eddie Ray Routh case began near dusk at the shooting range at the resort outside Dallas/Fort Worth on February 2, when the bodies of Kyle and his friend Littlefield were discovered in pools of blood with their backs riddled with bullets. A short time later Routh showed up at his sister and brother-in-law's house in a shiny black pickup truck. His sister said that he was behaving and talking strangely. He told them in an off-handed, matter-of-fact way that he and two other people were out shooting target practice and he couldn't trust them, so he killed them before they could kill him.

"I traded my soul for a new truck," he said.

Routh's sister, Laura Blevins, told police that her brother had been paranoid for a long time and thought everybody was out to get him.

"My brother," she said, "is out of his mind saying people were sucking his soul and that he could smell the pigs. He said he was going to get their souls before they took his."[93]

When Blevins asked Routh who he killed, he told her it was Christopher Kyle and a friend. She was shocked and pressed him for

[93] Ortiz, Erik. "'He Told Me That He's Committed a Murder': Sister of Accused Gunman Eddie Ray Routh Made Distressed 911 Call." *New York Daily News*, February 6, 2013. http://www.nydailynews.com/news/crime/sister-eddie-ray-routh-made-distressed-911-call-article-1.1256528.

more information, asking him if he was kidding, but he repeatedly affirmed the information. He had indeed committed the crime. Blevins urged her brother to turn himself in, but he said that he had to escape Texas authorities and get to Oklahoma. Routh, now knowing that he would be a hunted man, especially since he had confessed to his sister that he had murdered two people, had to escape. This would have been cataloged as a "mass murder" had Routh encountered more people at the shooting range.

Laura Blevins's 911 call was frantic, perhaps because she was afraid that her brother's demeanor was more menacing than ever before. She turned the phone over to her husband, Gaines, who laid out the facts as Routh had told them to his sister. He said that Routh, who was a strange-acting individual, was afraid that people were after him and had gone shooting with two people he believed were thinking about turning their weapons on him. So he shot them and took their truck. "I sold my soul for a truck," Routh reportedly said.[94]

Saturday night is usually pretty quiet in the Lancaster neighborhood where the Blevins family lives. But on February 2, 2013, neighbors were shocked to see dozens of police cars lining their street. They saw officers trying to negotiate with Routh, who had just pulled up in front of his house in the stolen black truck. For a survivor of war, Routh could hardly have done a worse job of escape and evasion, all but inviting his death when surrounded by police who were already warned of his dangerousness and military kill skills. He should have expected to be shot by the police. Officers tried to coax Routh out of Kyle's truck, but he refused, turned the ignition key in defiance, stepped on the gas, and sped off. His truck tires squealing, Routh ran over stop sticks, which did nothing to the large tires. The short chase ended when Routh rammed a police car along I-35 and Camp Wisdom. His escape attempt had come to an end, and he

---

94 Ibid.

was taken into custody. Searching his house, the police confiscated drug paraphernalia, a cell phone, and a semiautomatic weapon he carelessly left behind. The police easily checked ballistics on the gun and connected Routh to the double murder. They hoped to find some explanation of a motive on the cell phone, either photos from the range or text messages linking the victims with Routh. What the police uncovered was indeed disturbing.

Two days before Routh killed Kyle and Littlefield, he was discharged from the Dallas Veterans Administration Medical Center against the strong protest of his parents, who believed him to be way too sick and too dangerous to take home. This, we believe, was a minimization of his symptoms. He lived alone in the family house that was for sale, and his parents were not the ones to conduct a suicide vigil; they were terrified of him. Whoever made the decision to damn the torpedoes and send Eddie Routh packing from the VA hospital would have had to have heard of the family protests over discharging him. Yet Routh was released despite the warnings of dangerousness. Routh's eligibility at the VA hospitals is questionable because the Marines officially notified the press that he was on Ready Reserve status, which meant that he was still in an active category and not a veteran entitled to veteran's benefits. Although reservists and National Guard units have done much of the heavy lifting in Iraq and Afghanistan, it seems odd that a ready reservist would be eligible for certain military benefits, such as Base Exchange shopping access with considerable retail discounts but not medical services from the VA. It is unknown whether his probable ineligibility had anything to do with forcing the discharge without any follow-up case management reported.

What can safely be said, however, is that Routh was floridly paranoid—whether from a psychotic form of PTSD, a psychotic illness occurring while in the military, or a drug-induced aggravation of either is unclear. But it is safe to say that he was far sicker than the diagnostic labels attributed to him in the press, namely

PTSD. There have been rumors that he was a mechanic and was never in combat; however that is not true. Routh was deployed to Iraq in 2007, according to an article in the *Huffington Post*.[95] Then the Marine Corps said Routh was deployed to Haiti after the earthquake, which may have involved combat, but even if it had not, the exposure to the horrific damage to the landscape and loss of life among residents there could have caused PTSD. A reliable-sounding cousin described to the press a normal buddy who went off to war and came home a different person, one with emptiness in his eyes and uncharacteristic aggressiveness. Unquestionably, this was not the Eddie Routh known to family or neighbors. This was a seriously mentally ill patient who had to be tasered and strapped into a restraint chair when he became aggressive with guards after he would not give them back a food tray on the day after his arrest.

Routh's abnormal behavior, although probably at the extreme end for him, was nothing new. He was arrested for a DWI charge in January 2012 and was held in jail for two weeks. His bond was reportedly $1,500 at the time of his arrest. In May 2012, Routh was a suspect in the burglary of nine bottles of medication stolen from a neighbor's house. In September 2012, his mother told a 911 operator that her son had to be admitted to the Dallas VA Medical Center on an emergency basis, but she was unsuccessful in that effort. The police were then called to the Routh home because he had been drinking and was upset that his father was going to sell his gun. He said he would blow his brains out, and he allegedly made threats to kill his family. The police found Routh near the house, without shirt or shoes. They described in their report that he was crying and very emotional. He told them that he was a Marine veteran and had PTSD. Routh was taken into protective custody and transported to Green Oaks

---

[95] Brown, Angela K. "Eddie Ray Routh, Accused Killer of 'American Sniper' Author, Refuses to See Family and Lawyer: Sheriff." *Huffington Post,* February 6, 2013. http://www.huffingtonpost.com/2013/02/05/eddie-ray-routh-american-sniper-family-lawyer_n_2625387.html.

Hospital in Dallas. It is not clear whether he was admitted voluntarily or committed, but the Lancaster police had reportedly placed him in protective custody for dangerousness to self and others. That was the first time the police became aware that he suffered from PTSD from combat, but to this day it is not clear where Routh obtained the diagnosis or heard of it.

Routh was reportedly rehospitalized in mid-January at this same hospital, just two weeks before the murder, when his girlfriend called the police because she feared he would harm himself. She apparently expressed concern that he had shared his psychic pain with her and that his family did not understand what he had been going through. She may have also been afraid of him; the police had written a criminal trespassing warning for him after an apparent scuffle on the property. He was reportedly discharged quickly but somehow was admitted to the Dallas VA Medical Center shortly thereafter. Apparently, contrary to his girlfriend's observations, his parents did know months before that their son was coming unhinged but were helpless in obtaining any help for him. In fact, it is possible that they were so afraid of him that they moved away, put the house up for sale, and left Eddie behind in it. He was unemployed, and how he supported himself is unknown, but he may have done some carpentry work when he could. Routh was never threatening to the neighbors, although they did see him dressed in camouflage while walking his dog. One of them tried to share a family member's problems from deployment in Iraq and could not get Routh to talk about his own problems at all. Routh had even asked a neighbor to paint his red Volkswagen in camouflage colors.

Near the time of his final hospital admission to the Dallas VA Medical Center, Routh's mother happened to have noticed Christopher Kyle dropping off his children at the school where she worked as an aide. She hailed him before he drove off and asked if he could help with her son. This was likely after she realized there would be no medical help for him, because VA staff discharged him over her strong objections and fears for both her son's and others' safety. Understandably, she was at the end of her rope, but Kyle offered to help. His book had sold nearly one million hard copies and was number one on the *New York Times* bestseller list. Kyle was dedicating himself to helping fellow veterans by taking them to the shooting range. This was not VA-approved treatment, and specialists in implosion therapy for desensitizing combat veterans to the phobias acquired in war totally disown any unofficial therapy of this type, particularly shooting weapons. Sometimes they will allow a veteran to handle an unloaded weapon if they want to hunt again and are afraid to touch a weapon. But pushing a patient with PTSD so far so fast is not considered acceptable implosion therapy for combat-caused PTSD.

Kyle asked a neighbor where Eddie Routh lived. She pointed to the small, single-story frame house with the FOR SALE sign on it and red Volkswagen parked in front. Kyle must have found the Marine emblem on the back of the Volkswagen disarming. Eddie hopped into the truck, and they headed off to the skeet range for a nonprescribed treatment session of shooting targets. The police would find out that Kyle and Routh graduated from the same high school in Midlothian, but were fourteen years apart and likely knew each other vaguely at most. Kyle still lived in Midlothian, Texas, with his wife and two children. Routh's mother knew Kyle through the local public school district.

Former congressman and Republication presidential aspirant Ron Paul had posted a cryptic tweet about what was about to unfold that afternoon. The tweet drew a lot of criticism. "He lived by the sword and died by the sword," Paul wrote, as if denigrating the altruistic and passionate dedication Kyle had to the cause of helping his fellow veterans.[96] Christopher Kyle died as he could never have intended to, after having survived so many firefights in Iraq.

---

[96] Adams, Becket. "Updated: Ron Paul Account Tweets Shock Message about Former Seal Sniper's Death." *The Blaze,* February 4, 2013. http://www.theblaze.com/stories/2013/02/04/ron-paul-account-tweets-shock-message-about-former-seal-snipers-death/.

About three hours after Kyle stopped by Routh's house to take him to the shooting range, Routh unloaded his automatic weapon into Kyle's back and shot Littleton the same way. After searching Kyle's clothes for his truck keys and retrieving them from the blood-soaked garments, Routh ran for Kyle's truck, called his sister, and arrived on her doorstep shortly after to confess. It was over. The American Sniper did not die by the sword but by the treachery of a psychotic killer, who said he had traded his own soul for a black truck. Routh was not the typical veteran struggling with the phobias and nightmares of combat. He was clearly observed to be far beyond that. He had been grossly psychotic for many months, in fluctuating states of paranoid fear with homicidal impulses and suicidal despair. The police knew him well by this time, and the staff at Green Oaks evaluated him, diagnosed him, and probably prescribed medication for him. Jailers recently reported Routh to be better now that he was back on his medication. We do not know what that medication was, but presumably it was an antipsychotic that reduced his paranoid and aggressive agitation that had previously required four-point restraints and solitary confinement.

The personnel at Dallas VA Medical Center have studied Routh's records and have probably been debriefed on his case. They have much to be concerned about because he was discharged just two days before mowing down an iconic American hero. It is impossible to specifically interpret Routh's motives or intentions regarding the events of the murder of Kyle, especially if we take his coveting Kyle's pickup truck as merely a delusional statement. But it is not hard to add Routh to a gallery of suicidal mass murderers and their victims who were either at the wrong place at the wrong time, or, like Kyle and educational and medical staff, simply trying to do some good. It is unlikely that anyone else in the immediate area of this shooting range would have been spared the barrage of fire unleashed by this paranoid psychotic if anybody else had been there at the time. Thus, the body count in this case was two instead of the four needed to statistically qualify it for mass murder. In Routh's state of mind, however, it is likely that nobody within the radius of his paranoid radar screen would have been spared. Nobody else was there until a guide—by pure coincidence—came across the blood-soaked bodies near dusk. True, we do not have all the facts. We do not know whether Routh planned to escape and continue causing homicidal mayhem or whether he intended to die in a shootout with police, essentially a case of suicide-by-cop. We can only speculate, based on reliable reports of acquaintances and family about Routh's state of mind.

This was no plot to kill the American Sniper. This was no premeditative carjacking to abscond with an American idol's iconic black truck. This was pure treacherous, homicidal madness born out of serious mental illness. Only if this goes to trial might we ever know whether Routh was diagnosed with PTSD, another disorder more likely to cause paranoid psychosis, or even drug-induced psychosis. But we must assume that this Marine reservist was not considered to be this sick he was when discharged, or he would not have been in the Ready Reserves. The role of combat exposure and drug abuse are also wildcards at this time.

Another wild card in the great poker deck called public psychiatry and veterans affairs is the absence of case management of a known suicidal, homicidal, and psychotic young man who had easy access to lethal weapons and the skills, although not the judgment, to have them in his possession. Even his father knew that when he took his son's gun away from him months before. Why Marine Command, medical staff on three separate hospitalizations, the police, and Kyle did not know about the dangers Routh posed could remain a mystery.

What is Routh's state of mind now that he is less aggressive and agitated and back on his medications, as reported by jailers? Loughner expressed remorse when he was first medicated for psychosis and said he would not have committed the massacre at the Tucson Safeway Plaza if he had been on the antipsychotic medication that cleared his delusional mind, so he was determined competent to stand trial and agree to a plea that spared him execution. Perhaps Routh feels this same remorse. He now starts down the same pathway, adding one more portrait of neglected or failed treatment and case management to the gallery of the seriously mentally ill. Will he express a will to live or remain suicidal enough to get killed under jurisdiction of the state of Texas? Certainly, like James Holmes, there will be a price on his head for killing one of America's most revered military heroes who survived so many bloody firefights, only to be shot in the back by an insane man who did not even know him personally and who had gone to the same high school more than a decade later.

Chapter 8

Psychiatric, Sociopsychological, and Genetic Backgrounds of Violence and Aggression

Against the background of the epidemic of violence perpetrated by suicidal mass murderers, some common denominators define the underpinnings of their crimes. First, we know from records that almost all suicidal mass murderers are mentally ill and that their illnesses were detected years before their crimes. Second, we know that many suicidal mass murderers had gone through some types of medical screening, even forms of psychotherapy, and were diagnosed with various psychological or behavioral issues. Third, we also know that many suicidal mass murderers actually studied the crimes of other suicidal mass murders, for example, Adam Lanza's research into the crimes of Anders Brevik and Cho Seung-Hui's expressed admiration for Dylan Klebold and Eric Harris at Columbine High School and Cho's wish to copycat their crime. These three common denominators cause us to wonder whether Boston's Brothers Tsarnaev were also suicidal and whether they abandoned their plan to escape from Cambridge to confront the police to commit suicide-by-cop in a firefight rather than allow themselves to be caught. We know now that Dzhokhar, the younger brother, was caught on a police helicopter—mounted FLIR camera while hiding and bleeding out under a tarp in a boat in a private citizen's backyard, taken into custody, and charged with using weapons of mass destruction. He was hospitalized and is recovering from gunshot wounds after the confrontation with the police. He told interrogators that he and his older brother had planned to escape from Boston with improvised explosive devices they were going to plant in New York City in coordinated terrorist attacks. This is scary.

The commonalities that link suicidal mass murderers include, first and foremost, mental illness, an illness so profound that the perpetrator, although he might appear logical and methodical in his behavior, is living in a world of his own fear and fantasy that shuts him off from reality. Each of the subjects covered in this book share this form of mental illness, usually schizophrenia, a splitting off between the subject's delusional world of reality and the actual world of reality. It is no surprise that almost every one of the mass murder perpetrators we hear of has at one time or another either been deemed mentally ill by a psychiatrist or psychologist or has displayed the behavioral symptoms of someone going through a crisis of mental illness, even if that behavior is only vaguely apparent to the outside world. In fact, one of the most frustrating things about someone who acts strangely in a friend's or neighbor's description is post mortem—because most of these individuals wind up committing suicide—a line connecting the dots of the person's behavior and actions comes up as if it is a treasure map written in invisible ink held over a flame or hot light bulb. A pattern suddenly appears and makes sense, yet at the time of the perpetrator's crimes, the dots were simply dots: points on a timeline that bore little relationship to each other. We can see this in Tamerlan Tsarnaev's timeline because of his personality shift after he was told he could not compete for the US team in amateur boxing and became aware that his American citizenship application was held up for further investigation. Absent official American citizenship, the only sense of acceptance he could find was in radical Islamic jihad, much to the consternation and concern of his parents.

Serious mental illness may come in a variety of forms, but it is almost always progressive, ending up with the person feeling hopeless, in pain, and aggressive toward a world that seems neither to understand nor care. If and when the mentally ill person becomes suicidal, that is when violence itself is most likely, as we have seen over the course of mass murders since Charles Whitman in the Texas University bell tower almost forty years ago. Suicidality and mental illness go hand in hand.

The myth about mental illness is that it is static. If a person has schizophrenia, the person is mentally ill and may only get better through treatment. But what most people do not realize is that if left untreated, a mental illness progressively gets worse until, like Adam Lanza, what was just a person's fear that something may be wrong with his mind becomes a creeping paranoia walling off the person from the rest of reality. Thus made vulnerable by his mental illness, the perpetrator-to-be is prone to react to and from any stimuli that would not normally be a call to deadly aggression for the rest of us. The perpetrator falls victim to his own neurobiology as well as the external stimulus such as violent video games, television shows, or motion pictures portraying scenes of extreme and graphic violence.

The Neurobiology of Aggression

Question: Are Patients diagnosed with schizophrenia more likely than the general population to commit homicide? If so, what is the evidence?

A robust body of evidence demonstrates an association between psychoses and violence, most significantly between psychosis and murder. Substance abuse comorbidity increases this correlation between serious mental illness, violence, and suicide. Comorbidity is the presence of disorders in addition to the underlying illness, such as frequent attacks with bipolar affective disorder. Thus, people with mental illness are sometimes substance abusers or display symptoms of other diseases. Thus, the increased risk associated with this comorbidity is of a similar magnitude to that in individuals who have only substance abuse problems. This finding would suggest that violence reduction strategies could consider focusing on the primary and secondary prevention of substance abuse rather than solely targeting individuals with severe mental illness. This strategy would be like working from the outside in to remedy as many of the antisocial behaviors (often, outward manifestations of aggression) as possible to get to the core problem. Aggression is defined by hostile, injurious, and destructive behavior often caused by frustration. It can be categorized as impulsive or premeditated. Impulsive aggression is accompanied by over-reactivity to a stressful trigger, such as being insulted, and is accompanied by negative emotion and autonomic arousal, such as palpitations, sweating, and fast breathing. The autonomic responses to a stressful trigger bypass the brain's cognitive or rational assessment and involve reactions not immediately under the person's control. This is similar to a fright reaction when something startles a person, who then screams even as he recognizes that whatever startled him is not a threat. In people who gain control of their emotional response, autonomic reactions are quickly rationalized and the person returns to a state of emotional balance. Premeditated murder, however, is cold-blooded because it is planned with motive and not accompanied by autonomic arousal or caused by triggering stress. Contributors include political, cultural, socioeconomic, and neurobiological factors, the last of which we know more about.

Impulsive aggression occurs when the imbalance is top-down among insula and amygdala and anterior cingulate and orbitofrontal cortex—structures in the brain that control body reactions. The insula, for example, controls the hunger reflex and cravings. The amygdala area is part of what neurologists used to call the "old brain," where emotions are processed, an area that governs both fear and pleasure responses. These are also called "visceral" responses because the body responds autonomically, beyond rational mediated control to perceived threats such as frightening or threatening experiences. The amygdala and insula assess threat in context of an experience stored in the amygdala, which is similar to a repository of prior stimuli that have triggered both fear and pleasure. The body's responses to these feelings are also stored in the amygdala. Think of a stored set of deep threats, such as buried memories of childhood abuse or sexual abuse. Those memories can be stimulated by an event that falls into the same threat category of the prior abuse, hence a potential basis for post-traumatic stress disorder. The orbitofrontal and cingulate areas assess situations in terms of reward or punishment consequences for action on impulse. Thus you have a signal, cognitive processing of it, and regulatory response to processing. This neurological subsystem acts as a primary switchboard to connect perceived external events to a type of yes/no or good/bad response. It assesses the likelihood of a reward or a punishment for a specific action so that the person can judge how to respond. If this system is broken, and there are a variety of ways it can become dysfunctional, the person's response to external stimuli may seem awkward, inappropriate, or simply strange. For example, a combat veteran from the Vietnam War may have an abnormal fear-based response to a simple walk in the woods because, in his experience, walks among jungle-like foliage may evoke memories stored in his amygdala of bloody ambushes that killed members of his unit. Thus, he has a heightened sense of fear even decades after the event itself.

Neuromodulators are just what their name implies: chemicals that work on neurocircuits, the networks of nerve cells in the brain, whose uptake affects moods and information processing. These chemicals include glutamate (an amino acid that acts as a messenger chemical in transmitting information to neurons, too much of which is toxic to the neurons), GABA (a member of the amino acid family that regulates the excitation of nerve cells in the central nervous system), NE (or norepinephrine, a neurotransmitter that regulates the body's arousal mechanism from hunger and mood control and operates in the central nervous system), DA (or dopamine, one of the primary transmitters for mood reactions, particularly within the limbic system), serotonin (another neurochemical controlling mood and sleep functions), neuropeptides (chemical signals within the neurocircuitry of the brain controlling physiological reactions), and acetylcholine (a neurochemical that helps mediate memory and learning and is an important brain signaling chemical). Serotonin appears to be the major mediating neurochemical that affects much processing in the brain.

And here's how these chemicals work together. Glutamate is a generalized neurotransmitter operating throughout the brain and is mainly responsible for stimulating neurons. For example, the limbic brain cells might fire up to the cerebral cortical frontal lobe cells and activate them. Therefore, you should become more alert and think faster. But its counterpart, GABA, inhibits this activity. Thus, the balance between GABA and glutamate is increasingly important today for potential therapeutic targets of drugs to both activate certain regions of the brain or inhibit them, but mainly to balance them. Acetylcholine is necessary for memory. Hence, by blocking it with anticholinergic drugs and then experiencing something, you won't remember the experience.

Acetylcholine does many other things throughout the brain and the body, including stimulating the gut and regulating pupil size. Norepinephrine (NE), dopamine (DA), and serotonin are, like glutamate and GABA, widely dispersed throughout the brain and regulate much brain activity, but in a more specific way than simply increasing or decreasing activity of a cell. NE is necessary for interest and attention, but its dysfunctional transmission is also responsible in part for depression. DA is necessary for pleasure and energy, but its dysfunctional transmission is also responsible for depression and attention deficit disorder when deficient. But amphetamine psychosis and psychosis from bipolar to schizophrenic illness are found to have excessive dopaminergic neurotransmission in the limbic system. Neuropeptides are small molecules that operate inside and outside the cells, but they are the building blocks of proteins necessary for structure and function of the brain. DNA, for example, is a series of neuropeptides.

Serotonin, dopamine, and norepinephrine do not activate cells directly, as apparently does GABA, but, rather, they work through a second messenger system inside the brain cell, informing the DNA to produce different proteins, both for structure of brain tissue and neurotransmission. These chemicals affect protein production within the brain. Thus, a protein's improved production because of these neurochemicals via neuropeptide manipulation actually works like a fertilizer for brain cells, making them grow, sprout branches, and direct these branches and growth in the right direction. In schizophrenia, they are all tangled up; thus, signaling is chaotic.

When there is a dysfunction in the generation and uptake of chemical neuromodulators, the factors include cognitive impairment, psychosocial impairment, sensory impairment, and distortions of sensory perception by drugs and alcohol. You can see how, even though the human neurological system is resilient and has its own defense mechanisms, events that disturb the balance of chemicals and functions of various parts of the brain can have a huge effect on behavior. For our purposes, we focus on impulsive aggressive behavior.

Impulsive aggression can occur as the result of bottom hyperactivity in insula and amygdala, encoded for experience, and hypoactivity in the orbitofrontal cortex and anterior cingulate cortex—limbic music of hyperactivity or cortical hypoactivity, respectively. Cortical hypoactivity due to lesion, reduced brain volume, or aberrant information processing is dependent on serotonin for regulation and can be dysregulated by DA and NE. This means that if there is a dysfunction in the uptake of serotonin, a brain modulator, caused by any number of events, such as brain injury, lesions resulting from seizures, or reduced brain volume resulting from, for example, long-term alcohol abuse, the brain reacts aberrantly. If an at-risk individual, primarily a patient suffering from schizophrenia, is left untreated because of a misdiagnosis, lack of access to health care, or simply because parents or teachers do not understand that a child may be mentally ill, the long-term effects of brain dysfunction are progressive and the individual retreats into his or her own world devoid of external reality.

The amygdala, located deep inside the brain, provides emotional responses to stimuli involving basic emotions such as fear and flight. Generally, within a healthy neurological system, the amygdala stores long-term memories of emotional experiences and compares external stimuli to stored memories to generate a response. In a healthy amygdala, there is ample room for memory storage. However, there are instances of reduced amygdala volume resulting from emotional hypersensitivity or because of repeated stimulation—usually negative stimulation—a form of amygdala overload resulting in something akin to a dumping of long-term emotional memories into the conscious mind. Constant emotional pounding on the amygdala, caused by repeated threatening experiences, can actually reduce the volume of the amygdala to store memories. When that happens and a memory dump results, even a slow-drip leak into the conscious mind, the person's mind is flooded with something we call "limbic music," something akin to a waking dream state in which the person cannot differentiate between dreams and external reality.

Think of Adam Lanza, deeply psychotic, immersed in violent, single-shooter video games, sliding deeper and deeper into a waking dream state, albeit within the digital world of his computer while safely ensconced in his room. However, if his comfort zone is disturbed by even the slightest jarring, or if he feels threatened to the point of his perceived destruction, what might his response be? For a long-term schizophrenic, who has little or no grip on external reality, that response might take the form of a waking dream. Awash in limbic music, Adam Lanza, who may have once been able to differentiate right from wrong and might be aware of his immediate surroundings, acts as if he is in a dream in which he is the single shooter in *Call of Duty* who methodically eliminates all the threats to his avatar in the video game session. Only it is not a video game session and Lanza is not the avatar. This is real life. He is the real shooter, and he shoots real bullets. He eliminates his targets in his internal dream state. First, his mother, whom he sees as the cause of the disruption of his comfort zone because she is moving the family out of Newtown. Then it is the school he attended, the grade he attended, and the children, whom Lanza perceived to have threatened him with touching or other forms of social contact and who have now become his alias targets, standing in for those children who had bullied him over a decade earlier. And, finally, after less than five minutes of shooting, during which he expends more than 150 of the .223 rounds from his Bushmaster AR-15, he turns the weapon on himself. Game over. But it was never a game for all of us in the real world.

What we are seeing from Adam Lanza or James Holmes, and particularly from Jared Loughner, is pathological aggression, all too common in some psychiatric and personality disorders that may share risk factors with psychiatric disorders. Psychopathology may be a risk factor where there is an incorrect dosage and inadequate follow-up of antipsychotic medications or even cross-reactions between different medications. Manifestations of pathological aggression may also depend on genetic vulnerability, with cognitive impairment leading to deviant behaviors such as serial killings and murder.

For example, imagine someone like notorious serial killer Ted Bundy: intelligent, a volunteer at the University of Washington rape crisis center, and a first-year law student with important political connections. Yet, deep within his psyche, Bundy had no ability to relate to other people in a healthy way. He was a sociopath, brooding and angry, completely unable to respect physical, emotional, and social boundaries because his mental illness, his paraphilic compulsion for sexual homicide, also called "lust killing," and his psychopathic personality had made him blind to them. Everyone and everything belonged to him because everyone and everything was simply an object over which he must exercise control. He was a sex offender, a thief, and a cat burglar. Within his victim target group, he may have seemed harmless at first, sympathetic, friendly, and in need of assistance from his prospective victim. Then he struck, knocking his victim unconscious and strangling her to death. Then, after secreting away his dead victim, he exercised complete sexual control over the dead body—no need for social niceties or relationship management. His victim belonged to him even as she decomposed in some remote location in a northwestern primeval forest. The body disposal site itseslf, Bundy once told the police, was sacred to him.[97] Bundy, of course, was found guilty of murder in Florida and executed. But

---

[97] Keppel, Robert D., and William J. Birnes. *The Riverman*. New York: Pocket Books, 1995, Reprint, 2005. See also Liebert, J., MD. "Contributions of Psychiatric Consultation in the Investigation of Serial Murder." *International Journal of Offender Therapy & Comparative Criminology*, 1985.

what his real pathological motivations were, we can only guess. His secrets died with him. All of this having been said, offenders like Ted Bundy, Gary Ridgway, Jeffrey Dahmer, or Arthur Shawcross are not suicidal mass murderers. However, they may share the same limbic dream state as offenders like Adam Lanza during the commission of their crimes.

Among at-risk, suicide-prone individuals, susceptibility to aggression might be caused by co-occurring psychopathology, such as cognitive impairment, a form of deviant violence that can result from the neurological inability of the at-risk individual to respond to any perceived threats with even a marginally rational response. Think of James Holmes as he realized that he was sinking deeper and deeper into a world of fear and aggression. While under therapy at the University of Colorado, he was unable to participate in that therapy because he could not converse with the therapist for numerous possible reasons, including being locked off campus after he had flunked out. He could only descend deeper and deeper into his psychotic dream state until he, like Adam Lanza, inhabited the role of his avatar, only in real life. He became the Joker, even though there is no Joker, except on the screen or in comic books. But it is a role that allowed him to manifest his psychotic aggression in the comfort zone of a character and not the real James Holmes.

In this case, we have actually witnessed the terror of a fragmented mind coming together, glued like pieces of a jigsaw puzzle into a mosaic of horror. The biology of dysregulation, hypersensitivity, and hyperreactivity may result in impulsive aggression in borderline personality disorder (BPD).

BPD, though not considred to be a mental illness, is a very broad spectrum of enduring lifelong personality traits, frequently and mistakenly diagnosed because of a cross-sectional view of a patient without a longitudinal, or long-term, history of the necessary signs and symptoms. The underlying psychopathology is usually overlooked as well; it can include polymorphous perverse sexuality, specifically, gender identification instability and long-standing paraphilias, otherwise known as sexual perversions. There may be a history of what is called "splitting," wherein there always have to be good nurturing and bad nurturing figures, such as a good parent and a bad parent. The third element is called polyneurotic symptomatology. This element entails the presentation of multiple neurotic complaints, such as undiagnosable pain sensations, pseudoseizures, vague illusions mistaken for hallucinations, and other complaints that almost always have no physiological component. In other words, someone constantly complains about pains in his or her joints, but ultrasounds, MRIs, and X-rays indicate that there are no injuries and nothing to cause the pain. Thus, the pain may be deemed psychosomatic in origin. Although this triad of psychopathological elements is not Axis II criteria, which means it should establish a diagnosable basis for a mental illness, the triad should be sufficient to make BPD a diagnosis that has the reliability, specificity, and validity it needs for studies as serious as attributions of violence. Of course, there are severe narcissists and psychopaths—particularly sexual psychopaths—who do fulfill the criteria for BPD. Many patients with PTSD unfortunately fulfill the criteria as well. Therefore, BPD is often associated with PTSD, making things even more complicated when it comes to establishing a diagnosis.

Individuals with the Axis II personality disorder known as BPD have an extreme sensitivity to disappointments, perceived challenges, insults, and frustration. They have very low resiliency, a low tolerance for negative external stimuli, and an inability to cope with life's setbacks. At the more extreme edge of BPD, individuals display an impulsive aggressive reaction to challenges and disappointments and aim that aggression at target groups, but this aggression is not limited to just those groups. BPD sufferers can also become suicidal at the extreme range, and this form of suicidality is also aggressive. Thus, mass shooters such as Christopher Dorner, who commentators have said was an "injustice collector," drew disappointments into himself.[98] That inward struggle ultimately resulted in his violent aggressive homicidal and suicidal acts and displayed some of the classic symptoms of impulsive aggression of BPD, although his manifesto is a classic flight of ideas from a manic depressive patient, too. Inasmuch as we don't know his history of military service in the Middle East, his apparent BPD could have also been untreated PTSD. Perhaps some of the motivations underlying aggression in BPD sufferers are a need to restore a sense of balance to their lives and to reestablish equilibrium in their neurocircuitry by enacting what they see as justice to remedy their perceived injustices. This is what is known as projective identification, wherein the sufferer justifies his or her murderous rage based on a perception of the antagonist's aggression. Such projective identification defensive operations are necessary in warfare so as to justify killing a faceless enemy who, you are told, seeks your death. Projective identification is the foundation stone for paranoia. This explains such things as the Unabomber's manifesto, Breivik's manifesto, and Dorner's online manifesto about the injustices he claims were heaped upon him. Dorner drew some of his language both from the Unabomber Ted Kaczynski and from Breivik, whose manifesto echoes statements made by Kaczynski.

We don't know if Adam Lanza was diagnosed with BPD on Axis II, but serious mental illness in children, such as bipolar affective disorder and schizophrenia, can be mistaken for borderline personality disorder, for which there are no effective psychopharmological solutions. Treatment for such misdiagnoses can lead to dangerous extensions of duration of untreated psychosis until it is too late, as we have possibly seen in Lanza's case and certainly with Cho Seung-Hui. The child's or young adult's life comes to an end with

---

[98] Griffith, David. "Chris Dorner: The Injustice Collector." *Police Magazine,* March 5, 2013. http://www.policemag.com/channel/patrol/articles/2013/03/chris-dorner-the-injustice-collector.aspx.

suicide, intractable addiction, or incarceration after conviction for the commission of a felony.

Because those who have BPD are almost always emotionally disruptive—the least little thing will set them off if it is a perceived slight—family members of those with BPD are also at a loss to find a remedy to the person's behavior. Thus, imagine that you are a parent of an adolescent with BPD, who is awash in self-hatred and experiences remorse over his life, but who also has bipolar tendencies that make him or her swing from mania to an almost inconsolable depression. The manic highs can be marked by extreme aggression, while the lows are marked by self-mutilation or even suicidal ideations. For this reason, psychiatrists sometimes report that family members of those suffering from BPD describe the person as "mercurial" because of his or mood swings. These mood swings would be almost charming if the extremes of that bipolar behavior were not destructive or self-destructive. Furthermore, what can be so perplexing to family members is that a loved one who has BPD may be able to camouflage his behavior so that, to the outside world, the person may seem to act a little strange but is not perceived as a threat. This is how many potentially dangerous BPD sufferers can fly below the radar, especially because those few people close to the patient may not understand the disorder or its symptoms. Moreover, many parents of children with BPD may interpret the hyper and morose periods of behavior as a form of emotional growing pains. This is especially true among adolescents struggling with puberty, the flow of neurochemicals and hormones, and the stresses of either conforming to the outside world or being an outcast. Think of Adam Lanza trying to cope with his fears as the demands of the outside world threatened to disrupt his private comfort zone and closed in on him from every angle.

The neurobiology of BPD seems straightforward even if there has not been enough research to pinpoint the exact cause of the disease. There seems to be reduced activity in the frontal cortex of BPD sufferers, implying that the mediating function of the higher-level brain may be impaired, while the limbic region of the brain seems more active. That means that many BPD sufferers may be partially in a waking dream state with their conscious brain flooded with memories and emotions that may influence their wildly swinging moods. Also, the lack of uptake of the neurochemical serotonin probably plays an important role in BPD, because serotonin is the chemical that mediates mood swings. Some people with aggressive impulsivity have been found to have reduced levels of serotonin in their spinal fluid, thus possibly reducing the capacity of the frontal cortex to function properly. Medications that increase the flow of serotonin and that can promote greater activity in the frontal cortex generally improve the behavior of those with BPD, particularly among adolescents and young adults, who are most prone to violent mood swings.

Lack of empathy in psychopathy and Asperger's syndrome—called a behavioral disorder and not a mental illness by groups advocating a greater understanding of the syndrome—has been labeled a factor in the aggressive behavior of those afflicted with the disorder. Others have said that high-functioning victims of Asperger's are incapable of emotional empathy and therefore, under the influence of violent stimuli, are more prone to committing crimes of violence than those who do not suffer from the disorder. As reported by *USA Today* on December 10, 2012, Geraldine Dawson, the chief science officer at Autism Speaks and a professor of psychiatry at University of North Carolina at Chapel Hill, wrote that studies have challenged this view, saying that individuals with Asperger's or high-functioning autism do not perpetrate violence at levels greater than those who do not have the disorder. This was also reported by CNN.[99] However, if

---

[99] Robison, John Elder. "Autism Link to Violence Is a Myth." CNN.com, April 7, 2013. http://www.cnn.com/2013/04/06/opinion/robison-autism-violence (accessed December 12, 2013).

what is identified as Asperger's is actually childhood schizophrenia or a premorbid schizophrenia, the emotional withdrawal typical of an Asperger's sufferer can easily be confused by clinicians not well-versed in diagnosing psychotic behavior. BPD is not a psychotic disorder, although BPD patients can become transiently psychotic. It is likely that the lack of social empathy typified in Asperger's sufferers lends credence to the popular belief, whether true or not, that Asperger's sufferers are more prone to commit crimes.

It also seems evident that there is a genetic component to the current suicidal/mass murder epidemic. The genetic component does not mean that people can be born violent. It means that there might be a genetic predisposition to forms of brain dysfunction or neurological dysrhythmia that may make the person susceptible to certain types of environmental stimuli that contribute to psychiatric disorders. If an individual has a genetic predisposition to reduced function of the frontal cortex or a dysfunctional amygdala, thus leaving the individual prone to limbic music, which is the flooding of the person's consciousness with unmediated emotions from the amygdala, the person could be more prone to impulsive responses to those stimuli he or she perceives as threatening, even when they would not be threatening to an emotionally resilient individual.

Part of the biological basis for different types of aberrant behavior, particularly among psychotics, lies in the way the brain processes "reward" stimuli. The reward sensation is processed in the striatum, an area of the brain located inside the cortex, where abnormal activity can produce abnormal behavior. For example, if there is hyperactivity in the striatum and the activity in the mediation function of the frontal cortex, the subject may not be able to control his ability to process a reward reaction. The reward reaction resulting from the action of the neurochemical dopamine on the striatum may also result in aberrant behavior with a loss of impulse control, so violent responses are not impeded by the logical functioning of the brain.

On a related note, and this may have applied to Adam Lanza, adolescents with autism spectrum disorder (ASD) may experience cortical and limbic hypoactivity, meaning that the logical functioning of the brain and its ability to process and store memories are impeded. Although there is no dispositive medical test to diagnose ASD, many pediatricians point to behavioral clues that become evident in toddlers as young as a year and a half. Indicators include the inability of the child to recognize nonverbal clues from parents or family members, difficulty in maintaining eye contact, obsessively repetitive activities, and extreme adverse responses to changes in environment and routine. If we look at what might have upset Adam Lanza's equilibrium–his mother telling him that it was time to move—we can see that even in a young adult with behavior and developmental issues and, likely, schizophrenia, the possibility of a change in a routine that had become his comfort zone was so emotionally wrenching that it drove him into a panic-fueled frenzy of violence.

Before parents with ASD-diagnosed children express their unhappiness at our grouping their children with possible mass murderers, or at our including the autism spectrum, it is important to insert this caveat: autistic children are not automatically violent, nor will they ultimately become Adam Lanzas. In fact, they may be more likely to become victims of violence or, at the least, bullying. We describe ASD as a behavioral disorder because we are describing an equilibrium problem among the different processing centers in the brain whose relationship to each other is a major factor in mediating primal reactions to external stimuli. For example, to get a child to accept a family's moving to a new location where he or she will have to make new friends, adjust to a new school environment, and acclimate himself to completely new surroundings can be upsetting. But for children with behavioral and developmental disorders, such a move can be absolutely traumatizing.

Attention deficit hyperactivity disorder (ADHD) is a real disorder in which the child or adult not only has an inability to focus and maintain that focus, but the resulting lack of focus generates an increased level of activity often inappropriate to the situation. Because the brain uses various chemicals to help send messages across the nervous system, an imbalance of these chemical messengers may result in the inattentive and hyperactive or impulsive symptoms of ADHD, a condition that may also have reduced frontal lobe inhibition. This condition also results in increased impulsivity and a loss of impulse control. Another caveat: neither children nor adults with ADHD automatically turn out to be suicidal mass murderers, but ADHD contributes to other disorders that may result from the person's inability to adjust to what he may perceive to be hostile or threatening external situations. ADHD is also a problem in classroom situations because a student (especially a child) suffering from it may be inattentive and disruptive in class, resulting in poor grades, a sense of failure, frustration, and even behavioral issues as the child acts out to express frustration and anger. But ADHD can be treated symptomatically in a variety of ways, particularly with psychopharmaceutical medications.

Treatment for ADHD also focuses on improving cortical inhibition by increasing the flow of serotonin and reducing limbic hyperactivity with anticonvulsants. Stimulants can improve cortical inhibition, while clozapine and other atypical high-dosage medications increase serotonin at 2a receptor in cortical areas for inhibition and reduce dopamine in limbic dysfunction.

In treating ADHD, we are balancing drive with inhibition to increase focus. Genes do not cause ADHD, but they determine processes within brain systems that produce behavior, such as violence, as a manifestation of PTSD. Like many of our subject suicidal mass murder offenders, such as Loughner, Routh, Holmes, and Lanza, it was not genetics per se that turned them into the people they were. However, it easily might have been that somewhere in the genetic mix that makes each of us an individual, composed of the many variants we inherit from our parents and their parents and those in our bloodline who came many generations before us, are chromosomal combinations that might impair or impede one or more types of neurological connections resulting in aberrant forms of behavior. How these forms of aberrant behavior are addressed, either by parental guidance, social institutions such as school, or medical intervention, can prevent an at-risk individual from falling through the biological safety net that keeps the individual from catastrophic harm.

Nature interacts with nurture, and it is that form of positive nurture that we believe may be on the wane.

Chapter 9

Toward a New Biology: Violent Stimuli against the Background of Human Psychological Development

The television commercial for an online video game begins with a man getting up to prepare for his drive to the office. He opens the cabinet to get his can of morning coffee, which falls out and spills all over the counter. He finally makes his steaming pot of coffee, but he spills it all over himself. Everything is going wrong. His jaw is clenched, and his eyes roll back in their sockets. The camera finally comes in for a close-up, and we see that not only are his eyes bright red, flaming in fury above his set, angry jaw, but his pupils are completely dilated. His face has an expression of menace as if he is the embodiment of an evil avenger. Now that he has lapsed into what looks like a psychotic fury, the promotion for the single-shooter game he is about to play comes up on the screen. That is the message. When you are so angry that you are completely bereft of all rational thought, that is the time to exorcise your inner demons by playing a violent video game. The man's biology has merged with that of his avatar in a digital world in which there are no social restrictions against sadistic and cold-blooded murder and mayhem. It was a message Jared Loughner, James Holmes, Cho Seung-Hui, Anders Breivik, and Adam Lanza all embodied. They were all mentally ill young adults lapsed into a digital world of cruel and violent frenzy.

Click forward to 2013. President Obama made a stunningly bold announcement in early 2013 about his ambitious $100 million initiative to begin a study to map the human brain; $50 million would be funneled through the Defense Advanced Research Projects Agency (DARPA)—those same wonderful folks who brought us drones, nonlethal weapons, and the Internet—to support the brain-mapping project headed up by the National Institute of Mental Health. The president cited the program as vital to an understanding of the working brain and vital to finding solutions to PTSD, ASD, psychosis, and, one of the holy grails of neuropsychiatric research, Alzheimer's disease. Although we can identify star systems millions of light years away from Earth and smash subatomic particles together in the large particle collider buried outside of Geneva, we "have not unlocked the mysteries of the three pounds of matter that sits between our ears," President Obama said. This is an important undertaking that might make it through the federal budget approval process and open up new approaches to finding treatments and cures for mental illness by exploring the activity of neural networks inside the brain and ancillary structures, such as the neural activity lodged in the human heart.

The president's announcement, one of the promises he made after the Sandy Hook Elementary School shooting to study mental illness, is important because as of early 2013, approximately two or more completed or attempted mass murders/suicides occur per week—sometimes one or more per day. These events include family violence, workplace and schoolhouse murders, and even random murders in which children and teenagers in playgrounds and in their own homes are hit by stray bullets. If this violence resulting from what we believe is mental illness and remedial behavioral disorders were an actual virus, it would receive one of the highest priorities to find a cure, because stopping the spread of viruses is one of the essential worldwide health endeavors to eliminate deadly illnesses. Think of the research into HIV, the frenzy over breakouts of Ebola and the Marburg virus, and the panic over the bird flu. Think of the search for the pathogens that cause these deadly viruses. Mental illness is no exception, but where is the search for its biological and psychosocial causalities? The epidemic of violence includes teenage and young adult perpetrators, military veterans, and enraged former employees seeking revenge on those who fired them. The violence continues unabated while lobbyists on all sides of the violence prevention and gun control issue battle over ideologies concerning the Second, Fourth, and Fifth Amendments. Yet the shooting continues, and more and more children are dying in playgrounds, in school classrooms, and even in their own front yards. It is as if the violence is not abating but leaving police and public safety agencies at their collective wits' end. How did we get here? And now that we are here, how do we get out of this?

We believe there is a perfect storm of causality behind the landscape of violence that has America in its grip. The fascination with violence pervades the media. Images of graphic violence embed themselves in the neurocircuitry of at-risk, vulnerable individuals with a weak grip on reality and a low resiliency to trauma. This graphic media violence is reinforced by the wide marketing of violent, bloody, single-shooter online video games. The idea that individuals can indulge their most sadistic fantasies in violence online is pursuant to the rampant culture of guns in a modern society fed by fear promulgated by firearm manufacturers, who argue that even those at risk should arm themselves.

Family structure is also an issue in a situation in which the entire concept of family has evolved from the multigenerational farm families of the early twentieth century before the Great Depression to the latchkey, single-parent household of today. What we believe to be a new form of pathogen, a "psychopathogen," is spreading virally through the media, including social media, just like an epidemic of the plague through modern society. The first element of this new pathogen is the culture of violence in the petri dish of the media, a culture that, for very legitimate entertainment reasons, extols the mythos of the hero fighting against overwhelming odds to bring about a victory. This is a tradition that goes back much farther than Wyatt Earp at the O.K. Corral, Gary Cooper facing down the bad guys at high noon, or John Rambo violently resisting the designs of a corrupt sheriff. In the "monomyth" of Western culture, as Joseph Campbell has written,[100] we extol the virtues of the hero even when the hero has to employ extraordinary violence to combat evil. Think of Odysseus plunging the pointed spear into the single eye of the Cyclops. Think of Beowulf ripping Grendel's arm from its socket during the bloody struggle at Heorot. And think of the slaughter at Thermopylae as Leonidas and his three hundred Spartans held off an onslaught from Xerxes' Persian warriors to protect the Hellenic city-states. Two movies have already been made about this last story, one of which was made with advanced CGI and is more like a video

---

[100] Campbell, Joseph. *The Hero with a Thousand Faces*. New York: Pantheon Books, 1949.

game than a film with real human characters. This adoration of violence is not going to change, although there is a much greater number of at-risk viewers who fail to make a clean distinction between what is on the screen and what is real life.

There is fictional violence, and then there is violence as a form of reality, such as the viciousness of cage fighting or even the morality play of professional wrestling, where might almost always makes right. We know that this kind of television is having an effect on some viewers because of the stories of children and adolescents who try to mimic what they see in televised professional wrestling but without the safety net of pretense. Child psychiatrist Dr. Michael Rothenberg proved this theory nearly a half-century ago in his landmark University of Washington study of the effects of violent TV shows on children.[101]

Kids can and do get hurt when they carry out knee drops and punches to the throat in emulation of their favorite professional wrestling heroes. Essentially, violence, albeit fictional, has become a form of art, but an art without artifice, no longer mimetic but all too real for the most psychologically vulnerable. The fictional violence, particularly violence against women and threats to children, we see on television and in motion pictures is almost paradoxical to the lip service we pay to child victims of schoolyard shootings and to the political landscape that argues for the Violence Against Women Act, which affords female victims of violence greater protection under the law and greater access to legal remedies. Fictionalized violence is titillating, which is why films are becoming more graphically violent, but even though repeated violence on television may generate its own neural network among viewers, it is still designed to be a passive experience. Interactive digital video gaming is not and suggests a new type of neurobiology even though, as Johan Huizinga has written,[102]

[101] Rothenberg, MD, Michael B. "Effect of Television Violence on Children and Youth." *Journal of the American Medical Association, Vol. 234, No. 10* (1975): 1043–46.
[102] Huizinga, Johan. *Homo Ludens: A Study of the Play-Element in Culture.* New York: Roy Publishers, 1950.

play is not a product of culture; it precedes culture and defines it. Digital gaming is new, however, because it blurs the line between play, which is something one can leave, and interactive play, which becomes a part of consciousness.

What is fascinating about interactive digital gaming, particularly single-shooter, battle-oriented gaming, is that it satisfies at least two psychological motivations: first, it is an outlet, albeit a dangerous one, for aggression. A gamer can express feelings of frustration and anger by blowing away digital enemies, spattering their blood all over the screen, and convincing himself that he has saved the planet from its enemies. This healthy gamer can leave that fictional world and return to society as one would leave a dream. His score is saved in the "cloud" and not hanging in his consciousness as he navigates his way from his cubicle to the coffee machine. But what happens when the gamer is already in a waking dream state, his consciousness flooded by limbic music, a core dump of unpleasant memories from an overloaded and overwhelmed amygdala? What happens is that the game becomes reality, part of a waking dream of wreaking violence on proto-enemies that trains the gamer to eliminate foes, even if he projects those foes onto otherwise innocent people in their real lives, and even when it invites a psychotic and embittered child to navigate through the halls of school mowing down kids and teachers in the game *School Shooter,* which Adam Lanza had in his blackened computer room of horrors.

The second major factor affecting gamers is the reward mechanism. This makes perfect sense and explains part of the attraction for otherwise emotionally challenged gamers. Imagine the frustration of dealing with life's adversities for those such as children with ADHD, prodromal schizophrenia, bipolar affective disorder, a variety of ASD, or Asperger's. None of these children are actually mentally ill; they are behaviorally challenged or at risk for serious mental illness. Now imagine that for many of these individuals, the amassing of player points, the advancement from one level of gaming to another, and the accolades from other online gamers as the scores of successful players are posted are a form of reward or pleasure. We know that the pleasure center of the brain, the nucleus accumbens, is stimulated by the neurochemical dopamine, which is released from dopaminergic neurons in the ventral tegmental area of the brain. Therefore, in our model, the reward mechanism of video gaming is a stimulant, almost as addictive as methamphetamine, ringing the pleasure center bell of the nucleus accumbens, so that the gamer is attracted to the process of the game itself in the hopes of experiencing greater and greater pleasure from the rewards he receives from scoring points by blowing away the enemy. Remember those Parkinson's patients treated with L-dopa to supplement their insufficient dopamine in the ventral tegmental region of the brain? They start gambling for the first time in their lives.

You do not have to be a psychiatrist to figure out how online single-shooter gaming can become a honey trap. For the at-risk individual, however, the honey trap can easily become more trap and less honey. The game becomes a dopamine-stimulating drug. Among the seriously mentally ill, it is a propsychotic that stimulates psychotic behavior by locking the gamer into a perpetual dream state in which he or she cannot separate the game from reality—hence, James Holmes playing the Joker to seek revenge upon all of society and the Joker's enemies. The reward factor is even more important to gamers in light of how they can create characters and project their avatars into situations that can be death-defying if not just plain challenging in the game world. The more these avataristic projections succeed by eliminating enemies and avoiding catastrophic attacks upon themselves, the greater the reward mechanism that stimulates the pleasure centers. Therefore, the game can be a cycle of violence, success, and reward, all of it inside the chassis of a computer, a tablet, or even a smartphone, while the gamer himself has merged neurobiologically with the internal circuitry of the device and withdraws and morphs in isolation from reality.

Online gaming also relates directly to impulse control, particularly among the at-risk players. Because the player gets points for as many kills as he can achieve, the normal dampening function of the prefrontal cortex for impulse control and the logical restrictions of decision making are subsumed into the alternate fear and reward mechanism of the thrill of the hunt and the kill. More simply stated, the player finds a reward in not being forced to mediate decisions based on violence. Instead, the methodology of the game lies in the tactics and strategy of the hunt and the kill. For an at-risk player or one who is marginally at risk, this is a type of combat training but with a major difference. In a digital game, the player need only kill without facing the real-world consequences of taking a human life. Imagine if the lack of moral or legal consequence in a game were transferred to real life with real victims shedding real blood, as is the problem in real combat, whether in the Middle East or even on a street corner in downtown LA or in Times Square. This is one of the primary issues of online violent gaming for the at-risk or mentally ill player. The player loses the distinction between the digital world and the real world. In a depressed and delusional state where the player perceives the real world to be an antagonistic threat, the threat response transfers from the game to the real world. Importantly, for the decompensating young adult losing his core identity to the ravages of schizophrenia, gaming fills in the vacuum of chaotic signals and organizes them into a coherent construct for his cacophony of aggressive impulses. The gaming construct is better than the horrors of chaos of threatening signals and fragmentation of the young man's "I," his sense of identity or ego. Nature abhors a vacuum. So does a person whose identity is fragmenting into the black hole of psychosis. Game on. He is now in control. As we have seen, the control can be lethal to him and anyone else who happens to be in the wrong place at the wrong time, whether theater 9 in Aurora, Colorado, or a youth camp in Utøya, Norway.

Finally, two other mechanisms are at work in the world of online gaming that relate to real-world violence. First is the basic neuromuscular pattern of firing at what appear to be live targets. It normally takes many repetitions of point, aim, and fire to hit targets. The military and police training methodologies support the building of the neuromuscular network to enable officers to point and shoot to kill once after they have determined that a threat exists. For an at-risk player who is losing or has lost a grip on reality, this training can be extraordinarily dangerous to innocent victims because the neuromuscular pathways are trained to fire and kill even though the target may be a threat only in the shooter's mind. Breivik reportedly learned military skills by solitary gaming after having been rejected for military service by Norway's draft board.

What threat did a six-year-old first grader pose to Adam Lanza? None, except in his own delusional world of projecting upon those children all of his fear-driven anger. He saw these children as the representation of the child he never was nor could ever have been and by whom he had perceived himself, accurately or not, to have been relentlessly bullied. These were the children who shunned him when he was a first grader at Sandy Hook. These were the children from whose presence, even from whose casual touch, he withdrew as he slunk along the corridor walls of Sandy Hook Elementary, or in high school, clutching his computer, his back to the lockers, fearing human proximity. These were the children, according to friends who remembered Lanza's elementary school years, who had made fun of him and likely bullied him to the point where Nancy Lanza had planned to file a lawsuit against the school. School officials did try to prevent bullying, going to the extreme of assigning a school nurse to him for his protection. But perception is everything for the decompensating psyche. Hence, in his delusion-driven fury, Lanza imagined that the children had become the enemy he had trained himself to kill via his obsessive immersion into violent video gaming.

The other factor at work in violent video gaming is the graphic nature of the explosion of body parts and blood spatter. Human beings have to be trained to overcome a natural and healthy abhorrence to violence and gore. However, repeated exposure to violence and gore and the training to create gore through the instrumentality of violence can inure the gamer to what he would shrink from naturally. For an at-risk player on the borderline of mental illness, repeated immersion in digital violence, with the consequent graphics of exploding gore and bloody victories that generate a reward to excite the pleasure mechanism in the brain, becomes a Pavlovian-type conditioning apparatus that also likely dumbs down the insula's sensitivity to horrible sensations, thus creating the dehumanized adolescent, who is known to be a homicidal threat. Instead of salivating at the sound of a bell because of the expectation of food, the gamer is conditioned to feel pleasure or a release from pain at the successful elimination of a target—the gorier, the better. If thus inured to the abhorrence of violence and gore and rewarded for creating it, the at-risk delusional player, awash in the hopelessness of suicidal ideation, can, for the period of time immersed in the game, take himself right to the limit of threat and danger, turn those feelings into pleasure at confronting his fears, and then become addicted to those chemicals flooding his brain. How easy is it then to transfer those feelings to real life with real weapons at the ready? If you think that is far-fetched, look at the video gaming backgrounds of Adam Lanza, Cho Seung-Hui, James Holmes, Anders Breivik, and Jared Loughner, all of whom were seriously mentally ill and probably walking through their respective dream states. It would not be surprising to learn that the Brothers Tzarnaev conditioned themselves to dehumanize their American enemies by gaming. The older brother was a pugilist, but how did he dehumanize his younger brother? Was it through gaming or through the same type of conditioning that the Beltway Sniper John Allen Muhammad used with his accomplice, the seventeen-year-old Lee Boyd Malvo? To make things even worse, suicide is a reward in games, too, which might have been the point in Loughner's babbling that words mean nothing, life is a scam, and a final "good-bye."

The other side of the neurochemical-driven pleasure principle is the depression that follows when the neurochemical dopamine is not flowing. We have seen this type of bipolar reaction in methamphetamine addicts, whose behavior progressively deteriorates when they are not high on the drug. Methamphetamine operates on the brain by replacing dopamine on the neuronal reuptake pumps, then replacing it inside the neuron and flooding the synapses with the dopamine. The altered reuptake pumping of dopamine floods the brain with this activating neurochemical and arouses the brain's pleasure sensors of the nucleus accumbens. Flooding the brain with dopamine conditions the neurocircuitry to expect that level of arousal and fall into the opposite of a reward state when the chemical is no longer present. Hence, insofar as violent video gaming may stimulate the flow of dopamine, the game itself, especially for an at-risk mentally ill population, could be as addictive as speed. Psychiatrists are becoming increasingly aware of patients with chronic schizophrenia who likely have too much dopamine in their limbic system and too little in their frontal lobes. In fact, this is the very dichotomy sought with designer drugs for schizophrenia—a dichotomy known as "atypical" or "novel" for the new generation of antipsychotics.

Those psychiatrists working with this population through the decades are well aware of the addiction to cigarettes, emblematically displayed by the yellowed fingers of their patients. Newer antipsychotic medications do not block dopamine and norepinephrine in the frontal lobes, as did the older generation of antipsychotics, such as Haldol, which blocked dopamine receptors throughout the brain. In fact, the newer generation of antipsychotics, such as Geodon (ziprasidone) may in fact increase dopamine in the frontal lobes while blocking it in the limbic system, for a win-win reduction of limbic music and reduction of patients' cravings for nicotine.

Because gaming may act like a powerful drug, should the government, as a function of its powers to provide for public safety and the general welfare of its citizens, take steps to regulate it? Ideologically and legally, the attempt to regulate free expression runs right up against the First Amendment. If games and even some expressions of violence in the media act as pseudopharmaceuticals stimulating neurochemicals that can incite violence, does the exclusion of incitement speech from First Amendment protection act as a wedge for the federal government to set up communications restrictions? And if we discover that, in fact, violent games do act just like drugs in stimulating parts of the brain, might not the US Food and Drug Administration want to look at setting regulations for degrees of violence? In that case, the game is no longer a First Amendment–protected form of expression but an actual drug. Video gaming is not an isolated phenomenon limited to the at-risk population and the mentally ill. Is it not reasonable to argue that after the president and first lady personally expressed their deep sadness at four memorials of victims from suicidal mass murder, the time has come to use the bully pulpit at least to seek legislation to ban the game *School Shooter* in the wake of the SHES massacre?

According to the American Medical Association (AMA), about 75 percent of all households play video games.[103] Those immersed in video gaming, especially online multiplayer games, play more than two hours per day. In 1983 US Surgeon General C. Everett Koop linked media violence, which includes video games and violent scenes and stories broadcast over traditional media and violence in feature films, to aggressively violent behavior on the part of viewers and players, especially insofar as it concerned family violence.[104] For

---

[103] Elliot, Victoria Stagg. "AMA Meeting: AMA Concerned about Video Games' Impact on Youth." *American Medical News,* July 16, 2007. http://www.amednews.com/article/20070716/profession/307169962/7/ (accessed December 11, 2013).

[104] Brown v. *Entertainment Merchants Association,* 564 US 08-1448 (2011).

its part, although the AMA found that there are potential advantages to video gaming, such as improving hand-eye coordination, enhancement of logical thinking and decision making, benefits to victims of stroke, and teaching methodologies for students and even for the military, there are many potential detrimental health and behavioral effects.

In essence, the AMA suggested that there is evidence linking exposure to violent video games to antisocial behavior, aggressive affect, and what they describe as physiological arousal, which is the physical stimulation of fear/aggressive self-defense/flight stimulation in the autonomic nervous system. In other words, the violently aggressive stimulation of violent video game immersion bypasses the logical or meditative faculties of the frontal lobes and the limbic system's regional uncus neurons, transmitting directly to our animal defense and attack instincts. The AMA said that even independent researchers found that the "preponderance of research from both sides of the debate does support, without controversy, the conclusion that exposure to violent media increases aggressive cognition, affect, and behavior, and decreases prosocial behavior in the short term."[105] Therefore, does it seem obvious that Holmes, Lanza, Cho, Breivik, and Loughner, all of whom were immersed in violent video games, might have been conditioned to the point of initiating the violence in real life that they participated in on their computers? That conclusion can be drawn from the AMA report, particularly if the players we cite here are mentally ill to the point where they are experiencing hallucinatory paranoid suicidal ideations and not motivated by social interactions of gaming, which is, more likely than not, the case with these rampage murderers.

---

[105] Elliot, Victoria Stagg. "AMA Meeting: AMA Concerned about Video Games' Impact on Youth." *American Medical News*, July 16, 2007. http://www.amednews.com/article/20070716/profession/307169962/7/ (accessed December 11, 2013).

The Spread of Mental Illness: A Psychosocial Phenomenon?

As more background is revealed about the mental health system encounters of James Holmes, Adam Lanza, Jared Loughner, Anders Breivik, and Cho Seung-Hui, the more one can see that mental illness progressively got worse within their minds and shaped their realities. One can look at other instances of suicidal or attempted suicidal mass murder to discover that every one of the perpetrators was in a state of hopelessness, a despondence without remedy, from their perspective, except for death, and filled with anger over the belief that happiness would always elude them. That kind of demoralized state breeds anger, not just against the self, but against others the individual perceives as the enemy. The question is, what is it about certain forms of psychosis that leads to violent behavior? Certainly, psychiatrists and medical researchers have found that hopelessness, the absolute despondency of dragging through each day as a victim of relentless depression, feeds a seething anger and irrational guilt that results in violence to oneself, even if not immediately to others. However, mental illness is progressive, with anger spreading like a toxin through water, permeating everything with which it comes into contact. In a world without rewards or success, even the smallest positive stimulus can have an extraordinary effect. Thus, when a mentally ill individual suffering from depression or extreme anxiety from losing his mind can reward himself through success in a violent video game, that level of stimulus can be transferred to other objects of the person's anger: himself and those he believes are persecuting him. This is projective identification for paranoia that can scare you walking through the park when the homeless man shouts at you, but more ominously ticks like a time bomb of the well-organized, stealthy paranoid like Breivik. Thus, in the paranoid schizophrenic's mind, the irrational thought process might be, "I am seething with homicidal rage. I find a person who seems offensive. I perceive that other person has homicidal rage towards me. I react aggressively." Thus, both paranoid schizophrenics and those with borderline personality disorder project their rage onto another person, which, in their dysfunctional thought process, is a form of retaliation that justifies homicidal violence.

Mental illness also instills fear inside the decomposing mind of the sufferer. Fear also breeds anger at being afraid, anger at those who are perceived as causing fear in the individual, and anger at being at odds with society, even if being at odds is only in the mind of the individual. Every other person's success, no matter how insubstantial, is a reminder to someone who is suicidally mentally ill that life may be good for others but not for him. That thought instills hostility to those on the outside, a hostility that grows until a mentally ill person with significantly reduced impulse control finally strikes out in a moment of self-destructive violence, taking as many with him as he can.

In these ways, psychosis can feed violence, particularly when that violence begins with an unrelenting desire for self-destruction. Delusions of persecution combined with feelings of hopelessness tend to generate rage or an urge to strike back. Even in a decomposed mind flooded with delusions, there is a pseudological assumption that the person has nothing else to lose. For example, Navy-Yard shooter Aaron Alexis wrote on his rifle butt that the massacre at the Navy Yard was the only way to stop the thought control from the microchip implanted in his brain, most likely, in his mind, implanted by the United States Navy. Therefore, why not lash out at the targets perceived as persecutors? Alexis finally did, after his more appropriate and rational attempts to obtain medical help for his despair failed. Hence, when depression is linked to even minor acts of violence, violence against inanimate objects, such as destroying one's car with a sledge hammer, or cruelty to animals, can, among the mentally ill, be gross predictors of potential dangerousness that requires medical scrutiny. We have seen this with Holmes, Cho, Breivik, and Loughner, even though we still have seen neither Lanza's nor Holmes's complete medical records. What we can tell from anecdotal evidence about Lanza's behavior is that when the delusion-bound mentally ill person feels threatened, the person strikes against the source of the threat. In Lanza's case, that source was his mother, Nancy, and the evil child, whether helpless in the classroom or within himself.

Simply said, threats, whether real or illusory, generate anger. Anger generates rage, which can lead to violence among the mentally ill, whose minds are flooded with delusions not mediated by the logical functions of the brain. But why is there such an epidemic of suicidal mental illness? Is something going on beneath the surface of our collective awareness that has eluded the news media? We look at the landscape of our culture and can see that at the margins of American society are children, adolescents, and young adults who are at risk with various types of behavioral disorders, not limited to ADHD, ASD, or Asperger's, which are not manifestations of a serious mental illness in themselves. However, because disorders can become progressive as the individual reacts with societal institutions around him, the behavioral disorders can wind up at odds with those institutions. The resulting friction may further exacerbate what began as a behavioral disorder into a full-fledged psychiatric disorder complete with delusional thinking, auditory hallucinations, and a paranoid delusion that society itself is the enemy. Consider the most recent attempted suicide/murder by Los Angeles Airport shooter Paul Ciancia, who carefully targeted TSA staff in the most brutal way. He wasn't even a frequent flyer. But he wrote that he wanted to die after the kill of at least one.

We know that emotional issues in a child's home life that arise can affect a child's ability to perform in a classroom. Children from single-parent families have a difficult time relating to conventional subject matter in which traditional two-parent families represent the values of society. Worse, teachers found that when there is emotional turbulence at home from either divorce or separation or when the loss of a parent through death or disease compromises the child's view of reality, that child can fall seriously behind his or her peers. If that child is subjected to bullying or disdain from other children, and personal or physical attacks are not remedied by intervention from teachers or school counselors, the child's emotional stability, already compromised by learning difficulties resulting from problems at home, can become a behavioral disorder, which can then metastasize into antisocial psychological reactions. At the extreme, we have children from deeply disadvantaged neighborhoods exposed to actual threats to life every day from drive-by gang shooters. We speculate, therefore, that as society changes with respect to family structure, those changes can heavily impact what goes on in the classroom and schoolyard. And unless educational administrators are aware of these trends, not only could emotionally impacted students continue to struggle, but schoolyards themselves could become the new violent battlegrounds at the frontier of a changing culture. Even Maricopa County, Arizona, Sheriff Joe Arpaio has armed posses now riding the local schoolyards.

We know that certain populations are at risk for psychiatric impairment because of psychosocial risk factors. Poor, single-parent families with an adult son at home, for example, are at particularly high risk for having one of the 14 percent of patients who are afflicted with the most serious psychiatric disorders. In fact, R. Kessler's Kentucky epidemiological studies of family analysis predicted future psychopathology in 82 percent of cases.[106] These are lethal odds.

Among older members of society, particularly those who served in the military, perhaps in combat in Vietnam or the Middle East, there is another syndrome at work: PTSD, a progressive condition that

---

[106] Kessler, R., et al. "Lifetime and 12-Month Prevalence of *DSM-III-R* Psychiatric Disorders in the United States Results from the National Comorbidity Survey." *Archives of General Psychiatry,* Vol. 51, No. 1 (January 1994).

impairs the sufferer's resilience and his or her ability to react to stress in a healthy way. We find that individuals suffering from this disorder also experience friction with societal institutions and, unless treated, can wind up with a serious mental illness as memories of their past trauma flood their consciousness. This is also the case with young veterans, for whom cohort suicide rates are increasing. Politicians, now willing to chop pensions of civilians in the wake of the Detroit bankruptcy, have turned a blind eye to these combat veterans, now a million man and woman march to VA claims examiners for PTSD and traumatic brain injuries. These veterans suffering from varying degrees of PTSD and traumatic brain injury are a high-risk group for suicidal mass murder, like Navy Yard shooter Aaron Alexis and Eddie Ray Routh. This group is also at high risk for domestic violence.

Is our society inevitably and hopelessly degenerating into a violent generational conflict, or are there definable elements to the epidemic of self-destructive violence now rampant in our society? We believe that by looking at trends in the evolution of our society, as well as our own biological evolution, we can find some clues to what is happening and possible ways to halt the slide.

The Seismic Shift in Family, Economy, and Society

It seems clear that crimes of murder and suicide are more than a trend toward violence. Even as murder rates in general seem to have declined in most major cities, particularly in New York, incidences of suicidal mass murderers, depending upon how we define mass murder, have increased to an epidemic level. News of suicidal mass murderers breaks to the headlines on a regular basis, sometimes two or more times per week. We have to wonder whether these crimes have become a manifestation of something much deeper in American society, perhaps an outcropping of the clash of an ongoing seismic transformation in our society itself from the beginning of the twentieth century to the present. If that is the case, what are the pieces of evidence that point to such a societal transformation?

The evidence suggests, albeit oversimplistically, that human psychosocial biology has not evolved to where society itself has evolved over the past hundred years and is therefore locked in a conflict with the world itself. Our society is propelled by the forces of technology, mass population shifts, and a socioeconomy that has transformed so radically over the past century. Therefore, parts of America do not recognize the change or see it as threatening to their lifestyles. We have only to look at the policy arguments and resulting legislation over gay marriage to see the disparate ideological views regarding societal change. Even the Supreme Court, in oral arguments over the Defense of Marriage Act and California's Proposition 8, which banned same-sex marriage in the state (which has now been overturned by the United States Supreme Court, along with the Defense of Marriage Act), was locked into an ideological conflict over what marriage means. When we look at the transformation of American society since just before World War I, what we see looks as if we as a species have been shoehorned into a world that has socially and technologically gone beyond us. Sure, there is a younger generation that has grown up with the Internet, interactive games, and social media. But as a species, we have not yet evolved to a point where we can fit into the society we have created, although that society was created by default as a byproduct of technological innovation. Thus, if we argue that the violence that we see is a form of turbulence on the edges as our species evolves, still constrained by biology and unable to fit into its new reality, how can we measure that? We argue that what we are not getting what we need as members of a society, and the result is violence against those around us whom we perceive to be mortal enemies. Like Pogo, we meet those enemies, but they are we.

However, there is an app for that: an explanation.

In a January 2012 article in *Vanity Fair* magazine, economist Joseph Stiglitz, in interpreting data supporting the real underlying causes for the Great Depression of the 1930s and comparing it to the Great Recession between 2007 and 2009, argues that transformation of the American economy from a rural agrarian one to an urban industrial one was the primary underlying reason for the decade-long Great Depression. As the economic structure of America evolved in the period after World War I, jobs moved to the cities and disappeared from the farms. People either had to move to the cities to get jobs in manufacturing, find jobs on the large farms and orchards in California, or stay out of work until the United States went to war, absorbing the huge unemployment into the military, and borrowing money to reinflate the economy for war materiel production. Similarly, Stiglitz said, the transformation of the American economy from product manufacturing to services, leaving manufacturing workers out in the cold, is part of the reason for the ongoing recession today. The jobs have gone to developing Third World countries where labor is cheap and the cost of manufacturing is lower than in the United States. We can gnash our teeth over the Great Recession and the loss of manufacturing jobs, but until we can lure manufacturing and the capital that supports it back to the United States, manufacturing and the jobs it supports will be gone until American manufacturers feel they can make money at home again.[107]

As a consequence of his economic argument, we believe that Stiglitz identified one of the major transformational events in our own evolution as individuals within a too-quickly evolving society during the twentieth century. Our premise here, which Stiglitz pointed out, is that American society itself evolved from agrarian and mainly rural to industrial and super-urban. We believe that such an evolution also involved the transformation of the American family structure

---

[107] Stiglitz, Joseph E. "The Book of Jobs." *Vanity Fair,* January 2012. http://www.vanity-fair.com/politics/2012/01/stiglitz-depression-201201.

within the home from a multigeneration farm family to a nuclear double- or even single-generation family living in an urban setting. In other words, we've gone from *The Waltons* to *The Simpsons* in just about seventy years: the speed of light in evolutionary terms. Why is this so crucial to our understanding of modern sociopathic and psychopathic behavior, the extreme and the ultimate forms of which are mass murder/suicide, whether in the form of psychotic murder and mayhem in cases of Adam Lanza, James Holmes, Cho Seung-Hui and Anders Breivik, or terrorism in the form of the Brothers Tzarnaev in the Boston Marathon bombings? We believe it is part of a social evolution, and we can see it in our schools and colleges. Look at it as an engineering problem in which you have to account for what kind of structure or structural architecture can handle load-bearing stress, in this case, load-bearing emotional stress on the child. We hypothesize that structure to be the multigeneration family unit, the basic farm family in which all generations from grandparents to children participated in a common family goal; it collapsed under economic pressure and the migration to cities and then to suburbs. A completely unanticipated sociobiological transformation took place as well. Jack Kerouac prophetically saw this and described it in his first novel *The Town and the City*.[108] If one thinks of child development as partly an engineering case study in how the family handles the load-bearing stress on the developing child, one can see the valuable role a large multigeneration family plays in bearing that load and gradually leveraging it onto the growing child. Grandparents or even great-grandparents can intercede when tensions between parent and child exceed the ability of the parent/child relationship to bear them. Simplistic? Yes, but it makes a point. Parents who are under emotional stress in their own lives sometimes have little resiliency when it comes to dealing with the stresses of their growing children. That is when their parents, the children's grandparents, play an important role.

---

[108] Kerouac, Jack. *The Town and the City*. San Diego: Harcourt Brace Jovanovich, 1950.

But first a caveat about how television—and feature films, to a large extent—project a refraction of social ideals and values, whether negative or positive, onto an audience whose members, to a significant extent, share those ideals, hopes, and fears. We are contrasting two television series depicting life in two different societies, not as if they are documentaries but as if they are projections of social ideations that a viewing audience probably must share to understand the continuity of the stories.

On the old television series *The Waltons*, even during the tough times of the Great Depression, as the parents faced the stress of just putting another meal on the table and keeping the family farm from going bust, Grandpa and Grandma Walton eased the burden on their grandchildren by parenting their own son in times of difficulty and interceding with the grandchildren. As an engineering case study, to use our analogy, the load-bearing stress on the children was handled in large measure by grandparents, whose own egos and projection of their joint selves were not at stake in the parent/child interaction.

Sometimes, because parents see negative aspects of their own personalities manifesting in their children, they confront those aspects in their children's personalities when they are unconsciously confronting those aspects in themselves. The result: intergenerational conflict. Not so much when it comes to the grandparents. Grandpa and Grandma Walton, a projected refraction of what we idealize as grandparents, kept tradition alive by functioning, among other things, as a family encyclopedia, because they were the link between earlier farmers on Walton's Mountain and the children who were destined to inherit the family land. The Walton parents held up under the struggle because they were parented as they parented their children. Is ours now a cry for the good old days, tearing down the cities and heading back to the farms? No. It is simply an example of how society projects its own image of how it perceives the way things might have been or were supposed to be. It is a projection of perceived values. We do not see this in today's society.

In today's somewhat distorted projection of the comedy of an American family, as represented by *The Simpsons,* we see an entirely different picture: a father strangling his son or shaking him until his eyes bulge out, a father trashing his own father—depicted as a demented, physically challenged, and angry old man—while trying, but failing, to ease his way through life at his job at a leaking Three Mile Island–type nuclear power plant. The cartoon says a lot about how we recognize the foibles of a family as they fight over the last table scraps on pork chop night. Where is the multigenerational family when a grandparent with barely a grip on reality is relegated to a nursing home? It is nonexistent. And we have not even brought up the social values embodied in ABC's *Modern Family,* whose tagline is "one big (straight, gay, multicultural, traditional) happy family."

To our point, though, if we compare the agrarian, multigenerational family structure to what an urban child might face today in a single-parent environment or in a no-parent institution, we see that the child must shoulder the complete stress of growing up in society all by himself. That is hard enough. Even worse, what if growing children from single- or no-parent families find their family structure within the structure of a gang or a terrorist organization?

To make matters worse still, now add the additional stress of a dysfunctional parent taking out his or her frustrations on the child: an additional level of stress that a growing child must bear. A child of an alcoholic or violent substance abuser will most likely grow up dysfunctional, too, with little or no resiliency to stress and is at high risk of turning to violence as a first resort and winding up in the criminal justice system. This child will probably turn to violence as a first resort. We know from fifty years of research that children of abusers grow up to become potential abusers themselves. The abusive behavior they have learned feeds into whatever genetic predisposition may exist. If looked at from a transformative societal perspective, however, one can see the magnitude of the issue.

We presuppose a basic biological and developmental neuropsychological rationale for the inability of some of today's young adult children to cope with and to shoulder the stresses of what society, domestic violence, endless wars, and economic hardship place upon them. And we aggregate this trend with the fact that the human being is one of a tiny number of species whose neurological system continues to develop postnatally. As the human brain specializes in its functions from birth through age five, neurological pathways develop and allow for the learning of predicative language—grammar, syntax, and vocabulary—and ultimately socialization brought about by the imposition of protological structures within the asymmetrical brain. Rewiring of the brain accelerates during adolescence into the early twenties, a particularly vulnerable time for the young to be traumatized by crime or combat.

Parent-Child Bonding in an Alienated Society

During the early years and in concert with the internal neurological development of the young child, the child faces its first Eriksonian crisis: the crisis of borders and trust in which the child must discriminate between self and non-self and develop a sense of trust in the non-self.[109] This major developmental event, described by psychologist Erik Erikson, helps establish a healthy balance in the way a child looks at the outside world as it seeks to control its own bodily functions. In essence, from infancy through age four, the child's confidence and germ of self-esteem gestates from his ability to develop trust in world that is outside of himself and his immediate physical control. This is a primary boundary issue—a control issue—the child's primitive discovery that good biological fences make good neighbors and biological control builds self-esteem. Instilling in the child the distinction between self and other, "me and not me," is the physical establishment of biological boundaries and

---

[109] Erikson, Erik H. *Childhood and Society*. 1950. Reprint, New York: Norton, 1993.

the residing of trust in an entity that is a "not me" by skin contact with the parent. Research into ways parents can ease the emotional disturbance of children with ASD has revealed that autistic children respond to a sensation of pressure on their skin. Wrapping autistic children in a blanket, holding them close, or having them wear garments of a heavier weight so that they feel pressure on the skin helps the autistic child relax, feel secure, and not repeat some of the obsessively destructive behaviors that reinforce the need for physical contact. For example, Adam Lanza shrank from the touch of others when he was a student at Sandy Hook, but he pressed himself against the walls of school corridors. This might have served a double function as he reacted with visceral fear of contact with others while reassuring himself of a boundary by pressing his body against a wall.

The developing infant's important skin contact is common among mammals. Ever watch a cat with her newborn kittens? She licks them, not only to clean away the afterbirth, but to stimulate the skin, the part of the body with the greatest amount of sensors. Watch a female dog with her newborn litter or a chimpanzee with its newborn. Watch the closest biological relatives to human beings groom their young, stroking and licking and constantly stimulating the outer skin. Our biology and their biology are not so different.

Because the human skin contains the greatest amount of sensors, it enables the child to experience the sensation of benevolent contact to nurture its developing neurological system, which is shedding nerve cells as it specializes to conform to its environment. It is referred to in postmodern parlance as "attachment parenting," but it is a fundamental part of child-rearing from the dawn of human society. Parents must be in physical contact with their children in such a way that the sensors in the child's skin are stimulated. That stimulation helps develop the child's entire neurological sensory system while at the same time biologically demonstrating the distinction between what is the child and what is the outside world. Even more, it helps the child place his trust in the parent and thus reside trust in the presence of the outside world. Developing a native understanding of what is self and what is not self is vital. Failure to develop that understanding means that the individual will not distinguish between himself and others, not establish healthy boundaries, fail to integrate socially with peers, and wind up with some degree of psychosocial pathology in which the individual regards to some extent everything as his own. It does not mean that every child who fails the first Eriksonian crisis turns into a sociopathic killer like Ted Bundy or Jeffrey Dahmer. It does mean, however, that barring some form of external intervention from family sources or even school, the child may be at risk to develop antisocial criminal or asocial isolative tendencies. Now, if we place this child within the context of a modern two-career or single-parent family where a child is in day care and preschool and does not experience much physical contact with the parent, that child may find himself at odds with his peers and within the social system, especially when it comes time to demonstrate empathy or sharing.

We have found this out by observing very young children in day care or nursery school settings, wherein children assert their ownership of items by refusing to share. However, in conformity with classroom rules, older children from ages seven to ten do demonstrate the ability to share and to sympathize with other children. Unhealthy children do not demonstrate these things and from a very early age find themselves in conflict with the classroom rules of behavior. Does this mean that they will all grow up to be suicidal mass murderers? No, but it does mean that learning to share and participate with others in a social structure will be difficult for them. The prevalence of conduct disorder is 10 percent in males and 2 percent in females. Follow-up research on three hundred children who were referred to a child guidance clinic in St. Louis for antisocial behavior (conduct disorder) showed that in thirty-five years, 71 percent were arrested and 50 percent had multiple arrests and incarcerations. Nearly one-third in this group were diagnosed with antisocial personality disorder in adulthood, while almost all committed four offenses and went on to adult criminal careers. Only 16 percent were ultimately found to be free of psychiatric illness.

The severity and number of antisocial behaviors in childhood conduct disorder predict adult behavior better than any other variable, including social class and family background. And it is known that comorbidity between conduct disorder and ADHD is so high that the neurobiological linkage cries for large-scale research.

Time for another caveat: sociopathic behavior, like some forms of psychopathic behavior, exists along a spectrum. We can identify a Ted Bundy or a Gary Ridgway as extreme examples of sociopathology. They exerted the most extreme form of control over their victims, who they believed they possessed, by killing them, sometimes dismembering them, and thus making sacrosanct their burial places so that they could return to perform sexual acts upon their corpses. Necrophilia is the ultimate form of control over another's body. But the pathological need to control and to dominate others and the playing field on which they operate can be seen in all aspects of society: from the brutal supervisor spewing toxic criticism on all of those hiding in their respective cubicles at work, to the teacher who demands more than just respect from students, to members of law enforcement agencies who use their authority to exploit others. Sociopathic behavior exists at all levels of society, from mildly disturbing social transactions to crimes of sexual abuse and murder.

Consider the at-risk child who has not established healthy borders as he or she emerges from the toddler years. Raise that child in a television and video game environment, especially one that demands that the child shift his attention instantly from thing to thing—called "smash cuts"—to watch violent images so that, in a "clockwork orange" type of scenario, the child may be inadvertently programmed toward violent reactions to the stress of repeated sudden psychological attention shifts. At the very least, a child will develop a natural tendency for ADHD and a resistance to what would be the natural abhorrence to violence in such a way that violence becomes a first, rather than an ultimate, resort. As an example, just take any wartime video game or even professional wrestling, which many children imitate without regard to the injuries it can cause. For an already at-risk child, inculcation to violence can be a lethal psychological mix. Absent the nurturing and mitigating presence of older family members, grandparents, or parents, there is nothing to bear the load of the stress the child is experiencing.

As we have described it, generations of children after World War II and the subsequent generations of children they bore were simply not biologically or developmentally ready for this shift in the family structure. The family in which Theodore "The Beaver" Cleaver thrived is no longer. As our troops, the children and grandchildren of the post–World War II cohort, return from the Middle East, the problem we describe threatens to escalate to gargantuan proportions.

The Psychopathogens of an Epidemic

If we are in an epidemic and we are calling suicidal mass murder a syndrome, how is the syndrome spreading? Diseases are contracted because pathogens enter our bodies. The great Black Death that spread across Europe from the fourteenth through the seventeenth centuries was spread by infected fleas that fed on the blood of rats. The bacteria was transported in the bloodstreams of the rats and carried by fleas into the human population. It could not be stopped in England, until the reign of Charles II, when the great fire of London destroyed the population of disease-bearing rats. The pneumonic plague, another form of the disease, was spread in the air from infected person to infected person. We believe we know, and have entire organizations to study this process and intervene medically when necessary, how disease spreads and how to try and control it. But what about the disease of suicidal and homicidal mental illness?

From the records that have been pieced together about the life of Adam Lanza, investigators learned that he was an avid follower of the Anders Breivik case. For his part, Anders Breivik was an avid follower of the Unabomber, Ted Kaczynski, whose manifesto and other writings inspired much of the "rage against the machine" movement. If Lanza followed Breivik and Breivik followed Kaczynski, we can see how violently antisocial messages can spread—and that certainly comports with the First Amendment—and influence at-risk individuals who cannot partition an anger-driven rant from a homicide. Similarly, from what investigators learned about Cho Seung-Hui, he wrote a high school essay after the Columbine shooting in which he expressed his admiration for shooters Klebold and Harris and said that was exactly what he wanted to do. Even in high school, Cho was articulating his suicidal and homicidal ideations but objectifying them in the Columbine High School massacre. In the latest case of a mass attack in Texas by Lone Star College student Dylan Quick, who went on a stabbing rampage against students, we learned not only that had Quick been planning the attack for years, according to the Harris County, Texas, sheriff's office, but that Quick had studied books about serial killers and mass murderers. He was a student of psychopathic and sociopathic behavior.

Psychopathogens are spread by media. Within the context of video games, violent entertainment, and graphic news coverage of mass shootings, the pathogens are spreading among the most vulnerable and at-risk individuals. The suicidal mass murderers, while certainly not being extolled in the media, are objects of fascination and wonder. Photos of wide-eyed Adam Lanza, smirking Jared Loughner, and dazed James Holmes with flaming red hair are indeed media-catching. These horrendous suicidal mass murders are happening with too much frequency, are grouped too closely together, and share too many commonalities to be occurring coincidentally. We believe that violence does breed violence, but the way it is bred and spread has coalesced into a perfect storm among the most vulnerable and the most preconditioned to violence. One can combine the influences of media-borne psychopathogens, the influence of violent video games and media, and the growing population of undiagnosed, untreated, and unmanaged seriously mentally ill people and look at it within the context of the transformational societal shift. We can then see that there is an evolutional inability to catch up to that societal shift, and the problem of an epidemic of murder suicide becomes more dire. This perfect storm of suicidality is one of the root causes of the problems of apocalyptic and episodic rampage violence we face today. It is violence that threatens to engulf the very public agencies we rely on to protect us, and if not ameliorated, this violence will result in a draconian governmental reaction that will make anyone born before the twenty-first century wonder where the good old days went.

Chapter 10

Best-Practice Approaches

One of the first things society has to do is destigmatize mental illness and self-harm, whether non-lethal, self-inflicting wounds or suicide itself. Or at least we have to sensitize ourselves to mental illness as a real illness and not just a quirk or harmless neurosis that people laugh about, as they did in the old *Bob Newhart Show*. Does society stigmatize physical illnesses such as the flu or a virus? We now know that mental illnesses such as schizophrenia and paranoid delusions have a biological basis in reality and are not either failures of a person's will or matters of weird thinking. We know that suicidal ideations do not mean that the person has a spiritual flaw, but the flow of specific neurochemicals can predispose an individual to certain moods, particularly when specific neurochemicals interrupt interneuronal connections from the meditative portion of the brain. This reconsideration of the nature of mental illness was brought to public attention recently with the suicide of Matthew Warren, the son of California pastor Rick Warren, whose book *The Purpose Driven Life* inspired millions of readers. Matthew Warren's suicide has begun to spark many in the evangelical community to rethink the nature of mental illness and to look at it as a medical problem rather than a manifestation of lack of faith. Taking a completely objective and nonprejudiced look at certain lethal manifestations of mental illness as a form of pathogen is certainly a major step toward understanding why individuals suffering from suicidal delusions decompose into committing violent acts. For example, the incidence of bipolar disorder is increasing to 10 percent of our population, increasing the suffering of those struggling with it, and causing others to suffer as well. How can we even begin to identify and treat individuals suffering from the suicidal ideations of mental illness with psychiatric disorders at risk for suicide?

Certainly not by Senate Majority Leader Mitch McConnell's attempts to use mental illness as a political wedge, as Senator McConnell did in his re-election campaign against the undeclared candidate Ashley Judd, who has since said that she will not run for the Senate from Kentucky. And just months after Mitch McConnell's strategy session to play the mental illness card against a potential, though undeclared, candidate, and amidst the jubilant laughter of his staff, he actually voted against bringing an expanded background-check measure up for a vote in the Senate and then voted to sustain a filibuster, even though a majority of senators sought to bring up the measure for an up or down vote. Laugh at mental illness, but make sure that procedural safeguards to keep guns out of the hands of the dangerously mentally ill are voted down. And we wonder why the government cannot make a dent in stopping American mass murders perpetrated by the mentally ill in America.

Although in today's environment there is no absolute way to identify a potentially dangerous individual, medicine is making progress. As more studies of brain function and the biology of the brain improve our understanding of the neurobiological mechanisms that can go wrong, public institutions such as school districts and law enforcement are looking at ways to make preliminary presumptive identifications of potentially dangerous individuals to allow for early intervention in the lives of at-risk young people.

However, the new gun control bill holds some good news even though it was dead on arrival in the House. The bill was proposed in the US Senate, where a cloture vote short-circuited a promised filibuster by Senators Rubio, Cruz, McConnell, and Rand Paul, who, as a medical doctor, seems to have forgotten his oath to "first do no harm," because he was more responsive to the wants of gun manufacturers than he was to the victims of those manufacturers. The gun control bill, according to press reports, pays for constructing additional community mental health centers and funding grant money for teachers to be trained in spotting early signs of mental illness. This is something we have been advocating for years, because teachers, especially in the elementary grades when early signs of mental illness camouflaged by strange behavior tend to turn up in classroom social interactions, are among the earliest potential first responders or alerters to serious psychopathology needing early intervention. They can alert parents to what they see in the classroom and provide a cautionary advisory to parents to check in with their children's pediatricians. The new proposal also makes more Medicaid dollars, paid through state grants, available for mental health care. Funds for new mental health programs, particularly funding for teacher training in mental illness recognition, are also included in President Obama's 2014 budget. The president's budget proposal earmarked $50 million to train more specialists in mental health care, including psychologists and school counselors. Perhaps we can argue that the budgetary provisions should include funding for psychiatric training for medical school entrants and support for residency in psychiatry, but at least the president has advocated financial support for psychologically informed services at a community level.

Perhaps among the most important provisions in the bill is the new awareness of suicidal behavior as a sign of dangerousness.

The bill calls for the development of new approaches to suicide prevention and advocates a methodology to support counseling and other interventions for children who have experienced trauma. Perhaps, if new approaches to post-traumatic intervention can be developed as a function of public health under the new gun control measures, these types of interventions, whether they be formal therapy or other approaches, can be utilized by the military, which is now facing a flood of potential PTSD victims returning from the Middle East war zones.

Senator Debbie Stabenow of Michigan was quoted by the *New York Times* as saying that bills to address the problems of mental illness in this country, coming, as they do, under the rubric of gun control legislation, are the types of proposals that can garner the support of both Democrats and Republicans from the most liberal to the most conservative, who, she said, could come together on this. Senator John Cornyn of Texas joined Senator Stabenow in her support for the legislation. Senator Cornyn's advocacy is important because dealing with the problem of the mentally ill in America as a function of gun control can become a kind of refuge for legislators who want to seem open and sympathetic to the problem and want to find a policy fix for the growing number of violently mentally ill in America, but who do not want to be seen by Second Amendment advocacy groups as supporting legislation to infringe on citizens' constitutional right to keep and bear arms.

The shootings at Sandy Hook Elementary, though a single event on a single day in a skein of mass murder suicides and attempted suicidal mass murders over the past decade, galvanized those in support of a better public health policy for dealing with mental illness. Even though people might argue that a single event should not be the only reason to look for solutions to the mental health problems in America, being as linked to gun violence as Sandy Hook is, the event became the objective correlative of the problem: a public manifestation of what can happen when violence results from an untreated mental illness.

Even Senator Harry Reid of Nevada, a supporter of the legislation, remarked about his father's suicide by means of a firearm.

According to Ronald S. Honberg, the legal director for the National Alliance on Mental Illness, as quoted in the *New York Times* report: because Holmes, Loughner, and Lanza were not adjudicated as mentally ill, they would not have turned up on a list to prohibit them from purchasing firearms.[110] However, only James Holmes had been in the mental health system, even if he had been seen only by a psychiatrist or psychologist. Loughner is not documented as seeing anyone with "mental health" credentials until he was sent to Springfield Medical Facility in the Federal Bureau of Prisons following the massacre. We don't really know what clinician Lanza saw, although it was somebody who did behavioral therapy, according to the Connecticut attorney general's report. That could be anyone, and the psychotropics could have been prescribed by a family doctor or nurse practitioner. In the case of Holmes, the psychiatrist decided not to report Holmes in the state of Colorado, because she believed him to be non-committable due to absence of a police record of prior violence. Cho Seung-Hui was in a different category because he was picked up by Virginia Tech campus security and remanded to the custody of the psychiatric facility at a local hospital for seventy-two hours. He was later released early on his own recognizance after a minimal psychiatric and psychological evaluation of less than twenty-four hours and involuntarily committed to Cook Counseling Center for outpatient treatment. Loughner was tossed out of Pima Community College and visited by campus police who told him to stay away. But Honberg's larger point is that if there were a system to address mental health problems, more individuals at risk would be identified early and perhaps even before a psychotic break.

---

[110] Peters, Jeremy W. "In Gun Debate, No Rift on Better Care for Mentally Ill." *New York Times,* April 12, 2013. http://www.nytimes.com/2013/04/13/us/politics/senators-make-bipartisan-push-for-mental-health-care.html?ref=jeremywpeters&_r=0.

A caveat, however: just like the Behavioral Emergencies section EMS Systems legislation, these new measures have to be funded or else, despite all the good intentions and need for public safety, nothing whatsoever will be done. If this program is subjected to the budget cutter's meat cleaver like other programs have been, it will only serve to make members of America's extreme right wing beat their chests in victory while their children remain potential targets. Most of the time, you have to pay for what you want and not just give it lip service.

The Los Angeles School District's Model Approach to Intervention

In the best of all possible worlds, school-aged children who are exhibiting strange behavior or acting dangerously toward their peers can be identified early and receive help through an intervention program ideally involving parents or caregivers. Dr. Tony Beliz, director of the School Threat Assessment and Response Team Program for the Los Angeles Unified School District was recently quoted by the *New York Times*:[111] "Some school gunmen— Mr. Lanza, for example—have already left school when they turn to violence, and such cases are the most difficult to identify and prevent." He is absolutely correct insofar as school guidance or intervention programs are concerned. But if students like Lanza were still in school, Dr. Beliz believes that counselors in school can help.

"We'll stay with these people as long as we can, and it makes a difference, because we're knocking on their door or their therapist's door," he said. "That's the missing piece in some of these school shootings. They were in engaged in some sort of way, but dropped out and no one really thought to follow them."[112] Adam Lanza, One L Goh, who shot and killed seven people at Oikos University

---

[111] Goode, Erica. "Focusing on Violence before It Happens." *New York Times*, March 14, 2013. http://www.nytimes.com/2013/03/15/us/in-los-angeles-focusing-on-violence-before-it-occurs.html?_r=0 (accessed December 13, 2013).
[112] Ibid.

in Oakland, James Holmes, Boston Marathon bomber Tamerlan Tsarnaev, John Schick, who opened fire inside the University of Pittsburgh Medical Center and was killed by police, and Jared Loughner were all suspended from or dropped out of college.

Dr. Beliz directs one of the most aggressive school programs in the nation to identify and assess the potential for school violence. It is an innovative approach but one that holds a lot of promise because the program amalgamates input from Los Angeles County mental health resources and law enforcement agencies such as the Los Angeles County Sheriff's Department and the LAPD. Developed initially by the LAPD in 2007 after the Cho Seung-Hui mass shootings at Virginia Tech, Dr. Beliz expanded the program to all schools in the county. This is an example of local government seizing the opportunity to review the potential for violence within county public school institutions and is one of the best practices that can easily become a model for counties and school districts throughout the country. Just imagine if such a program existed in the Newtown, Connecticut, public school system. Might Adam Lanza have been identified early? Might the municipality have tried to work with Nancy Lanza to find ways to address her son's early behavioral abnormalities? After a shooting rampage, all we can do is look at the possibilities from the perspective of hindsight and perform a suicidal autopsy based on best information available, mostly circumstantial and hearsay, with informed clinical speculation. We need to evaluate the young before such necessary, but inadequate, postmortem assessments.

Dangerousness Identification Protocols

In all the rampage murders we have studied, there are powerful testimonials from witnesses acquainted with the shooters. These testimonials speak of a history of mental illness, obvious suicidal threats, or personality change with strange behavior. For parents at their wit's end in figuring out what to do with children acting strangely, a protocol for decision making may be as accessible as the nearest hospital emergency room. Most emergency rooms have racks of protocol sheets to help hurried and harried staff in documenting their findings and dispositions of hundreds of patients evaluated and treated every day. These sheets are quite standardized and considered standards of care in emergency medicine, and they are known in emergency medicine as "presentation-based clinical assessments." These protocols are remarkably consistent in naming presentations and rules for necessary diagnostics, treatment, and post-discharge clinical management, whether that is admission to a hospital or outpatient referral. The names of these protocol sheets tagging clinical presentations are most relevant for any violence prevention program, such as Dr. Beliz's pioneering program in Los Angeles. ER doctors, under the federal law EMTALA, have to examine the patient and select presentations and document diagnosis and treatment. They select from a menu of paper presentations or electronically in their electronic medical record standardized clinical presentation template titles, such as the following:

"Appears Intoxicated"
"Strange Behavior, Verbal"
"Strange Behavior, Nonverbal"
"Burns"
"Skin Lesions"
"Suicidal"
"Seizures"
"Head Injury"
"Mental Illness History"
"Overdose"
"Poisoning"
"Wounds"

When discovering that such racks of protocols tagged with broad names for problems—rather than actual diagnostic codes for which research and reimbursement can select patients or reimburse for services, respectively—are pieced together, they can be all-inclusive for diseases and psychiatric disorders with the risk for death and disability, whether for the patient or others. Another way of saying this is if a person's presenting problem(s) cannot be tagged by one or more of these presentation-based protocol sheets, that person is not a patient. The protocols are that inclusive and can be adapted for any institutional use, including Dr Beliz's school nursing offices.

Ideally, a certified first responder, including police, fire, and rescue squad personnel, can be trained to rule in as many of these problems as possible during pretransport and transport phase in any encounter where there is apparent disability or threat of violence to self or others. Of course, emergency room clinicians cannot be everywhere, and they are an increasingly scarce resource as 20 percent of our emergency rooms have been shut down since 9/11 and are increasingly overcrowded with patients needing care elsewhere, such as in psychiatric hospitals that are also being closed faster than architects can even dream of building better ones.[113]

What is not discussed in Dr. Beliz's program is the critical need for close liaison with emergency medicine and its community physician extenders, emergency medical technicians. Even such inclusiveness still does not sufficiently extend the critical loop of emergency clinical services required by the School Threat Assessment and Response Team Program—or any violence and suicide prevention program. Dr. David Boyd recognized the need for expanding the loop for emergency services when he drafted the original Emergency Services Act nearly half a century ago. He most prophetically recognized the need for all first responders to learn and apply best practices in behavioral emergencies. Although his visionary inclusion of this physician extender into the community to essentially do what LAPD is now trying to do remains law, Congress created scarcity of

---

[113] Ostrow, Nicole. "Hospitals Eliminate 1 in 4 U.S. Emergency Rooms Since 1990, Study Finds." *Bloomberg News*, May 17, 2011. http://www.bloomberg.com/news/2011-05-17/hospitals-eliminate-1-in-4-u-s-emergency-rooms-since-1990-study-finds.html (accessed December 11, 2013).

services right from the beginning by failing to fund the behavioral emergencies section of the Emergency Services Act, responsible for founding EMS Systems. Of course, we know how the Emergency Services Act saved many lives through its operational component, which we now take for granted as 911 and EMS Systems. But these lives were saved by faster and better treatment of strokes, major trauma, obstetric and pediatric emergencies, and heart attacks. Overt stigmatization of the mentally ill in Washington, DC, simply deleted the behavioral emergencies section from the act.[114]

Whether police chiefs know it or not, this failure to equitably and intelligently fund EMS Systems conspired with deinstitutionalization of the seriously mentally ill, who were transferred into community mental health centers that were concurrently soft targets from which financing was also easily drained at both state and federal levels. Then, "seriously mentally ill patients" became "eccentric" people at best, a less dangerous and more acceptable term, and criminals at worst under court decisions like the Lessard ruling in Washington. And over-legislating the rules for involuntary commitment holds out little hope for diagnosing, treating, or managing cases of behavioral emergencies. Police officers and most first responders are not trained in behavioral emergencies, but the many toxic political and social cross-currents gushing through our public health and safety systems in the wake of returning public psychology and mental health services to the dark ages in less than fifty years ironically dumped the system on police chiefs. Psychiatrist E. Fuller Torrey presented this current historical public health crisis and conundrum treatise to the American Psychiatric Association in "Bedlam Revisited," Promised Approaches to Mental Health under the Affordable Care Act.[115]

---

[114] NAEMT. "History of EMS." http://www.naemt.org/about_ems/EMShistory.aspx (accessed December 11, 2013).

[115] Torrey, MD, E. Fuller. "Bedlam Revisited: Jails, Police, & Mental Health Courts as the New Psychiatric Care System." Presentation to the APA Annual Meeting, Philadelphia, May 6, 2012. http://www.treatmentadvocacycenter.org/storage/documents/2012-bedlam-revisited-slideshow.pdf.

President Obama has asked the CDC to focus some attention on mental illness and the prevalence of mental illness in American society. The president has also called for a $100 million brain-mapping study. The medical community certainly welcomes both initiatives, but on an immediately local level, what will these initiatives accomplish in the short term to identify and then treat those potentially dangerous mentally ill individuals? And who will pay for those families without the means to pay for their own mental health care? The question drives commentators into an apoplexy over public health costs, but what is the cost–benefit balancing test between the human and financial cost of mopping up after a mass murder/suicide on the level of what happened at Sandy Hook Elementary and the cost of funding an emergency mental health initiative? We expect that public funding will be less expensive over the long term and that the human cost, in terms of deaths of loved ones and community trauma, will be vastly reduced.

According to the US Census Bureau's 2010 report, "The proportion of Americans without health insurance is the highest it has been in a decades. As the president's 2014 budget proposes, cuts will be implanted under Medicare Part B and D, meaning cuts to senior benefits. And under the Affordable Care Act (ACA), as payments to doctors are cut, the impact on lower-income families will be harder to bear. Under the current, pre-ACA system, today's quality measures are not necessarily driven by service optimization, the optimal effectiveness of treatment with highest level of cost efficiency.[116] Results demonstrate that it is not working for either effectiveness or efficiency. Managed care has had massive impact on clinical practice in the United States but not necessarily optimized service. The Affordable Care Act promises solutions, but the anticipated relief from its implementation has faded with the

---

[116] US Bureau of the Census. "Health Insurance—Highlights: 2011." http://www.census.gov/hhes/www/hlthins/data/incpovhlth/2011/highlights.html (accessed December 11, 2013).

nation's fiscal crisis and worst economic recession in history; since its passage, everything has become worse. There are more people who are uninsured, and likely more on the way, as business gets out of the health care benefits market and leaves its employees to the unexplored realms of health insurance exchanges.

How Will the Health Care Revolution Finally End?

Within this decade, according to Morris Collen, MD, we may be reading one of two different headlines, mainly in the business and trade journals. Either the managed care industry buys out physician-controlled medical practices, effectively corporatizing the private medical practice, or physicians' groups themselves will incorporate their own industry, effectively imposing their own management constraints upon an industry whose costs no one seems to be able to control. Alternatively, in a scenario of rampant spread of mental illness, the media-borne spread of psychopathogens, and the social devastation that results, we could be looking at the federal government's modifying of the ACA into a single-payer system, bringing with it medical evaluation panels, payment restrictions, and medical malpractice settlement caps that reduce the cost of tort litigation. Is that something we want? Furthermore, might there be a solution to identifying and diagnosing the mentally ill under pending initiatives to computerize all medical records, thus providing a health tracking system under the ACA?

Medical center databases of patient information hold not only clues to patient retention but patterns of practice and morbidity affecting legal risk. Although the average American consumer of medical services might be adverse to universal health-care databases containing private patient information, in an environment where pending background check gun control legislation might mandate a database for the mentally ill, a policy of public safety might trump individual concerns over privacy of medical records, with the exception that patient records for legal intervention would be protected by due process under the Fifth and Fourth Amendments so that it would require either a court or magistrate order to obtain privacy information from a patient record.

However, the massive overhead required to implement nationwide digital health records at all levels, from private upscale hospitals through health maintenance organizations to community and county-funded medical care facilities, may mean that integrated digitized mental health records, available to doctors on demand, may be over a decade away because of what we are seeing as a disconnect in information technology (IT) integration. What do failures in IT integration have to do with these massive disruptions among longstanding and world-famous freestanding medical centers? We will see what is disgorged in the media as the ACA's requirements clash with the VA's attempts to computerize medical records. At first, it could be a giant boondoggle with massive system disruptions that will bring up the pressing question for US teaching hospitals: How can their state-of-the-art IT departments set up a standard for best practices and teach the new generation of clinicians to screen for mental health? From a strictly IT perspective, this will be more complex than the format wars between Betamax and JVC in the 1970s.

The push for universal mental health electronic records raises another question regarding who will have routine access to those records. This is an especially relevant question as Congress debates the new cybersecurity bill within the context of cyber attacks from foreign countries and from groups within the United States. How that database of valuable patient information is selectively mined for either purely financial goals or for optimization of clinical services becomes crucial. How information is shared via web-based systems and local area networks within medical centers' wide area networks rather than via the traditional governance of committee meetings, staff meetings, utilization review, and medical records will also be an issue.

For example, Stanford University announced that its neuroscientists have developed a procedure for creating transparent images of a working brain in a live subject—in this case, a mouse—but they can also view parts of a human brain. Suddenly, the actual process of human consciousness may become visible: the tracking of thoughts and emotions in various parts of the brain as represented by which areas turn on and the intensity of the electron flow along the brain's wiring in real time. The diagnostic capability this provides to neuropsychiatrists and neurosurgeons will be enormous, but the entire development comes with a potential downside as predictions of mental illness make their way into patient databases.

Ostensibly used only for the purposes of background checks for gun control, brain mapping and transparent brain technologies could also be used by the military, by law enforcement, and by the courts to monitor a witness's mental state at the time of testimony. What does a brain display when a witness is lying? What does truthfulness look like? These are questions that could possibly have answers within the next five years. Those answers will go a long way either to allay radicals' suspicions at both ends of the political spectrum, from extreme left to extreme right, that most psychiatrists are the enemy or confirm the predictions of universal health-care advocates that a society can maintain privacy over sensitive personal medical records.

Computer Diagnostics and Treating the Mentally Ill

Computer-enhanced diagnostics could advance the current art and practice of clinical medicine, particularly for the mentally ill or those exhibiting strange behavior, by supporting selection of both diagnostic and therapeutic technologies in a significantly more objective and effective manner than the current state of practice. Computer-enhanced diagnostics within the medical services industry promise both cost control and improvement in quality of care, again, particularly for the potentially dangerous mentally ill, who are routinely underdiagnosed and underserved in our society. Imagine how history would have changed if the University of Colorado, Pima Community College, and even the Newtown school system and the University of Connecticut had flagged and diagnosed Holmes, Loughner, and Lanza before their respective mental breaks. Even now, gatekeeper physicians, backed by tight internal control of clinical pathways and high deductibles for out-of-network providers, are technically capable of reducing health-care costs without imposing a maximum for any benefit or violating privileged communications. Both quality and cost control, however, require diagnostic innovations that focus on service optimization (the medically necessary enhancement of patient selection for advancing procedures and treatments). Service optimization, particularly for the constant diagnostic screening in both triage and continuous tracking along clinical pathways, is key to operational success for both cost and quality control in managed care. As both the brain imaging and brain mapping initiatives open up new areas of research into mental illness and traumatic brain injury, the push to computerize all medical records will ideally help pediatricians and the parents of their patients discover problems early to prevent violence and self-destructive behaviors.

For neuropsychiatrists, the advent of successful discoveries of biomarkers to improve diagnostic reliability and validity promise an improvement in practices of great need for advances in neuroimaging of dreaming-in-sleep studies, the prediction of losing impulse control following detention for, or assessing violence potential in, psychotic and suicidal patients.

The promises of identifying complex genetic variants lead to promises of personalized psychiatric medicine, which is now a best practice in first-line treatment for breast cancer. We know that certain genetic variants reliably correlate with psychopathology. Specifically, a pediatric neuropsychiatrist might look at similar or influencing behaviors between parent and child to see whether there might be a genetic component to the child's strange or aberrant behavior. In that case, the issue could be addressed through treating both the parent and the child. For example, a functional polymorphism in the catechol-O-methyltransferase (COMT) gene moderated the influence of adolescent cannabis use on developing adult psychosis. According to *Medscape,* carriers of the COMT valine158 allele were most likely to exhibit psychotic symptoms and to develop schizophreniform disorder if they used cannabis.[117] Imagine that both parents were using marijuana along with their adolescent child. If the child was carrying the COMT valine158 allele, we would have a predictor of that child's potential behavior as an adult. Cannabis use had no such adverse influence on individuals with two copies of the methionine allele. Therefore, these findings provide evidence of a gene–environment interaction and suggest that a role of some susceptibility genes is to influence vulnerability to environmental pathogens.

Computer-Assisted Diagnostic Interview

Studies have reliably demonstrated that primary care clinicians have a significant daily need for more information than they access in their current practices. You can see also "Unity in Health Care: The Toyota Way—Can Lean Engineering Fix North American Health Care?"[118] for a fuller explanation.[119] Drs. Weed, Klein, and Westberg, cited in that article, have unequivocally emphasized the need for enhanced availability of diagnostic and treatment information for service optimization. As R. Miller says, "Fortunately, practitioners are capable of reasoning with incomplete and imprecise information and often make clinical judgments at times when they have unfulfilled

[117] "Is COMT a Susceptibility Gene for Schizophrenia?" *Medscape.* www.medscape.com/viewarticle/528487,4.
[118] Liebert, MD, John. "Unity in Healthcare: The Toyota Way." February 2008. http://www.johnliebert.com/johnliebert/pdfs/ToyotaWay_BulletinFeb2008.pdf.
[119] Ibid.

information needs."[120] However, at this time, we cannot state that clinical computing is more valid for service optimization than the significant and current seat-of-the-pants, state-of-the-art, or some other enhancement of clinical decision making, such as consultation or clinical and continuing clinical education. But IT has probably already reached an irreversible critical mass within the health-care industry. Clinical educators will have to find a way to make it the ultimate solution to ongoing and potential damages that stem from ignoring the proven information needs of primary care clinicians and also make sure that diagnostic decision making is not completely machine-driven. This is particularly urgent for health professional educators when considering that the next-generation Internet will speed the transition of informatics from a support for health care to a means of transforming health care. The need to communicate medical information over large networks will require an enhanced broadband distribution. Laser fiber optics, for example, will furnish more acceptable rates of transmission of images between multistate medical facilities, making telemedicine a more practical and routine mode of care delivery.

"IT will penetrate every aspect of professional practice as small and inexpensive Internet-linked notebook computers pervade clinicians' offices, examination rooms, nursing stations, procedure rooms, bedsides, clinics, and patient homes. These devices will become as familiar and as indispensable as the pen, the telephone, and the pocket calculator as means for recording, communicating, and extending the individual's ability to recall, find, calculate, store, and process information as informatics becomes fully integrated into health care delivery and management."[121] However, we know that computers themselves are not the ultimate answer in telemedicine: the data are.

---

[120] Westberg, MS, Edward E., and Randolph A. Miller, MD. "Medical Diagnostic Decision Support Systems—Past, Present, and Future: A Threaded Bibliography and Brief Commentary." *Journal of the American Medical Informatics Association,* Vol. 1 (1999): 8–27.
[121] Weed, L. L. "Problem-Oriented Medical Information System (PROMIS) Laboratory." In G. A. Giebin & L. L. Hurst (eds.), *Computer Projects in Health Care.* Ann Arbor, MI: Health Administration Press.

Progressive Computer-Assisted Screening: Innovation for Service Optimization

Geographically distant case managers, supported by programmed algorithms, already determine clinical choices, but doctors working with clinically reliable algorithms and protocols can take the lead. Patients still want and need their doctors to control their care, but for this to happen, their case managers and clinicians must communicate from reliably standardized protocols and semantic mapping. Now case managers track their patients' care via telehealth. The electronic medical record in ambulatory care is in its infancy and rarely clinician-driven, despite its widespread implementation demanded by the Affordable Care Act health-care reform law and testimonials by computer companies with marketing, sales, and lobbying power to get the lucrative contracts. The state of Arkansas mandated, for example, that all family practitioners reimbursed by certain insurance companies such as BlueCross/BlueShield or Kaiser chart their cases via an electronic medical record, which is selected by the insurance company. The family practitioner either learns how to use it or does not get paid by the insurer. More consensus needs to occur between managed care case managers and frontline clinicians, or patients will inevitably be stuffed into cookie-cutter protocols and managed clinical pathways.

A "patient- and clinician-friendly" diagnostic screen can efficiently and uniformly assist triage of patients entering the health-care system at all points of entry, including the corrections system. The incredible costs of underdiagnosing and attendant denial of treatment for the complex needs of mentally disorganized and psychic-impaired patients will eventually demand revolutionary approaches at the points of entry to health services. Whether that point of entry has the form of clinical offices, public health services, emergency rooms, or jails can ultimately make no difference because that is where the at-risk individuals present for the infrequent opportunity of comprehensive, computer-enhanced diagnostic assessment.

Computer Software Can Model the Clinician's Triage Decision Process

Here is where the rubber meets the road in terms of using IT and knowledge databases combined with good clinical decision making to speed the diagnosis and treatment process. On an emergency-room level, in trauma centers, and in the military, clinicians are faced with the question: What is triage in medicine?

In disasters with multiple victims and in battlefield surgical hospitals, incoming patients are triaged according to the severity and life-threatening nature of their wounds or traumas. Triage, therefore, is the process of sorting out patients according to their immediate need for urgent care. It was developed by a military surgeon in Napoleon's army but it is now commonplace in civilian medical treatment, particularly in trauma centers. In the 1960s, triage was used to allocate scarce resources for kidney dialysis treatment in cases of renal failure. It is also used today to qualify patients and establish queues for organ transplants. Modern emergency medicine requires the clinical discipline of triage, a word used all the time in many different contexts and usually associated with urgent clinical practices and response to disasters. The public was first made conscious of "triage" as a discipline in civilian surgery when it was profiled in the 1965 NBC documentary *Who Lives? Who Dies?*

The documentary focused on the bioethics of Dr. Belding Scribner's pioneering work in renal dialysis at the University of Washington Medical Center in Seattle. When new medical technologies, such as organ transplants and kidney dialysis, emerged as practical life-saving treatments, choices had to be made in US medicine. There were not enough viable organs or dialysis machines available to all who needed them. Therefore, committees had to be set up to determine whose life was worth saving. "Triage" emphasized the value of a life saved and biases in the selection criteria of the committee evolved. These biases triggered a lasting and sometimes strident debate about the ethical propriety of such a triage process. Thus, the contemporary public first learned of triage as a judgment process for rationing scarce health-care resources for the greatest good of the greatest number. For example, in a world where there is a long list of patients needing kidney transplants and a limited amount of kidneys, evaluation boards at kidney transplant hospitals have a selection criteria for patients who should receive kidneys. In a multiple-vehicle traffic accident on a freeway, those patients with life-threatening injuries will usually be treated first because incoming patients are triaged in emergency rooms according to the severity of their injuries.

Now the politically polarized publicity of so-called "death boards" confounds implementation of new health-care reform legislation. Nowhere are the needs of triage as great as they are in the Department of Defense and the VA. The young wounded warrior competes for traditionally scarce resources on the battlefield and then returns to compete with civilian peers, retired military, and veterans of other wars for scarce resources at home. Although the organization and distribution of care in military medicine is only sporadically called triage, the discipline is embedded into actual practices. Physician assistants and nurse practitioners, for example, have vastly more diagnostic and treatment discretion than they do at the Mayo Clinic or at most other civilian health care facilities. Such embedded triage is exactly what former Congressional Budget Office director Peter Orszag proposed under new legislation for reforming health care. It is the trend now visible with the coming of health-care reform, because there are simply not enough doctors to diagnose and treat every patient under universal health care—nor is there enough money to pay them. Some cynics have termed this practice the "dumbing down" of medicine to the point where real medical intervention could be shifted into categories by individuals who are not qualified to make those decisions. Therefore, one of the real-world issues becomes the issue of who is in charge of the triage mechanism.

The levels of competency, credentialing, training, and consistency of supervision are huge issues in malpractice trials, such as those against the military. The pyramidal structure of clinical care, when cracked, can implode. In some cases, you have one psychiatrist working in an administrative office with responsibilities for psychologists, practitioners, and nurses. This psychiatrist prescribes complex psychotropics and perhaps delegates the supervision of physician assistants with bachelor's degrees to nurses with extra training as nurse practitioners. Now that the state has made a preliminary rejection of James Holmes's offer to plead guilty in exchange for a life sentence without parole and has asked for the death penalty, one might expect to see a similar extreme leveraging of scarce clinical resources, which is the common standard of practice on college and university campuses. Those campuses were home to grossly psychotic students who later committed devastating acts of murder and mayhem. Some of these students are described as follows:

Terry Joe Sedlacek at Southwestern Illinois College suffered from Lyme disease that likely impaired his brain function. He randomly murdered a minister with whom he had no personal connection.

Jared Loughner was suspended from Pima Community College for disruptive behavior before the 2011 Tucson shooting that disabled Representative Gabrielle Giffords and killed many others, including a federal judge and a young girl.

Radcliffe Haughton was a student at Milwaukee Area Technical College and was in transition to their school of nursing when he committed suicidal mass murder at a salon in Brookfield, Wisconsin.

Cho Seung-Hui was an involuntary treatment patient of Cook Counseling Center at Virginia Tech before he committed suicidal mass murder in 2007.

James Oliver Seevakumaran withdrew from classes at Central Florida University before planning to commit mass murder. Instead, he killed himself.

Ross Ashley, a student at Virginia's Radford University, randomly killed a campus police officer at Virginia Tech and then killed himself on the Tech campus.

Steven Kazmierczak, a graduate of Northern Illinois University, returned to his alma mater with a firearm to kill five people and injure another twenty-one before committing suicide.

James Holmes flunked out of his graduate neuroscience program at the University of Colorado and committed mass murder at an Aurora multiplex.

Let's reverse-engineer this conceptual framework as if Dr. David Boyd's plan for emergency medical services had actually been funded for behavioral emergencies. What would the landscape look like for the LAPD and the Los Angeles School District's Dr. Beliz? Let's dissect the conceptual framework of triage practice piece by piece. In reverse-engineering each element, we can reinvent a more civilized and far less violent landscape for all of us to live, shop, and go to school without having to fear being shot. The steps to reverse-engineer each element are as follows:

1. Incidence, demographics, epidemiology, and clinical aspects associated with these critical patient categories was mandatory for a systems approach that could be addressed in relation to emergency medical services, regional planning, and operations.

2. General and specific planning for regional emergency medical services' response to the routine overall and particularly critical target patient groups to provide a system of care for critical medical conditions and other emergencies, including behavioral emergencies, so that all would receive better care and benefit from sound regional emergency medical services planning and operations.

3. Responsive system plans and operations in the general and critical care areas provide a basis and an opportunity for evaluating these goals and creating with an aim toward prevention.

All those who have called 911 at least once in their lives should have an idea of what a simple three-digit number has done for medical emergencies. Response times are faster. There is no need to hunt for a phone number for a first-aid squad or police. Smartphones have an automatic dialer for 911. Most of us know the kinds of emergency care and transport that a 911 call brings. Now let's see what a 911 call could do for behavioral emergencies such as a Jared Loughner in Pima County, Arizona. Are there resources to deal with cases like Loughner or Holmes? Will resources become available in the future?

Behavioral emergency services were never funded, although they were mandated in EMS Systems legislation to enhance emergency response, stabilization of the sick and injured, and transportation. To make matters worse, the introduction of antipsychotic medicine during the 1950s has led to the dumping of psychiatric patients on the unfunded resources of local communities. State and federal governments are pulling out as fast as they can, wherever and whenever they can, from dealing with emergency psychiatric cases, because not only are governments afraid of dealing with injuries they cannot see, they also have an underlying fear of psychiatry in general. Thus, it is no surprise that behavioral emergencies are framed as criminal justice matters rather than health-care issues—that is, when the derision stops. Public derision of psychiatric issues might have caused a Nancy Lanza not to aggressively pursue any help for her son. In the absence of a public emergency health protocol at a local level for the mentally ill acting strangely, jail increasingly becomes the solution of choice.

If criminalizing the mentally ill acting strangely is policy, how will we afford it? The Cook County jail, for example, is the second-largest psychiatric hospital in the United States. And the United States, as *Salon Magazine* has reported, now has more people incarcerated in jails and prisons than any other nation on Earth, supporting, in the process, a privately outsourced prison system business.[122] How many of those prisoners are actually dangerous? From 1994 on, our prisons held two hundred thousand combat veterans from Vietnam, mostly for drug-associated convictions, and their replacement with Gulf War I veterans was accelerating so that over the ensuing decade, Vietnam War and Gulf War I veterans comprised 39 percent of federal prison inmates and 36 percent of state prison inmates.[123] Also the Bureau of Justice Statistics estimates that we are likely approaching that number of incarcerated combat veterans from the wars in Iraq and Afghanistan as previous generations of incarcerated veterans decompose in mind and body or perish within the criminal justice system.[124] The mandate for parity in emergency response and management of behavioral emergencies is all but forgotten in the archives of the Congressional Record, both in the Emergency Services Act for civilians and the Forgotten Warrior Program for combat veterans, which should not be confused with the charity the Wounded Warrior Project.

Having emergency medical technicians trained in dealing with behavioral emergencies is a good thing, but convincing hospital emergency rooms of that is another matter. Why receiving hospitals would question emergency medical technicians' prediagnostic opinions may seem odd on the surface, but receiving hospitals might not want too much documented about a newly transported patient in the event that they decide to transfer the patient ASAP to another hospital for any number of administrative reasons: shortages of staff during periods of a flu epidemic or the patient's lack of medical

---

[122] Lennard, Natasha. "US Has More Prisoners, Prisons Than Any Other Country." *Salon*, October 15, 2012. http://www.salon.com/2012/10/15/us_has_more_prisoners_prisons_than_any_other_country/ (accessed December 11, 2013).

[123] US Department of Justice. "Veterans in State and Federal Prisons, 2004." By Margaret E. Noonan and Christopher J. Mumola. NCJ 217199 (Office of Justice Programs, May 2007). bjs.gov/content/pub/pdf/vsfp04.pdf (accessed December 12, 2013).

[124] US Department of Justice. "Veterans in Prison or Jail." By Christopher J. Mumola. NCJ 178888 (Office of Justice Programs, January 2000). http://bjs.gov/content/pub/pdf/vpj.pdf.

insurance. The last thing a hospital administrator wants to face is a deposition from an indigent patient's lawyer filing a seven-figure lawsuit against the hospital because of refused treatment that caused the death of a patient during transport to another hospital.

Rudimentary computer-assisted diagnostics that support emergency medical technician patient care are certainly better than nothing, because now ambulance drivers calling in transport emergencies to local receiving medical centers at least know what the regional bed census is in many metropolitan regions and can divert en route rather than pulling up, wheeling the patient in, and being told to go somewhere else. Some of those who call themselves experts in computer aided dispatch (CAD), who did not think that psychiatric patients made up a large percentage of emergency room visits where they work, admitted that they had counted nine out of fourteen patients on just their nights on duty. These were primary psychiatric patients for whom the staff had "emptied the candy jar." The "candy jar" is medical slang for prescribing a lot of Lorazepam tranquilizers.

It is reported that less than 7 percent of ER visits are primary psychiatric patients, but upon closer inquiry, the numbers turn out to be far higher.[125] This means that we can do better in identifying the primary psychiatric patient population overutilizing hospital emergency rooms. Relying on emergency room services for psychiatric treatment is bad for the patient, bad for emergency rooms, and bad for emergency medical/surgical and trauma patients, whose care is sometimes triaged behind a violent psychotic patient. Therefore, first responders and the lay public alike must have more knowledge to cull the at-risk and known violent people from home and community. Clinical staff at all points of entry to our health-care system today, particularly our emergency rooms, must be "epidemiologically informed."

---

[125] McCambridge, Ruth. "Psychiatric Patients in Emergency Rooms Wait and Wait . . . and Wait." *Nonprofit Quarterly,* January 23, 2013. http://www.nonprofitquarterly.org/policysocial-context/21674-psychiatric-patients-in-emergency-rooms-wait-and-waitand-wait.html (accessed December 11, 2013).

The Constitutional Arguments

The obvious argument that arises when psychiatrists advocate that, in the interest of public safety, the state should have a greater authority to order involuntary commitment for observation for individuals who manifest dangerous behavior, even if that behavior is not immediately threatening to self or others. The medical argument is not only for traditional bioethical reasons of doing the greatest good for greatest number. It is for the basic premise of protecting the patient and those with whom he or she may come into contact. Psychiatrists argue that there is a greater need for clinical observation of those whose behavior is threatening. What civil rights are spared when a person known to be dangerous commits the final act of violence that either puts him to death or away for life, particularly after that person has murdered others?

We will face that tragic display of justice in Denver when the prosecution pursues the death penalty for the defendant, whose visible mental deterioration and personality change took him from stardom in a National Institutes of Health–sponsored neuroscience doctorate program at the University of Colorado to murder and mayhem in Aurora. Holmes knew he was decomposing mentally; he sought help at the same time he sought guns. The help did not come, but the guns did. Now the state has to pick up the detritus of the disaster and explain why Holmes's execution will bring justice when the crime itself could have been prevented if the university had intervened before his complete mental breakdown. Had Colorado's new gun laws been in effect, the number of casualties might have been reduced because Holmes would have had to reload more than once. That is also a fact that seems to have made no difference to the NRA and its acolytes in the Senate.

The Holmes case is an example of what can happen when the decomposing mentally ill are left to their own devices and shunted away from the institutions they attended. They then turn their anger and frustration, which they cannot control without medication and therapy, toward the innocent public, or they wind up in jail because mental illness is also criminalized in our country. Therefore, what is saved financially by forcing nearly 22 percent of our population impaired with psychiatric disorders into clinical pathways promising bad outcomes? Too many unnecessary deaths and massacres have occurred to allow this trend to continue. Parity must be achieved for behavioral emergencies, and that means implementing the Seattle model for regional care of disrupted heartbeats by applying it to disrupted brainwaves. The science is as powerful in neuropsychiatry as it is in cardiology. Translational research in neuropsychiatry from lab to first clinical encounter with the impaired psychiatric patient holds great promise.

This is not as easy as it sounds because only 10 percent of Americans believe that behavioral emergencies emanate from abnormalities of brain function that are responsive to relatively effective and safe medications, according to clinician and School of Medicine faculty member at the University of California, San Diego, Dr. Stephen M. Stahl, an expert in psychopharmacology, who utilizes psychopharmacology to work on treatment-resistant cases.[126] In fact, even more ominous is how influential public-opinion makers manipulate epidemiological data to reinvent the antipsychiatry argument by touting what they claim are the adverse effects of psychotropic medications. They argue falsely that these medications actually cause behavioral emergencies, which they most assuredly do not when prescribed correctly. "Nearly Every Mass Shooting in the Last 20 Years Shares One Thing in Common, & It's NOT Weapons" reads a headline on ammoland.com.[127] This is a common argument the gun lobby likes to make to divert attention

---

[126] Stahl, S. M. *Essential Psychopharmacology: Neuroscientific Basis and Practical Application*. 2000. Reprint, Cambridge, UK: Cambridge University Press, 2008.
[127] Roberts, Dan. "Nearly Every Mass Shooting in the Last 20 Years Shares One Thing in Common, & It's Not Weapons." *Ammoland*, April 1, 2013. http://www.ammoland.com/2013/04/every-mass-shooting-in-the-last-20-years-shares-psychotropic-drugs/.

away from the real problem and point their fingers of blame elsewhere. This public outlook regarding mental illness and the dangers to public health must change to make our homes, neighborhoods, cities, and communities, whether academic, military, or civilian, safe from violence once again.

The public education and applied research of cardiology and emergency medicine embedded in training first responders and emergency medical technicians must be adapted for reduction of violence and suicide, too. A truly effective EMS Systems system therefore must provide an emergency medical response for behavioral emergencies as it does for emergencies such as heart attacks, strokes, and traumatic accidents.

What the current epidemic of violent crimes committed by the mentally ill also requires from regional emergency medical services planners is not only training of first responders to handle behavioral emergencies, but a program of training for nonurgent patient care. Once delivered to emergency rooms, nonurgent care patients must be promptly triaged to lower levels of care, even in cases of natural disasters such as Hurricane Sandy. Boarding of chronic mentally ill patients must cease in our emergency rooms. Emergency medical services must be as high a priority in American cities as they are for soldiers in Operation Enduring Freedom; the Times Square bomber case refreshes our memories that OEF and Homeland Security are, on principle, inseparable, although different department secretaries are involved and not often communicating well enough.

With demands of implementing health-care reform legislation looming over the White House, the administration will have to eliminate the dangerous gridlock of ambulance diversion, both in ordinary times and for disasters. If we look at what types of crimes the dangerously mentally ill are committing in the United States, and we say to ourselves that these crimes are simply not preventable, we are simply placing innocent citizens and our children in the crosshairs of individuals who have degenerated into avatars in a digital war game. What good is it to fight the Taliban in far-off Afghanistan for Operation Enduring Freedom, if we cannot provide either emergency medical services for citizens at home in ordinary times or emergency preparedness for another attack on the homeland, a disastrous flood in Nashville, killer tornadoes in Oklahoma, a Hurricane Sandy, or an epidemic in Seattle that has shut down emergency rooms? What social good is achieved by allowing at-risk youth and psychiatric patients to roam the streets of campuses, military bases, cities, and towns? What social good is allowing them to sleep on the streets like ticking time bombs while they plan their next strike? It was too late to intervene in the lives of all those college students we mentioned in this book.

Emergency rooms, although the last and only resort today—some even consider them the "new Ground Zero"—are not the answer; nor are jails and prisons or street justice meted out by overzealous and ill-trained police officers. Like any social and economic cycle, the promises of modern psychiatry were oversold in the community mental health movement of the 1960s; even the Republic of South Vietnam was to have extensions of our grandiose community mental health system. The pendulum has now swung too far toward a Puritanical vision of punishment and incarceration. We are only now reading that we cannot afford mental health care, and deterrence of certainty of punishment is only political rhetoric because only a fraction of violent assaults and threats are investigated. An even smaller fraction results in adjudication, whether through civil litigation or criminal prosecution.

Failure to identify and manage people with abnormalities of the brain is simply too long to wait to remove the wounded from the field, sort them via triage, and treat those who are treatable. Months are too long to remove the volatile and unstable soldier from the military base preparing troops for deployment and providing rest and relaxation for those returning. For the untreatable, unfortunately, secure and humane institutionalization is the only solution in civilian society. And for soldiers and the VA itself, this is a similar solution. This solution is true in both military and civilian medicine: long-term care for disabled veterans, like Navy Yard mass shooting perpetrator Aaron Alexis and chronic neuropsychiatric cases like Adam Lanza.

Triage has been performed for centuries. Triage diagnosis is even mentioned in Leviticus as the only method for dealing what is mistranslated in modern versions of the Bible as "leprosy," red or orange skin lesions oozing a discharge and indicating an inflammation or infection(Leviticus 12:1–15:33). A priest diagnoses the infected individual, who is quarantined from the rest of the camp of the Israelites and placed on a watch to see whether his sores dry up or continue to fester. If the priest deems that the infected person has an active case of leprosy, all of the person's possessions, including clothing and shelter, are burned to prevent reinfection and communication of the disease. Only then, after the skin lesions dry up, a purification ritual is performed, and a sacrifice is made, is the infected person allowed back into the camp.

Triage finally was officially given a title and operational diagnosis in World War I. Its meaning has developed with exigencies of the times, whether combat, disaster preparedness, or modern bioethics of expensive technologies and emergency medical services. Yet we lack the necessary discipline of standards of care for emergency medical triage or even regulatory restraints for when the discipline inferred by the term really applies. Ideally, these standards of care for behavioral emergencies will emerge from new gun control legislation and President Obama's mandate to the CDC to focus on a review of mental health issues. Board-certified surgeons perform surgical procedures under sterile conditions in operating rooms. But when it comes to triage, who does it? Where and how? From hospital to hospital, it seems catch-as-catch-can, and nobody seems to know. Insurance adjusters, some of whom are actual MDs or are posing as clinicians, invoke triage to deny care. The insurance adjusters may require prior authorization even to go to an emergency room, which would involve emergency triage. This use of the term "triage" to ration care is actually invoked to justify claims management to deny care at hospitals that refuse patients without insurance. However, those making the decisions are rarely clinicians, and, if so, they are thoroughly trained to think in terms of economics rather than quality of care.

Triage, in the context of insurance medicine, is not even performing the greatest good for greatest number. Rather, in today's emergency medicine, triage performs the greatest good for stakeholders in the insurance company. The VA and Social Security disability insurance, ironically the beacons of federally administered health care, are among the most arbitrary and capricious in their clinical decision making, which is oftentimes erroneously labeled as triage. The message within these insurance company medical claims offices is quite clear and unambiguous, whether for commercial or governmental compensation: deny if you can and pay as little as possible. In the world of medical insurance claims adjustors, particularly physicians in the role of forensic evaluators, one is an insurance doctor first and a clinician second. They are there to help manage claims, not to determine what is best for the patient. Simply stated, rather than taking the patient as he presents, they take the patient as they suspect he is and look for ways to deny what might otherwise be a fair and reasonable claim for compensation or care. Triage is thus bastardized into rationing health services. For the obviously at-risk juvenile delinquent and seriously mentally ill psychotic who might belong to the cohort that commits the vast majority of homicides today, triage is not done until time for prison classification; by then, it is too late to have protected the victims of the violently mentally ill convict.

The Clinical Discipline of Triage as It Applies to the Mentally Ill

Given what we are calling an epidemic of mass homicide perpetrated by suicidally mentally ill individuals, we have to look at triage as a preventive life-saving procedure. Triage has sufficient evidence-based rules and knowledge base to be a hard clinical discipline. A dysrhythmic and dysfunctional brain, a brain in which the neurocircuits are misfiring and altering the individual's perception of reality, is as lethal as a fibrillating heart, although the diagnostic technology lags in both translational research and practice for neuropsychiatry versus cardiology.

We know that triage should not be applied to the process of sorting out claims to be paid from those to be denied. Nor should it be reserved for classifying convicts within the penal system. Rather, it should have been used when opportunities for prevention of violence presented themselves in the lives of Jared Loughner, James Holmes, and Adam Lanza, all of whom had access to different forms of mental health services. Catastrophic neglect of the rules and knowledge base for classical triage is dramatically demonstrated in all three mass murder cases because each offender had encounters within the health-care system before ultimately perpetrating his crimes.

In the practice of medicine, specificity of diagnosis is only necessary for validity if it improves service optimization or medico-legal documentation. Thus, if a school counselor, say in Newtown, notices a child acting strangely by withdrawing from contact with others, not responding to attempts to communicate, or showing fear or a refusal to engage, that counselor should follow up with the parents. Perhaps if the counselor notices that there are guns in the parent's house and asks whether the weapons are secure, depending upon the parent's reaction, new decisions might present themselves.

How defensive is the parent about the child's behavior and guns in the house? Has the child seen a pediatric psychologist or psychiatrist? Is the child immersed in online violent video gaming? Is the parent aware of the prevalence of violence among at-risk adolescents who have access to firearms? These valid questions in no way even present a remote threat to the parent's rights to keep and bear arms under the Second Amendment. But it is the beginning of a form of triage to put that child under the school counselor's observation. There also should be a point at which the child's behavior triggers a more formal response from the school counselor, even if the child is not violent. Violence might not be manifested for years or even a decade later, as it was in the case of Adam Lanza. This is not a situation of "future crimes" out of *Minority Report*. It is a logical observation or decision-tree approach to looking for signs of strange behavior within the context of the family unit where there might be weapons that the child may ultimately have access to.

JAL Triage Algorithm

If a person whose behavior seems potentially violent presents either to first responders or to a clinician at an emergency room, user-friendly algorithms can model triage decisions to reduce the errors to avoid cases as devastating as those highlighted in this book. Time-determined clinical presentations are organized into the following four categories:

> Emergency
> Medical/surgery
> Dangerousness
>> Immediate to staff and ER itself
>> Future violence after discharged
>
>> Medical/surgical
>>> Neuropsychiatry
>>> Medical surgical
>>> State of mental disorganization
>>> Psychiatric impairment
>>> Codes such as malingering
> Suicidality

After ruling out obvious signs of injury, such as physical trauma, bleeding, shock, cardiac arrest, or cessation of respiration, violence is the major problem for medical personnel, particularly psychiatric staff and emergency room staff. This was evidenced by a homicide at Camp Liberty, Iraq, where a psychiatrist and others were killed by a mentally ill soldier named Sergeant John Russell in May 2009 who had mentally deteriorated.[128] Psychiatrists are under threat in stateside emergency rooms, and there is ample data to suggest that these attacks on all hospital personnel, particularly emergency room staff, inside medical centers. Emergency rooms are the second most dangerous work site in the United States because of patient assaults—second only to mines![129] Following the suicidal mass murder at the Urology Clinic in Reno and the surge in hospitals, at-risk specialists and other medical staff are arming themselves because they have come to believe that they have targets on their backs.

The JAL triage algorithm requires that by following the procedures of checking for obvious signs of injury and ruling out bleeding, breathing, or shock—rules many of us learned in basic first-aid courses—we should not then dismiss the possibility that the patient is safe to handle. In reality, seething beneath an otherwise nervous patient might be a hair-trigger response to what that patient perceives as a threat. Therefore, after a mandatory weapons check, usually facilitated by a metal detector, the emergency room clinician should evaluate any strange or aggressive behavior and triage that patient for psychiatric evaluation if there is any doubt.

Even the type of metal detector can raise issues of fairness and equality. For example, a racial debate can occur over fixed versus portable metal detectors in emergency rooms. Fixed detectors make no distinction with regard to who gets searched upon entering the medical facility because everyone, regardless of ethnicity, must pass through the same device. However, if a medical facility sets up a

---

[128] Smith, Elliot Blair. "Military Mental Health Crisis Exposed with Camp Liberty Killings." *Bloomberg News,* August 1, 2012. http://www.bloomberg.com/news/2012-08-01/military-mental-health-crisis-exposed-with-camp-liberty-killings.html.
[129] "DETER: Self Defense in the ER." Live Course, ED Violence & Self Defense. http://store.chall.com/productimage.php?product_id=138.

portable metal detector and uses it based on the ethnicity of the patient entering the facility, that medical facility has prejudged and done what amounts to racial profiling. The answer is to channel everyone through the metal detector, because just the hint of racial profiling or of prejudging a patient based on skin color or ethnicity will affect the way the patient will deal with medical personnel. One can therefore argue that triaging begins at the point of contact with the first screening device at the emergency room or trauma center. The recent suicidal mass murder at Pitt University Emergency Services by John Shick should be the clarion call for improved point-of-entry triaging for dangerousness.[130] In fact, Shick was not only well known in the community to EMS Systems first responders, but staff had been warned of his dangerousness by Shick's former physician. The Shick case fits the prototypical profile of a mass murder/suicide or attempted suicide: a person already judged to be potentially dangerous and behaving strangely upon entering a facility has a complete breakdown and commits a multiple homicide.

There is an ongoing debate whether to have armed guards, dogs, metal detectors, or all three at entrances to emergency rooms. Some reception desks in emergency rooms already have bullet-proof windows. The issue at Pitt was open entry for anyone—even patient John Shick. Ideally, it should be this way. But the potential for violence against medical staff is quickly changing the openness of emergency room access.

Are we simply to put up with such risks and favor what is politically correct and dictated by adversarial involuntary commitment laws? Was Dr. Fenton, the faculty member and psychiatrist who treated James Holmes at the University of Colorado's graduate school, restricted in what she could do to commit Holmes based

---

[130] Associated Press. "Pittsburgh Hospital Shooter Was Gifted, Troubled Student." *USA Today*, March 10, 2012. http://usatoday30.usatoday.com/news/nation/story/2012-03-10/Pittsburgh-hospital-shooting/53469700/1 (accessed December 11, 2013).

on Colorado's onerous commitment laws? Here was a young man acting out, expressing ideations of homicide, and trying to seek help even while he was actively planning his horrific crimes. Similarly, in the Oak Creek, Wisconsin, Sikh temple massacre, Wade Page's neighbor, a psychiatric nurse, viewed his dramatic personality change and strange behavior before he committed the suicidal mass murder at the temple. Did the nurse have any professional responsibility to sound an alert? Wisconsin also has very tight restrictions on involuntarily commitment procedures, which were set forth in the *Lessard* decision.[131] In *Lessard,* a federal court struck down Wisconsin's involuntary commitment law regarding patients whom doctors determined were mentally ill, imposing, on constitutional grounds necessitating a due process proceeding, a narrow definition of the patient's potential for "extreme violence" committed upon self or others and affording the patient a right to counsel as if the patient were charged in a criminal proceeding. In essence, the court imposed Fifth and Sixth Amendment conditions upon involuntary commitment proceedings. At the time of this writing, Dr. Fenton is currently being sued for not petitioning for Holmes's detention. Was she legally bound to do so? If Dr. Fenton believed that Holmes was a danger to others and himself, would she, under tort law, be liable for a breach of duty of care toward all those with whom Holmes might have come in contact? Would a reasonable mental health professional in her position come to the same or a different decision? These are questions for the court on motions for dismissal and for a finder of fact if the plaintiff case survives a motion to dismiss. Look at the position Dr. Fenton is in. Existing law does not preclude Holmes from purchasing firearms, even semiautomatic weapons, and large-capacity ammunition clips. The law does lay down strict rules for involuntary commitment for which a physician may be liable if the rules are breached.

---

[131] *Lessard v. Schmidt,* 414 US 473 (1974).

What is a doctor to do? In Holmes's case, Dr. Fenton did have his police record checked and found no history of violence, the major criteria upon which she could have petitioned for his commitment without fear of criminal or civil reprisals against her.

Most clinical staff in emergency room and psychiatry settings either will be or have been assaulted at the level of a felony. Signs in emergency departments now boldly warn, "Assaulting a health care professional in this state is a felony." Not only are emergency medical staff at the "new Ground Zero" in this post-9/11 world, they are right in the center ring of urban, campus, and military violence every hour of every day they work! This is not external workplace violence.

Clinical work in emergency medical settings, particularly acute-care psychiatric settings, is dangerous. Self-defense courses are now required for staff before working in many high-acuity hospitals that manage the seriously mentally ill patient population. VA emergency room nurses are ordered to check the bags of admitted combat veterans to prevent explosions in their psychiatric inpatient units. VA police stand by in case there is an explosion in the emergency room that blows up the nurse and others in her proximity. This is part of a trend in which medical professionals have to consider violent custodial management, such as defending themselves with weapons, as a prior concern before simply treating the patient.

Over the last couple of decades, violence against staff has increased. There are thousands of assaults in US hospitals every year, because of the high concentration of patients with primary or secondary psychiatric problems, drug and alcohol issues, or combined problems requiring far higher medical and psychiatric clearance. Patients in police custody sometimes use admission as means for escape. And the delays in treatment, because of reduced clinical resources, mean that psychiatric patients tend to become more agitated and even frantic waiting for help.

Emergency departments likely have a disproportionate incidence of violence against staff. It is well known that most mental health professionals, including psychiatrists, have been assaulted by their patients at the level of at least a felony during their careers. More than half of emergency medicine residents have been assaulted during their residency training as well. Both residents and nurses report fear of assault and injury as one of the primary concerns in the emergency department work environment. Such fear of personal harm can affect morale and performance of emergency department physicians and nurses, the latter of whom, along with "techs," are at the highest risk.

Self-Harm

In progressively screening from highest to lowest levels of lethality, the emergency screen prevents patients from leaving the point of entry when the screen predicts severe morbidity, violence, or deliberate self-harm for follow-up outpatient disposition. This means that the patient potentially dangerous to himself stops at the screening station and the patient is immediately placed on suicidal precautions and legally detained because he or she can cause other deaths in a moment of self-inflicted frenzy as a result of his suicidal ideations and despair.

Medical

Not all strange behavior means that a person is mentally ill, which is why medical screenings are important; they can detect medical problems affecting behavior. One can proceed through an entire psychological screening, but if the clinician fails to perform a simple blood glucose test as part of an initial encounter, she may miss that the patient may be hypoglycemic or have a severely low blood sugar count, probably because the patient's dosage was off or the patient failed to eat for a long period. Diabetics in a hypoglycemic trough may act strange and disoriented or even paranoid over their own inability to stabilize their hold on reality. They may become violent, frantic, lose impulse control, or even lapse into a noncommunicative state as they sink into the early stages of insulin shock. This is just one example of an encounter screening with a strangely behaving person that can turn fatal within minutes.

Behavioral Neurology (Traumatic Brain Injury)

Wars in the Middle East, punctuated by the use of improvised explosive devices or roadside bombs, and wars on football fields across America, punctuated by brain-jarring collisions, have brought to the forefront the debilitating long-term effects of traumatic brain injury (TBI). As medical practitioners come to understand more about how untreated brain trauma evolves—metastasizes is almost a better word—we are coming to see more about how a physical injury can manifest itself through psychological disabilities. Sufferers sometimes lose portions of their memories, can easily become disoriented, and can experience a sense of friction between themselves and the rest of the world. We see this in combat veterans whose return to civilian life is marked by a type of emotional instability from brain injury that leaves them less resilient to stress and confrontation than their uninjured comrades.

For children and adolescents who have suffered brain injury, the symptoms can become even more debilitating because the brain's neurocircuitry is still growing. We recognize the dangers of these types of injuries among young people and have translated that into a public policy wherein many states and municipalities require that cyclists, particularly young cyclists, wear helmets to protect them if they fall. Yes, people may protest the onerous burden of wearing a cycling helmet, but in reality a helmet protects the skull from the kind of brain-jarring damage that can affect the rest of a person's life. Just look at some of the debilitating effects of concussions and TBI suffered by NFL players, whose symptoms manifest even years after they have retired from the game. This policy of head-protective gear for cyclists is an example of how society, aware of a specific danger, takes steps to impose a rule to protect potential victims from that danger. Helmets do not stop every head injury, but they protect enough people that they reduce many dangers of head injuries. Now, in the wake of Newtown and mass shootings over the past decade as well as ongoing gun violence across America, public safety concerns require another step that many might call onerous. That step involves aspects of gun control.

Public Safety, Public Policy, and the Second Amendment

This is your jeremiad alert. You probably knew it would be forth-coming. And here it is in the wake of the Senate's refusal to vote up or down on extended gun purchase background checks and the frantic search and ultimate capture in Watertown, Massachusetts, for the at-large Boston Marathon bombing suspect, Dzhokhar Tsarnaev, who has now confessed to his role in the bombing.

When Jared Loughner ran out of ammunition during the Tucson shooting and had to stop to change one of his large-capacity clips, Patricia Maisch, a woman in the crowd, grabbed the clip from his hand while people in the crowd restrained him, kept him from reloading, and held him for the police. Representative Gabrielle Giffords, a federal judge, a young girl, and other people had been shot, many of them fatally. But for the nine-year-old girl who was killed by being shot in the back as she tried to flee, she might not have been killed had Loughner not had a large-capacity ammunition clip. Loughner did not steal the guns he used. But just imagine if Loughner, the actual firearm he used notwithstanding, had equipped himself with ammunition clips that held only seven or eight rounds because a federal law precluded the purchase of large-capacity clips. Imagine if he had had to stop and reload more times. Who would have avoided being shot? Would that little girl still be alive today?

Now flash forward to the first-grade classrooms at Newtown's Sandy Hook Elementary. If you were a parent and your child had been killed by the eleventh or twelfth round from Lanza's extended magazine clip—and information released from the police investigation showed that Adam Lanza deliberately chose extended clips over the smaller clips that were left behind in his closet—would you not have wanted a law limiting the size of ammunition clips? Your child would have most likely been spared if Adam Lanza had to stop to change clips more often. In fact, when Lanza did change one of the clips, a group of children escaped during the quick lull in shooting.[132] Had there been a federal law restricting the capacity of ammunition clips or the law now in place in Connecticut restricting ammunition clip capacity, some of the children's lives at Sandy Hook might have been spared. Does this not present its own logic? Smaller capacity clips mean that if there is a mass shooting, people may be able to avoid being injured while the shooter changes a clip. Gun advocacy groups argue that such a law would be an infringement of their Second Amendment rights.

If the University of Colorado had reported the distress messages that James Holmes had been sending to his therapist, or if the school had moved to commit Holmes for psychiatric evaluation, and if a federal background check law had been in place to prohibit Internet sales of firearms, ammunition, and weapons accessories to the seriously mentally ill, would Holmes's victims at the Aurora movie theater have been spared? Might some of them have been spared had there only been a law in place to prevent Holmes from acquiring his firearms and the one-hundred-round ammunition clip? Even the United States Supreme Court recognized that handguns and semiautomatic rifles are different, and the possession of them

---

[132] Mahoney, Edmund H., Dave Altimari, and Jon Lender. "Sandy Hook Shooter's Pause May Have Aided Students' Escape." *Hartford Courant,* December 23, 2012. http://articles. courant.com/2012-12-23/news/hc-lanza-gunjam-20121222_1_rifle-school-psychologist-classroom.

could be held to different standards under the law.[133] The Supreme Court recently turned down an appeal from gun advocates and a Second Amendment lobbying group to strike down New York State's requirement for a special permit for anyone who wants to carry an concealed weapon in public. The Court let stand rulings sustaining the New York State law, which further refines the Court's earlier decision in *Heller* that restricted striking down the ban that prohibited individuals from having handguns in their homes.

Background checks, which are legal for licensed gun store purchases, limits on concealed weapons, and the requirements for permits—which bespeak a type of registry themselves—are all constitutional unless the Supreme Court rules otherwise.

The point is simple. If there is a way to limit the damage caused by the mentally ill or by felons wielding firearms—a way that does not violate the Second Amendment — why not take it?

Manufacturers want to sell more of their product. Pump oil, sell oil. Assemble cars, sell cars. Manufacture guns, sell guns. But the problem is that when the lobby to sell guns impinges on public safety, commonsense rules to limit the damage those guns can cause should not be filibustered at the urging of lobbyists for gun manufacturers. Logic dictates that if you can save some lives, save the lives you can, even if you cannot save every single life from gun violence. We will probably always have to deal with sociopathic bullies in our society, just like we deal with terrorists like the Brothers Tsarnaev. Just keep as many guns out of their hands as possible.

Of course, psychiatrists and other mental health professionals have to be circumspect in their advocacy of gun control laws. As psychiatrists, we are always advised that mental health professionals have to focus on the data of mental illness and their relationship to gun control advocacy positions even more than lay members of society or the politicians who represent them. If we

---

[133] *District of Columbia v.* Heller, 554 US 570 (2008).

are arguing from an epidemiological perspective, the numbers have to be there to sustain an argument. While Freedman and Michaels cite that as of 2011, mass killings in the United States accounted for only 0.13 percent of all homicides, the disproportionate nature of the number of victims, and the victim profiles themselves—first graders at Sandy Hook and a member of the US House of Representatives—increase the public awareness of these crimes and the impact that the crimes have on the public.

Freedman and Michaels offer other caveats to members of the mental health profession. They suggest that lowering the legal bar for involuntary commitment of those acting dangerously or even acting strangely for the purposes of observation may be counterintuitive because individuals who are mentally ill but who have a fear of psychiatrists and of any encounters with the public safety and health-care systems would resist asking for help. Imagine members of the mentally ill population, so frightened by the prospect of involuntary commitment that they simply go underground and stay out of harm's way and public view until it is too late. Like New York's "mole people" who live in subway tunnels and beneath Grand Central Station, these mentally ill people may inhabit their own nether regions in twilight as their respective grips on reality decay more and more. We argue that what seems most obvious to advocates might not be the stuff of reason for mental health professionals who cannot allow their own personal views to color their scientific perspectives on mental illness and the violence that can result from it.

There are still some basic ways that allow us to address the problem of suicidal mass murder if we approach the solutions from the perspectives of public health, understanding the nature of mental illness (especially in children), and controlling the number of lethal firearms in circulation. The question is, are the solutions that seem so obvious to some of us beyond the capacity of our political system to tackle? For the collective sakes of those of us watching the epidemic of violence engulf society, we hope not.

Chapter 11

Practical Guidelines for Identifying Signs of Potential Violence

Strange Behavior: What to Look For

Social and political solutions, the result of budgetary allocations, are designed to solve the major problems over the longer term when it comes to addressing violence and mental illness. But on a more practical level, one has to ask what a parent or teacher should do when a child or student exhibits signs of strange behavior. We know what happened at Virginia Tech, Pima Community College, and the University of Colorado. The students in question—Cho Seung-Hui, Jared Loughner, and James Holmes—were all summarily removed from the campus community and dumped into a public safety network ill-equipped to deal with their dangerous behavior until after they had perpetrated their crimes. We believe we know what Nancy Lanza tried to do with her child, who was behaving strangely from an early age and who was the object of bullying when he attended Sandy Hook. She taught him all about guns. And then he turned the guns on her. We know what happened when former Navy SEAL and bestselling author Chris Kyle tried his own brand of immersion therapy on PTSD sufferer Eddie Ray Routh by taking him target shooting. Routh turned the gun on him.

This approach does not work and cannot work, but people still keep following it as if oblivious to the failure of their own pursuits.

How many times must a person ram his or head into a brick wall before looking into a mirror to see how much blood is running from the wound? Is it only Bob Dylan who can point us to the answer?

If we analyze what we know about a point of contact between an at-risk individual and a parent, a teacher, or even an educational administrator, we might be able identify red flags that parents and teachers can recognize to see whether the child requires heightened scrutiny or observation or if an intervention is called for.

Physical Abuse or Emotional Abuse.

Children who are abused sexually, physically, or emotionally are automatically at risk for either PTSD or emotional impairment as they reach adolescence. This is actually a no-brainer and one of the issues that President Obama has raised in his call for heightened awareness to children in trouble. Kids react to events at home, whether the events are the breakup of a marriage, the results of substance abuse, physical abuse inflicted upon them, or even sexual advances from relatives or neighbors. The results of these types of trauma turn up in a child's behavior, and we can see them as the following: marked behavioral differences over a short time, aggressive behavior toward others, lack of resiliency, lack of empathy, refusal to follow standard rules of behavior, outbreaks of emotional instability, or outbreaks of temper inconsistent with the stimulus.

Emotional reactions, sometimes violently self-destructive or even homicidal, can result from bullying and abuse at school. As reported by relatives of Nancy Lanza, Adam was bullied at Sandy Hook Elementary to the point where his mother had contemplated suing the school district. Recently in the news is the story of Audrie Pott, a fifteen-year-old student from Northern California who committed suicide. The teenager had passed out from drinking alcohol at a party and was raped by teenage boys. Videos of the rape were posted on social media, and the girl was bullied and tormented by other students who saw the videos. Audrie, seeing no way out, committed suicide. One can only wonder how attorneys will defend the teens accused of raping the victim.

Ideations of Violence

People who contemplate suicide, even violent suicide, will almost always find an outlet to express their ideations of what the suicidal moment might be. Christopher Dorner was explicit in describing what plans he had in store for those in the LAPD who he believed persecuted him. Cho Seung-Hui wrote an entire essay in high school about the Columbine high school shooting, his admiration for shooters Klebold and Harris, and his plans to emulate their crimes. He described it again in his writings in college. James Holmes expressed his ideations in letters to Dr. Fenton at the University of Colorado, and Anders Breivik wrote about his intentions in his manifesto. You do not need Dr. Phil, Dr. Drew, or Oprah to tell you that when someone explains exactly what he or she is going to do, you should take it seriously because you can bet your bottom dollar that he or she will do it.

Manifestations of Violent Behavior

Children will sometimes react aggressively if they or their territory is challenged. We can see this in nursery school or kindergarten settings before the teacher can communicate the rules of social behavior. However, a teacher will occasionally notice that a child

249

exhibits extraordinarily violent behavior toward another child. This is a warning sign, not just that something is wrong at home, but that the child has no resilience to whatever the challenge or stimulus was. Simple discipline, a time-out, or sitting in a corner is not enough. The warning sign indicates that something is wrong emotionally and needs to be followed up on, ideally by a school counselor who is trained in pediatric psychological counseling.

Sadism and Cruelty

We know that children can be cruel. But by the time a child is eight or nine and has been socialized to work and play with others in a classroom setting, the child tends to demonstrate empathy for others' feelings. However, children who are not only unsympathetic or unfeeling but who manifest cruelty to others and enjoy others' suffering are emotionally at risk. When those children immerse themselves in the types of video games that actually extol sadism and cruelty as virtues and amalgamate sadism and cruelty with the larger purpose of saving the planet from extraterrestrials, monsters, or terrorists, we are not talking about a simple game anymore. We are talking about a mechanism inculcating the habits of mass destruction.

Withdrawal from Others

If anything typified Adam Lanza in elementary school, it was his withdrawal from others. Nancy Lanza, however good her intentions might have been, failed completely in addressing the psychological problem that plagued her son and manifested into a full-blown psychosis. Children who display an aggravated level of fear-driven withdrawal also display signs of a behavioral disorder or emotional upset on which a teacher should follow up.

A Child Who Bullies

Bullying behavior is often learned at home from an early age. It is not just about striking out at other children or at the teacher.

It is about refusal to follow any rules and inability to deal with other children except in terms of bullying. It is about a level of cruelty toward others that defies any logic. Bullies learn abuse from their parents or caregivers and impose what they learn on others. Ninety-five percent of bullying behavior can be addressed and remedied in the classroom. But for those children who are at risk because they are victims of abuse at home, bullying might be their way of acting out. Consistent, sadistic bullying evidencing a level of cruelty toward others is a clear psychological problem that the teacher should report to a guidance counselor, who should bring in the parents sooner rather than later.

Indifference to Others' Pain

Sympathy toward others usually manifests itself in classroom interactions in children older than eight years. However, when indifference to the pain of others lasts beyond age eight and into the preteen years, it usually indicates that something is wrong and the child is disturbed in some way. This behavior does not pass away as the child grows older. It only gets worse as the stressful transition to high-school social and sexual interaction or competitive sports ramps up aggressive behavior. It is up to parents, teachers, and coaches to mediate this behavior and to discourage indifference to or enjoyment of others' pain.

Violent Mood Swings

Anyone who has raised a child remembers how that child could move from wild laughter and ebullience to a flood of tears very quickly in early age. Manic behavior followed by a collapse into sadness usually means, for children ages two to five, that the child needs a nap because weariness and fatigue have drained him of the ability to cope. However, as a child gets older, violent or dramatic mood swings may indicate something is amiss either chemically or emotionally. People who might be predisposed to violent behavior experience dramatic changes in mood from calm to violence with no provocation whatsoever. These hair-trigger behavioral swings often mean that an older child is under severe pressure at home, is suffering at school, or has a severe neurochemical imbalance or even type-1 diabetes. Any of those conditions might imperil the child's ability to cope with life's stresses. Most children grow out of this. But some do not, and these are the children school personnel need to observe.

Cruelty to Animals or Inanimate Objects

Some children exhibit extreme cruelty to animals, to the point where they feel that they cannot stop themselves because the emotion is somehow addictive and feeds upon itself. Animal cruelty is an indicator of potential violence, as is violence toward inanimate objects. The destruction of things, whether animate or inanimate, who pose threat indicates that the perpetrator of violence and cruelty has little or no impulse control, is controlled by violent emotion, and probably has little regard for the consequences of his or her actions. The person may simply be deriving a sense of pleasure from the destruction of something over which the person exercises control.

History of Violence

A history of violent or sadistic acts is also an indicator of potential danger. For older children and young adults, any history of unprovoked sexually or racially tainted assault is a real sign of dangerousness, particularly when the individual attempts to use weapons, including common tools for blunt-force assault, against others. A first resort to violence is a significant red flag, especially when combined with a lack of impulse control and a substance or alcohol abuse problem. This means that unless that individual is treated for lack of impulse control and substance abuse, he is likely to be at odds with law enforcement in the future.

Insatiable Sex Drives and Violent Sexual Fantasies

Although more in the category of episodic or serial sexual crime, fantasies that combine sexual urges with ideations of violence and violent control over the victim are indicators that the individual is on the spectrum of becoming a sexual offender. Fantasies, although not crimes, can be fed by pornographic and violent sexual material so that the individual pushes the envelope of engagement to the point of indulging in real-life versions of fantasies. What seem to be mere flirtations in the workplace can push the envelope of social acceptability and can quickly escalate to real sexual offenses.

Abnormal Fascination with Blood, Gore, and Death

This type of indicator usually goes hand-in-hand with immersion or addiction to violent video games. These dark nihilistic fantasies tend to be manifestations of the individual's own feelings of worthlessness and deep remorse, bordering on the suicidal. As we have seen in the cases of Lanza, Holmes, Loughner, Breivik, and Cho, the deeper and more obsessive the fascination with death and gore is, the more problems the individual will likely have in separating his fantasies from real life.

The Importance of Early Intervention

Because society is changing and childhood exposure to graphic violence and violent video games is prevalent, what once might have been considered hypervigilance twenty years ago should now be considered the norm. There is just too much violence in the environment for parents to ignore their child's fascination with it. A parent who suspects that his or her child is spending too much time interacting as a warrior avatar in a digital world should ask the child what he gets out of the game, rather than banning video games outright. Are there frustrations that the child is working out? Are there anger issues that crop up at school that can only be addressed within the four corners of an onscreen video game? Is the child being bullied or coerced into doing things that embarrass him or make him feel guilty? Or is the child so frustrated that pseudo violence is his or her only resort? And how is all this being reflected in the child's performance at school? Is the gaming more social, with visible friends seen talking about it, or obviously isolative? The latter is of far greater concern.

Consider for a moment how a school might look at procedures to follow if a child turns up in class constantly sick, constantly hungry, or even carrying what the school might consider to be a communicable disease. Would that child simply be ignored in the expectation that things will ultimately work themselves out with no intervention? Absolutely not. In fact, the school would involve itself directly with the family and even notify county or state child or family services if the situation was serious enough. The school counselor or social worker would become involved, and they would open up an official investigation. However, this is not a routine procedure for emotional problems, which is why school districts are becoming more vigilant about children manifesting significant emotional disturbance problems.

These seem like basic questions that might turn up in any television commercial. However, in many households where the burdens of raising the child, keeping up with bills, and holding onto a job can be overwhelming, it is easy to overlook or query what is going on in the inner world of a child's imagination or emotions. There are very early indicators of a child's difficulty in coping with issues in school or at home, some of which raise problems that even parents are sometimes too embarrassed to deal with. What if the child is having problems with a step-parent? What if there are issues of emotional abuse? Environments in which children can feel empowered to speak freely to parents, even if the child is bristling with hostility, are more healthy than those that are cloaked in silence.

If a child exhibits real signs of emotional difficulty, the earlier a parent or caregiver addresses these signs with the child's pediatrician and takes any advice to consult with a child psychiatrist, the better it is. This does not mean that every child who appears hyper needs to begin a Ritalin or Adderall regimen. It does mean that if there are neurological or emotional issues, the earlier they are dealt with in a professional context, the better.

We may never completely understand the dynamic between Nancy Lanza and her son. We may never be able to see whatever medical records exist about Adam's diagnoses or what a psychiatrist might have said about him. But the tragic outcome of the Lanza relationship and Adam's mental illness speaks for itself. Parents have to intervene early so that mental illness, which is progressive and not static, does not wind up so badly crippling the child's grip on reality that he is no longer able to differentiate between violent fantasies and real life.

Many Americans have built-in prejudices toward seeking outside help for their children's problems. First, there is a robust, albeit irrational, mistrust of psychiatrists because of the stigma of mental illness, regardless of the fact that a paranoid schizophrenic can purchase a gun on the Internet or at a gun show. There is no such stigma about going to a doctor for medicine to help a child get over the flu. Mental illness and emotional disorders are as medically legitimate as the flu. The more we understand the biology of the brain, the more we can understand that perception, or lack thereof, is essentially a matter of how the brain interprets signals. Because so much of the brain's interpretation of sensory data is based on electrochemistry and the flow of mood-altering neurostimulants, we should know that we are dealing with molecules, not a moral stigma. If parents and caregivers can be educated to accept that, we will have gone a long way toward solving prejudice over mental illness.

Success Is Often Achieved at the Margins

In Oliver Stone's 1999 feature film *Any Given Sunday*, Al Pacino's character, coach Tony D'Amato, gives a very compelling speech about how football imitates life because, like life, football games can be won on the margins. Control the inches at the line of scrimmage, and you control the yardage. Control the seconds on the clock, and you control the time you spend in control of the ball. Inches and seconds can translate into yards and minutes, which can translate to the dominance usually required for victory. How does this translate into real life?

Control the number of rounds allowed in an ammunition magazine, and you control the number of times a shooter has to reload. Force a shooter to reload more than once, and you give more potential victims the time to escape and police to arrive on the scene and disarm the shooter. You do not save every life, but you save some. And every life you save is precious.

Control the ways people can obtain guns through background checks for all sales, and you control the individuals on the edges who are either too sick or have violent criminal backgrounds. Again, maybe not every single mass murder will be prevented, but some will. And those mass murders that are prevented will save precious lives.

Now apply this to a child or young adult who is exhibiting strange behavior. The earlier the intervention, even if that intervention only amounts to a heightened state of vigilance, the less bioneurological overhead may be required to remedy an illness. We are not talking about drugging an entire generation of video gamers so that they can become social or lobotomizing them so they act like zombies from George Romero's *Night of the Living Dead*. We are talking about children and young adults at the margins who, because of a deteriorating mental state, are losing their grip on reality and replacing it with an inner reality fed by delusions, hallucinations, and the limbic music of the video games they are playing through their avatars: their extensions of self injected into a graphically violent digital world.

Conclusion

Even after the FBI, the Bureau of Alcohol, Tobacco, and Firearms, Massachusetts state police, and Boston police closed in around Watertown to catch Dzhokhar Tsarnaev alive and take him into custody, the stakes for our society are very high. It is not just the guns, the video games, or the instructions from bomb makers on the Internet to show wannabe terrorists how to construct an improvised explosive device out of fertilizer, a battery, and a pressure cooker. We can address the problem of firearm access to felons and the mentally ill through basic gun control legislation. It is likely that the current Supreme Court would uphold this legislation. We can also make more stringent the regulations covering video game distribution. We know that in dealing with forms of entertainment, we bump right up against the First Amendment's protection of speech. But that right to free speech is not absolute. It is governed by what the Supreme Court has called time and place qualifications. The content of speech, though subject to strict scrutiny by the Court, is governed by the notion of "incitement," that is, whether the speech incites listeners to immediate violence.[134] And the bar is very high for that as well, even though wannabe extremists constantly test the envelope of what incitement is. However, if that speech creates a neurochemical reaction in a listener or in a game player that incites violence directly attributed to the speech, it raises a possible qualification to the free speech protection the game manufacturer relies on. This is so particularly if the marketing to young children is reckless or willfully blind to the violence that the game can incite, which might

---

[134] *Brandenburg v. Ohio,* 395 US 444 (1969).

be another qualification on the game manufacturer's free speech. In the wake of Sandy Hook, might a court deem the game *School Shooter* as incitement speech? After all, if we can rethink the nature of absolute thinking and look at the vulnerability of our children and other potential victims of mental illness–inspired violence, we just might be able to stave off the kinds of draconian solutions that even Richard Nixon was afraid would have to be imposed if society degenerated into violence.

We can do this if we put our ideologies into the context of keeping our society and our citizens alive. We can do this if we can destigmatize mental illness, which modern brain imaging will help us do. We can do this if we realize that the pain of each one of the Sandy Hook parents is a pain that any one of us can experience if our children or grandchildren become the victims of an entirely preventable crime.

We can do this.

And we'd better do it soon.

Index

A

Above Top Secret (website), 113

Abuse
  bullying and, 251
  child, 157, 195, 248–249
  relationship with violence, 50
  substance, 42, 81–82, 156, 195

Acetylcholine, 158–159

Adams, Becket, 149n95

ADHD (attention deficit-
  hyperactivity disorder), 170, 178,
  188, 189

Adolescence, 12, 196
  Affordable Care Act (ACA),
    213–214, 215, 220

Aggression
  neurobiology of, 156–171
  online gaming and, 178, 185

Alcohol abuse. *See* Substance abuse

Alexis, Aaron, 187, 190

Alex, Johnson M., 26n10

Allan Memorial Institute,
  Montreal, 67

Alleles, 42, 43, 218

Allen, Nick, 71

Altimari, Dave, 243n131

Alzheimer's disease, 174

American Medical Association
  (AMA), 184–185

American Sniper (Kyle), 143

Ammunition clips, 242–243

Amygdala area of the brain, 157,
  158, 160, 168

Anger, 186–187, 188

Animal cruelty, 187, 252

Anosognosia, 15, 24

Anschutz Medical Campus, 86, 89

Anterior cingulate cortex, 157, 160

Antipsychotic medication
  Breivik, Anders and, 138–139
  family history of mental illness
    and, 39–40, 44
  Holmes, James, 95
  Loughner, Jared and, 13, 115–
    116, 125, 151–152
  new generation of, 183
  violence caused by nonadherence
    to, 24

Any Given Sunday (film), 256

Arkin, James, 72n35

Aronson, Elliot, 50

Arpaio, Joe, 25, 189

ASD. *See* Autism spectrum disorder (ASD)

Ashley, Ross, 10, 20–21, 28, 111, 224

Asperger's syndrome, 51, 56–57, 84, 167–168, 188

Assessments, psychological/psychiatric, 19–20

The Atlantic Monthly, 66

Attachment parenting, 197

Attention deficit-hyperactivity disorder (ADHD), 170, 178, 188, 199, 200

Auditory hallucinations, 12, 14, 64, 87, 110, 112, 128

Aurora, Colorado shootings, 2, 6. *see also* Holmes, James
  Fox News article on, 98–99
  Holmes' preparation for, 101–102
  magnitude of, 79–80
  911 call, 71–72, 73
  prevention of, 243–244
  sequence of events, 70–72

Autism, 56–57, 167

Autism spectrum disorder (ASD), 60, 169, 174, 178, 188, 197

Autopsy, suicide, 19

B

Background checks, 244

Bailey, Kaylan, 72

Bales, Robert, 20

Balt, Steve, 113n80

Barry, Dan, 107n72

Bates, Daniel, 82n44

Batman: Arkham Asylum (video game), 104

Becker, Jo, 107n72

Behavioral disorders, 167, 188, 189. *see also* Autism spectrum disorder (ASD)

Behavioral emergency services. *See* Emergency medical services, for behavioral emergencies

Beliz, Tony, 208–209, 210

Berger, Joseph, 52n22

Berzon, Alexandra, 109n75, 128n85

Best-practice approaches. *see also* Emergency medical services, for behavioral emergencies
  computer-assisted screening, 220
  computer-enhanced diagnostics, 216–218
  computerizing medical records, 214–216
  dangerousness identification protocols, 209–211
  early intervention, 204–205
  emergency medicine, 211–213
  gun control bill, 205–206
  Los Angeles school program, 208–209
  personalized medicine, 217–218
  triage decision process, 221–227
  universal mental health electronic records, 214–216

Big Book of Granny, 58, 60

Bipolar mood disorder, 101, 204

Birnes, William J., 12n4, 29n14, 80n42, 162n96

Black Death, 200

Blevins, Gaines, 145

Blevins, Laura, 144–145

Borderline personality disorder (BPD), 163–167, 187

Boston Marathon bombing, 1–2, 3, 5, 16, 34–35. *see also* Tsarnaev, Dzhokhar; Tsarnaev, Tamerlan

Boyd, David, 211, 224

BPD (borderline personality disorder), 163–167, 187

Brain

    ADHD and, 170

    amygdala in, 160–161

    bodily reactions to feelings and, 157–158

    borderline personality disorder and, 166–167

    chemical neuromodulators of, 158–160

    genes and, 42, 44–45

    methamphetamine and, 183

    transparent images of a working, 215–216

Brain injury, 241–242

Brain mapping project/technology, 174–175, 213, 216

Brain scans, 12

Brandenburg v. Ohio (1969), 257n

Breivik, Anders, 9, 15, 19, 21

    gaming by, 89, 181

    ideations of violence, 249

    influence of Klebold/Harris on, 154

    insanity defense and, 133, 135–136

    Kaczynski and, 66, 67, 132–133, 201

    Knights Templar and, 134–135

    Lanza, Adam and, 65–66, 67–68, 139, 201

    manifesto of, 131–132, 133–134

    marijuana-psychosis relationship and, 43

    mental illness of, 103, 135

    neologisms of, 113, 136–137

    Norwegian security and, 139–141

    parents of, 53

    prison sentence of, 138–139

    pseudocommando and, 42

    suicidal mission of, 20

    violent media and, 44, 65–66

    violent video games and, 174

Brookfield, Wisconsin, 223

Bullying, 49, 50, 169, 181, 189, 249, 250–251

Bundy, Ted, 162–163, 199

Bunker Hill Community College, 117

Bureau of Justice Statistics, 226

Byers, Colorado, 100

C

Call of Duty (video game), 65

Cameron, Ewean, 67

Campbell, Joseph, 176

Cannabis, 43, 218

Casper, Wyoming, 26

Castroville, California, 82

Catechol-O-methyltransferase (COMT) gene, 42–43, 44–45, 218
Cedar Creek Pub, 97
Center for Disease Control (CDC), 27, 28, 29, 213, 232
Central Intelligence Agency (CIA), 67
Chase, Alston, 66
Chestnut Lodge sanatorium, 136
Child abuse, 157, 195, 248–249
Child development
    bonding and, 196–200
    family stresses and, 195–196
    multigenerational family and, 193
Child-parent bonding, 196–200
Children
    cruelty of, 250
    cruelty to animals by, 252
    early intervention for, 253–255
    emotional issues in home of, 189
    manifestations of violent behavior in, 249–250
    mood swings in, 251–252
    school and classroom cliques of, 50
    who bully, 250–251
Cho, Seung-Hui, 7, 15, 30, 88, 111, 193, 209, 223, 247
    Columbine shooters and, 17, 68, 154, 201, 249
    delusion of passion in, 22
    duration of untreated psychoses and, 25, 115, 165
    ideations of violence in schools, 60
    investigation of case of, 28
    media influence and, 10
    mental illness of, 103, 186
    Pima Community College and, 13
    pseudocommando and, 42
    threat from, taking seriously, 17
    Tucson shooting and, 13, 116
    underdiagnosed mental illness of, 12, 14, 207
    victimization of, 21
    video to NBC News, 80
    violent media and, 44
    violent video games and, 174, 182
CIA (Central Intelligence Agency), 67
Cingulate area of the brain, 157, 160
Clan of the Cave Bear, 116
Cliques, school, 50
Clozapine, 44, 170
College campuses. see also individual names of colleges
    preventative actions by, 13–14
    psychotic students on, 223–224
    responsibility toward student safety, 121
    suicidal catastrophes on, 117
    suspensions or dropping out of, 208–209
    Virginia Tech trial verdict and, 120–121
Collen, Morris, 214
Colorado law, 75, 81, 94, 103, 238

Colorado Mental Health Institute, 79

Columbine High School shooting, 17, 30, 60, 68, 154, 201, 249

Comorbidity, 156, 199

Computer aided dispatch (CAD), 227

Computer-assisted diagnostic interview, 218–219

Computer-assisted screening, 220

Computer-enhanced diagnostics, 216–218

COMT gene, 42–43, 44–45, 218

Conduct disorder, 198–199

Connor, Tracy, 74n36

Cook Counseling Center, 207, 223

Cook County jail, 225

Cornyn, John, 206

Cortical hypoactivity, 160, 169

Crime statistics, 29

Cruelty, 250, 252

Cruz, Ted, 205

D

Dahmer, Jeffrey, 22, 75

Dallas Veterans Administration Medical Center, 146, 147, 148, 150

Dana, Joe, 115n81

Dangerousness identification protocols, 209–214

The Dark Knight Rises (film), 70, 96, 102

Dawson, Geraldine, 167

Death, fascination with, 253

De Clérambault's syndrome, 22–23

Defense Advanced Research Projects Agency (DARPA), 174

Defense of Marriage Act, 191

Delusions/delusional behavior, 22–23, 24

Breivik, Anders and, 103, 134–135, 139

diagnosing schizophrenia and, 37, 38

duration of untreated psychosis (DUP), 40

feeding violence, 187–188

Holmes, James, 70, 76–77, 101

Loughner, Jared, 128

violent video gaming and, 181

Denver Post, 70–71, 104

Diagnosis

computer-assisted interview, 218–219

computer-enhanced, 216–218, 216–219, 220, 227

schizophrenia, 37–38

triage, 232

underdiagnosis of mental illness, 12, 216–217

undiagnosed mental illness, 12, 13, 115, 116–117, 207

Diagnostic and Statistical Manual of Mental Disorders (DSM-IV), 39, 45

Digital medical records, 214–216

Digital video gaming. *See* Video games

District of Columbia v. Heller (2008), 244n132

DNA, 41, 42, 159

Dopamine (DA), 87, 88, 95, 158,
159, 160, 170, 179, 183
Dorner, Christopher, 7, 18, 32, 61,
126, 164–165, 249
Dreams, 110–111
Drug abuse. *see* Substance abuse
*DSM-IV (Diagnostic and Statistical
Manual of Mental Disorders)*,
39, 45
Dudee, Narander, 93
Duration of untreated psychosis
(DUP), 13, 25, 40, 115, 165
Dysphoric mania, 101

E
Electronic medical records,
214–215, 220
Elliott, Dan, 94
Elliott, Victoria Stagg, 184n102,
185n104
Eltman, Frank, 7n3
Emergency clinical services,
211–212
Emergency medical services,
for behavioral emergencies,
211–212, 213, 224–225
constitutional arguments,
228–233
incarceration and, 225–226
involuntary commitment and,
237–239
JAL triage algorithm, 235–236
for medical reasons, 240–241
911 call, 225
protocols for, 209–214
reverse-engineering elements of
triage, 224

self-harm and, 240
transporting patient to another
hospital and, 226–227
for traumatic brain injury (TBI),
241–242
triage decisions and, 221–224,
233–237
violence against staff and, 237,
239–240
Emergency Services Act, 211–212,
226
Emotional abuse, 248–249
Empathy, 167, 168, 198
Empire State Building event
(2012), 7
EMS Systems, 212, 225, 230
Emshwiller, John R., 128n85
EMTALA law, 210
Entertainment industries. *See*
Violent media
Environmental factors, genetics
and, 39, 42, 43–44, 168
Erikson, Erik, 196
Erotomania, 22, 128
Erotomanic delusion, 22
Extended clips, 242–243

F
Family. *see also* Parents
in contrasting television shows,
194–195
emotional issues in, 188–189
multigenerational, 193, 194, 195
Family structure, 176, 189,
192–195, 200
Fantasies
"acting out," 99

of Holmes, James, 94, 98
sexual, 253
Fear, 187
Fenton, Lynne, 80–81, 93, 94, 98, 237–238, 249
Ferner, Mark, 89n51
Fictionalized violence, 177
Fifth Amendment, 10, 103, 175, 214–215, 238
First Amendment, 8, 10, 125, 184, 201, 257
First-episode psychosis, 12–13, 14, 88
First responders
behavioral emergencies and, 211, 212, 230
emergency services training for, 230
Holmes, James and, 21, 77
Spengler, William and, 17
Flores, Robert S., 122
Flores, Roy, 120, 121
Fonzi, Kaitlyn, 69–70, 73, 77, 78, 102
Forelle, Charles, 109n75
Forgotten Warrior Program, 226
Foster, Jody, 23, 128
Fourth Amendment, 10, 17, 175, 214–215
Fox News, 80, 98–99
Freud, Sigmund, 111
Frosch, Dan, 79n39, 81, 81n43, 88n49, 90n53, 95n60, 100n68
Funding
for emergency mental health services, 211–212, 213, 225
for mental health training, 205

G
GABA, 158, 159
Gallagher, Ian, 89n52
Gaming. *See* Video games
Gang violence, 28–29
Gardner, Frank, 134n89
Gatian de Clérambault', Gaëtan, 23
Gaudiosi, John, 66n28
Genetic markers, 40
Genetics
aberrant behavior and, 170–171
computer-enhanced diagnostics and, 217–218
predisposition to brain dysfunction and, 168
Genetic testing, 38, 40–41
Geodon, 183
Giffords, Gabrielle, 13, 22, 104, 107, 108–109, 110, 120, 124–125, 126, 128–129, 242
Glutamate, 158
Goh, One L., 208–209
Goldman, Russell, 17n5
Goode, Erica, 18n6, 79n39, 81, 81n43, 85n46, 88n49, 90n53, 95n60, 100n68, 208n110
Gorner, Jeremy, 29n13
Graham, Caroline, 89n52
Grandparents, 193, 194
Gratehouse, Donna, 127n84
Great Depression (1930s), 192
Great Recession (2007-2009), 192
Green Oaks Hospital, Dallas, Texas, 147–148

Griffin, Alaine, 51n21, 56n23, 62n25
Griffith, David, 165n97
Gun control
    causes of suicidal mass murders and, 34
    new bill for, 205–206
    prevention of mass murders and, 242–245
    Tucson shooting and, 124–125
Gun lobby, 120, 229–230
Guns. *See* Weapons
Guth, Robert A., 128n85
Gye, Hugo, 82n44

H
Hallucinations, 24
    auditory, 12, 14, 87, 110, 128
    diagnosing schizophrenia and, 37, 38
    to harm others, 24, 25
    of Holmes, James, 81
    of Lanza, Adam, 64
    of Loughner, Jared, 112, 128
Hallucinogens, 81
Harris, Eric, 17, 21, 60, 68, 154, 201, 249
Hartford Courant, 50, 61
Hasan, Nidal, 20, 21
Haughton, Radcliffe, 223
Hawkins, Robert, 121
Head injuries, 241–242
Health care revolution, 214–216
Health care, triage decisions and, 221–227
Health insurance, 213–214

Healy, Jack, 79n39, 81, 81n43, 88n49, 95n60, 100n68
Hilscher, Emily, 22
Hinckley, John, 23, 128
Hitler, Adolf, 133
Hochsprung, Dawn, 54
Holmes, James, 7, 9, 12, 224. *see also* Aurora, Colorado shootings
    academic decline in, 96–97
    attempted suicide of, 80
    behavior in jail, 77–78
    biographical information on, 82
    booby-trapped apartment of, 69–70, 77, 78–79, 102
    calls for execution of, 19
    charges against, 104–105
    denied to University of Colorado campus, 98
    dropping out of college, 97, 208–209
    drug and alcohol use by, 81–82
    education of, 83
    escape and evasion plans of, 75–77
    failure to help, 228–229
    genes and, 41–42
    gun club and, 100
    hopelessness of, 15
    ideations of violence, 249
    indifference of, 73–74
    insanity defense and, 14, 74–75, 103, 104
    intentions of, 20, 21
    involuntary commitment and, 237–239
    last laboratory presentation of, 93, 94

medication and, 81, 94

mental health treatment and, 93–94, 98, 99, 163

mental illness of, 111

mood-swing disorder and, 101

motivations/intentions of, 21

neuroscience studied by, 86–88

outgunning police officers, 30

package sent to psychiatrist by, 80

personality and profile of, 88–92

personality of, 83

preparing for Aurora shooting attack, 101–102

at Salk Institute, 84–86

surrender by, 6

text messages with University of Colorado student, 95–96, 100–101

trial of, 102–103, 105–106

undiagnosed mental illness of, 13, 14

University of Colorado and, 86–87, 90, 91, 93–94, 98, 105

violent video gaming and, 44, 82–83, 89, 174

weapon and paraphernalia acquired by, 18, 92–93, 97, 98

Holstege, Sean, 110, 110n77

Homicides, prevalence of, 29. *see also* Mass murders

Honberg, Ronald S., 207

Hopelessness, 14–16, 186

Hough, Andrew, 66n29

Huffington Post, 7, 94, 99, 147

Huizinga, Johan, 177–178

Huntington's chorea, 14, 38, 39, 40, 41

I

Ideations of suicidal behavior, 16–17

Identification protocols, 209–214

Impulse control, 168, 170, 180, 217, 241, 252

Impulsive aggression, 156, 160, 167

Incarceration. *See* Prison

Information technology (IT) integration, 215

InfoWars, 34

Ingold, John, 104n71

In loco parentis, 110, 121

Insanity defense

by Breivik, Anders, 133, 135–137

Holmes, James and, 14, 74–75, 103, 104

Insula, 157, 160

Intervention. *see also* Involuntary commitment; Medication; Treatment

importance of early, 253–255, 253–257

Los Angeles School District's model approach to, 208–209

responding to strange behavior, 154–155, 208, 234–235

Involuntary commitment, 19

as counterintuitive, 245

Holmes, James, 81, 94, 99, 237–239

Lanza, Adam, 64

Loughner, Jared, 119

over-legislating rules for, 212
state authority for ordering, 228

J

Jacobson, John, 85–86
JAL triage algorithm, 235–240
"The jigsaw classroom," 50
Johnson, Jeffrey, 7
Joker character, in *The Dark Knight Rises*, 70, 72, 74, 77, 79, 83, 96, 104, 163
Jones, Alex, 34
Judd, Ashley, 204

K

Kaczynski, Ted, 31, 66–67, 104, 132–133, 201
Kazmierczak, Steven, 224
Keneally, Meghan, 82n44
Keppel, Robert D., 162n96
Kerouac, Jack, 193
Kessler, R., 189
Kiefer, Michael, 115n81
Kino campus, University of Arizona Hospital, 118–119, 122
Klebold, Dylan, 7, 17, 21, 60, 68, 154, 201, 249
Knights Templar, 134–135
Kovaleski, Serge F., 18n6, 81, 81n43, 88n49, 90n53, 95n60, 100n68
Kovner, Josh, 51n21, 56n23, 62n25
Kraepelin, Emil, 87, 91
Kyle, Christopher, 143, 144, 146, 148–150, 151, 248

L

Labor Party (Norway), 135
Landsend, Merete, 68n31
Lanza, Adam, 7, 9, 11, 12, 19. *see also* Sandy Hook Elementary School shooting
ammunition clip of, 243
borderline personality disorder and, 165, 166
Breivik, Anders and, 65–66, 67–68, 139, 201
bullying of, 49, 50, 249
decomposing mental state of, 58–61, 64
delusions of, 23
gaming by, 57, 65–66, 89, 174
as gun enthusiast, 54
head injury of, 53–54
hopelessness of, 15
"limbic music" and, 161
medication taken by, 63
mental illness of, 56–57, 111
in middle school, 50–51
mother's efforts to help/reach, 51–52, 63–64
online gamer chat session of, 57–58
physical contact with others and, 51, 56, 197
pseudocommando and, 42
relationship with mother, 47–48, 54, 62
Sandy Hook school district and, 52–53
schizophrenia and, 39
school intervention and, 209

social isolation of, 47–48, 49–50, 51, 56, 62–63

"strange behavior" of, 48–49, 65

threat of Sandy Hook children to, 181

undiagnosed/untreated mental illness of, 207

violent media and, 44

weapons used by, 17–18

withdrawal from others, 250

Lanza, Nancy, 23, 50, 56, 181, 188, 209, 225, 250, 255

  assault on, 61

  efforts to help/reach son, 51–52

  efforts to help son, 49, 60, 63–64

  multiple sclerosis of, 61

  relationship with son, 47–48, 54, 62

  shooting of, 53, 54

  son's gun access, 17–18, 51–52, 53, 61, 248

Lanza, Peter, 64–65

Lanza, Ryan, 65

LAPD (Los Angeles Police Department), 18, 32, 209, 224, 249

LaPierre, Wayne, 29–30

Ledger, Heath, 70

Lee, Michelle, 115n81

Lender, Jon, 243n131

Lennard, Natasha, 226n121

Lessard v. Schmidt (1974), 238, 238n130

Liebert, John, 12n4, 29n14, 80n42, 218n117

Limbic hypoactivity, 169

Limbic music, 160, 161, 168, 183, 256–257

Lippestad, Geir, 133, 136, 137

Littlefield, Chad, 143, 144

Los Angeles Police Department (LAPD), 18, 32, 209, 224, 249

Los Angeles School District, 208–209

Los Angeles Unified School District, 208

Loughner, Jared, 12, 223, 247

  activities and profile of, 107–108

  ammunition clip of, 242

  encounters with Tucson law enforcement, 126–128

  expelled from Pima Community College, 108, 116, 118

  Giffords, Gabrielle and, 107, 108–109, 128

  Internet postings by, 108, 114, 115, 117, 127–128

  "lucid dreaming" of, 112–113

  medication and, 13, 115–116, 125, 151–152

  mental illness of, 111, 112, 128–129

  paranoid delusions of, 22

  Pima Community College's failure to help, 118–119, 121–122

  psychosis of, 13, 87

  responding to warning signs in, 126

  schizophrenia of, 103, 114–115

  shooting by, 107

strange behavior of, 109–110
suicidal mission of, 20
thinking/emotion split in, 114–115
trial of, 125–126
undiagnosed/untreated mental illness of, 12, 13, 115, 116–117, 207
verbigeration in, 113–114
violent video games and, 174
Loughner, Randy, 126
Lovaleski, Serge F., 107n72
Luigi's Mansion (video game), 60
Luo, Michael, 107n72
Lysiak, Matthew, 49n19, 72n35

M
Mahoney, Edmund H., 243n131
Maisch, Patricia, 126, 242
Malvo, Lee Boyd, 182
Margiotta, Nick, 127
Marijuana use, 43, 218
Mass murders. *see also* Suicidal mass murders
    potential, since 2011 Tucson shooting, 26
    statistics, 175
Mayo Clinic, 222
McCambridge, Ruth, 227n124
McConnell, Mitch, 204, 205
McCoppin, Robert, 29n13
McDonough, Kate, 49n18
McGarthy, Garry, 29
McShane, Larry, 72n35
Media. *see also* Violent media
    impact on potential mass murderers, 10
    prevalence of violence in, 175–177
    spread of mass murders and, 201
    violence in, 175–176
Medical records, digital, 214–215, 214–216, 220
Medicare, 213
Medication. *see also* Antipsychotic medication
    for ADHD, 170
    for borderline personality disorder, 167
    gun lobby's blame on, 229–230
    Holmes, James and, 81, 94
    Lanza, Adam and, 63
    Loughner, Jared and, 13, 125, 151–152
    prevention of Tucson shooting and, 115–116
    preventive psychiatry and, 39–40
    psychotropic, 40, 44, 63
    Routh, Eddie Ray and, 151
    schizophrenia and, 44
Mengele, Josef, 67
Mental illness. *see also* specific types of mental illnesses
    of Breivik, Anders, 103, 135
    of Cho Seung-Hui, 103, 186, 207
    correlation between violence, suicide, and, 156
    criminal justice system and, 127
    early intervention for, 204–205
    genes and, 37–45

of Holmes, James, 13, 14, 72, 111
of Lanza, Adam, 56–57, 111, 207
leading to violence, 186–188
of Loughner, Jared, 110, 111–112, 115, 116–117, 128–129, 207
need for research on, 175
nonadherence to, 24
populations at risk for, 189–190
progressive worsening of, 155–156
rethinking nature of, 203–204
suicidality and, 155, 156
in suicidal mass murderers, 153, 154–155
underdiagnosed, 12, 216–217
undiagnosed, 12, 13, 14, 115, 116–117, 207
untreated, 87, 111, 155, 160
Mentally ill
criminalizing, 10, 225–226, 229
dangerousness of seriously, 23–25
digital medical records of, 214–216
emergency services for, 211–212, 224–225
failure to help, 228–229
Methamphetamine, 183
Miller, R., 218–219
Milwaukee Are Technical College, 223
Minshew, Charles, 71n33, 76n37
MKULTRA Program, 67

Modern Family (television show), 195
Montgomery, Bill, 127
Montini, Ed, 123
Mood swings, 101, 166, 167, 251–252
Moser, Ashley, 72
Moser-Sullivan, Veronica, 72
Mt. Washington Resort, Bretton Woods, New Hampshire, 62
Muhammad, John Allen, 182
Multigenerational families, 193, 194, 195
Multiple personality disorder, 114
Mumola, Christopher J., 226n122
Murray, Henry, 66–67
MySpace, 108, 117

N
Nager, Matt, 79, 85, 88
National Alliance on Mental Illness, 207
National Institute of Mental Health, 174
National Institutes of Health, 86
Neologisms, of Breivik, 113, 136–137
Neurobiology of aggression, 156–171
Neuromodulators, 158
Neuropeptides, 158, 159
Neuroscience, studied by Holmes, 86–88
Neverwinter Nights 2, 82–83
Newton High School, 56

Newtown shootings, 2, 9, 33. *see also* Lanza, Adam; Sandy Hook Elementary School shooting
New York Times, 79, 81, 206, 207
Nick's Liquors, Aurora, Colorado, 79
911 calls
    Aurora shooting, 71–72, 73, 74
    behavioral emergency services and, 225
Nixon, Richard, 258
Nolan, Christopher, 70
Noonan, Margaret E., 226n122
Norepinephrine (NE), 158, 159, 160
Northern Illinois University, 224
Norway massacre (2011), 131–141. *see also* Breivik, Anders

Oak Creek, Wisconsin, Sikh temple massacre, 18, 28, 33, 238
Obama, Barack, 122
    background gun checks legislation and, 1
    Boston marathon massacre and, 34
    brain mapping project and, 174–175, 213
    brain research initiative by, 174
    budget for mental health care under, 205
    CDC focus on mental health and, 213, 232
    CDC research and, 27, 28
    Sandy Hook and, 33
Obama, Michelle, 33

Oikos University shooting, 208–209
Online gaming. *See* Video games
Orbitofrontal area of the brain, 157, 160
Orszag, Peter, 222
Ortiz, Erik, 144n92
Ostrow, Nicole, 211n112
O'Toole, Mary Ellen, 76

P
Page, Wade, 7, 9, 18, 19, 32, 238
Pain, indifference to others', 251
Palin, Sarah, 120, 123
Paper Mario (video game), 60
Paranoia
    diabetics and, 240–241
    projective identification and, 165, 186
    of Routh, Eddie Ray, 143, 144, 146–147, 150, 151
Paranoia erotica, 22
Paranoid delusions, 22–23, 40, 101
Paranoid psychosis, 151
Paranoid schizophrenia
    anger and, 186–187
    Breivik, Anders and, 137–138
    Cho Seung-Hui and, 14
    genetics and, 38
    Holmes, James and, 13
    homicidal rage and, 187
    insanity defense and, 103
    Kaczynski, Ted and, 104
Parents. *see also* Family
    bonding with child, 196–200
    impact of dysfunctional, 195
    of Loughner, Jared, 126

monitoring child's access to violent media, 44

multigenerational families and, 193, 194

Pathological aggression, 161–162

Patrick, Deval, 1–2

Paul, Rand, 205

Paul, Ron, 149

People v. Holmes (2012), 71n34

Personalized medicine, 38, 40, 44, 217

Peters, Jeremy W., 207n109

Phantasy Star Online (role-playing game), 60

Physical abuse, 248–249

Pietz, Christina, 125

Pikmin (video game), 60

Pilkington, Ed, 30n15

Pima Community College, Tucson, Arizona, 22, 108

failure to help Loughner, 118–119, 121–122

handling of psychiatric emergencies and, 13

Loughner's behavior on, 109–110

Loughner's forced expulsion from, 8, 10, 116, 118, 119, 207

Virginia Tech massacre verdict and, 120

warning signs in Loughner and, 126

Pitkin, James, 108n74

Pitt University Emergency Services, 237

Polyneurotic symptomatology, 164

Post-traumatic stress disorder (PTSD), 11, 170

borderline personality disorder and, 164, 165

brain mapping study and, 174

intervention for, 206

Kyle, Christopher and, 143, 248

populations at risk for, 189–190

Routh, Eddie Ray, 146–147, 148, 149, 151, 248

Pott, Audrie, 249

Prevention of mass shootings, 8, 125. *see also* Best-practice approaches

Prison

Breivik, Anders and, 138–139

costs, *vs.* treatment of mentally ill, 127

criminalizing mentally ill and, 10, 225–226, 229

veterans in, 226

Privacy issues, 125, 214–215

Professional wrestling, 177

Projective identification, 165, 186

Project MKULTRA Program, 67

Proposition 8 (California), 191

Protocols, dangerousness identification, 209–214

Pseudocommandos, 42, 47–48, 53, 79, 134–135

Psychiatric emergencies, 13. *see also* Emergency medical services, for behavioral emergencies

Psychopathogens, spread of, 176, 200–202, 214

Psychose passionelle, 22

Psychosis/psychotic behavior.
see also Duration of untreated
psychosis (DUP)
borderline personality disorder
and, 168
brain mapping study and, 174
brain scans and, 12
disrupted signaling from neurons
and, 87
first-episode, 12–13, 14, 88
genetic testing and, 40–41
in Loughner, Jared, 13, 87
marijuana use and, 43
"reward" stimuli, 168
violence and, 187–188
wave of shared, 10
Psychotropic medications, 40, 44,
63, 82, 223, 229
PTSD. *See* Post-traumatic stress
disorder (PTSD)
The Purpose Driven Life (Warren),
203
Putin, Vladimir, 133, 137

Q
Quick, Dylan, 201

R
Radford University, 10, 28, 111,
224
Ready Reserves, 146, 151
Reagan, Ronald, 23, 75
Reid, Harry, 207
Residential facilities, 23
Rey, Dr., 19
Ribera, Angie, 96, 97
Riccardi, Nicholas, 94, 94n59

Ridgway, Gary, 199
Risperdal, 13, 24, 115
Roberts, Dan, 229n126
Robison, John Elder, 167n98
Rothenberg, Michael B., 177n100
Rotkovich, Glenn, 100
Rough Creek Lodge, Glen Rose,
Texas, 143
Rousseau, Lauren, 54
Routh, Eddie Ray, 126, 143–152,
190, 248
Rubio, Marco, 205
Ruffner, Kevin C., 67n30

S
Sadism, 250
Salk Institute for Biological
Sciences, 84–86, 91, 105
Salon Magazine, 226
Same-sex marriage, 191
Sandy Hook Elementary School
shooting. *see also* Lanza, Adam
bare details of, 53–54
impact of, 33–34
impact on finding solutions to
mental health problem, 206
Lanza, Adam attending, 49, 56,
181
Sandy Hook school district, efforts
to help Adam Lanza, 52–53
Santora, Marc, 52n22
Schizogenic DNA, 40
Schizophrenia, 103. *see also*
Paranoid schizophrenia
Asperger's syndrome and, 167–
168
in Breivik, Anders, 136–138

diagnosing, 37–38
genes and, 42
genetic marker for, 40
Holmes' studies and, 87
impairment of language and logic with, 114
Lanza, Adam and, 57
Loughner, Jared and, 111, 112
mass murders/murderers and, 103–104, 111
medication and, 44
neuron signaling and, 87
state of mind with, 111, 113
suicide and, 39
thinking/emotion split in, 114, 117
verbigeration of, 113–114
Schneider, Daniel J., 71n33, 76n37
School cliques, 50
School Shooter, 44, 48, 178, 184, 258
School Threat Assessment and Response Team Program, 208, 211
School violence, 208–209
Second Amendment, 10, 34, 243, 244
Secret Harbor, San Juan island, 23
Sedensky, III, Stephen J., 47n17
Sedlacek, Terry Joe, 223
Seevakumaran, James Oliver, 223
Serotonin, 158, 159, 167, 170
Seung-Hui. *see* Cho, Seung-Hui
Sexual abuse, 157, 248
Sexual fantasies, 253
Sexual homicide (lust killing), 162
Sexual perversions, 164

Sexual psychopaths, 164
Shapiro, Rich, 49n19
Shared psychotic behavior, 10
Shepes's Rincon, 90
Sherlach, Mary, 54
Shick, John, 237
Sickles, Jason, 76n38
Sikh temple massacre, 18, 28, 33, 238
The Simpsons (television series), 195
Single-parent families, 188–189, 195
Sixth Amendment, 238
Skin contact, with parent, 196–197
Slosson, Mary, 84n45, 86n48
Smith, Elliot Blair, 236n127
Societal changes, 190–196
Sociopathic behavior, 193, 198, 199
Solutions to suicidal homicide epidemic, 29–30, 31–33
Soto, Victoria, 55
Southwestern Illinois College, 223
Speck, Richard, 7
Spengler, William, 7, 9, 15, 17
Springfield Medical Facility, 112, 207
Stabenow, Debbie, 206
Stahl, S.M., 229n125
Stahl, Stephen M., 229
Stanford University, 215–216
Stiglitz, Joseph, 192
Stone, Oliver, 256
Strange behavior
   dangerousness identification protocols and, 209–211

identifying, 247–248
of Lanza, Adam, 47, 48–49
responding to signs of, 154–155, 208, 234–235
Substance abuse, 42, 81–82, 156, 195
Suicidal mass murderers. *see also* individual names
commonalities among, 7–8, 12–14, 153–154
fear and hopelessness of, 8
hopelessness of, 14–16
influence on eachother, 200–201
learning from eachother, 26–27
mental illness of, 153, 154–155
paranoid delusions among, 22–23
personal statements of, 18–22
Suicidal Mass Murderers: A Criminological Stuy of Why They Kill, 14
Suicidal mass murders
increase in, 29, 190
media impact and, 201–202
studying epidemic of, 2–3
typical scenario of, 6
understanding and responding to epidemic of, 26–35
Suicide-by-cop, 25, 154
Suicide missions, 20
Suicide/suicidal behavior
attempted, by Holmes, 80
borderline personality disorder and, 164–165
correlation between mental illness and, 156
hopelessness and, 15–16

ideations of, 16–17, 249
mental illness and, 155
in online video games, 182–183
rethinking nature of mental illness and, 203–204
schizophrenia and, 39
Sullivan, Veronica Moser, 72, 102
SWAT team, 30, 70, 71, 77, 102

T
Taibbi, Mike, 74n36
Teachers, early intervention and, 205
Television shows
contrasting views of family in, 194–195
violent, 177
Thorazine, 95
Torrey, E. Fuller, 212, 212n114
The Town and the City (Kerouac), 193
Transparent brain technologies, 216
Traumatic brain injury (TBI), 241–242
Treatment. *see also* Involuntary commitment; Medication
of ADHD, 170
computer diagnostics and, 216–218
costs of, *vs.* incarceration costs, 127
failure to provide, 115–116, 155
Holmes, James, 93–94, 98, 99, 163
Treatment Advocacy Center, 24

Triage decision process, 220, 221–227, 232–236

Tsai, Catherine, 99n67

Tsarnaev, Dzhokhar, 2, 7, 9, 257
    dropping out of college, 117
    execution of, 19
    gaming by, 182
    intentions of, 154
    suicidal mission of, 21

Tsarnaev, Tamerlan, 2, 7, 9, 19
    causes of death of, 6–7
    gaming by, 182
    green card acquisition by, 34
    personality shift in, 155
    psychological state of, 8

Tucson shootings (2011), 2, 107.
    see also Loughner, Jared
    gun control and, 124–125
    politics of, 122–123
    prevention of, 119–120
    proceedings following, 123–124

U

Unabomber. See Kaczynski, Ted

Underdiagnosed mental illness, 12, 216–217

Undiagnosed mental illness, 12, 13, 14, 115, 116–117, 207

United States Medical Center for Federal Prisoners, 119–120

Universal mental health electronic records, 214–216

University of Arizona, 122

University of Arizona Hospital, Kino campus, 118–119, 122

University of California, Riverside, 83

University of Colorado, 32, 80, 86, 90, 91, 95, 98, 105

University of Colorado Anschutz Medical Campus, 86

University of Colorado Counseling Center, 93–94

University of Illinois, 86

University of Texas Tower mass murder, 7

Untreated mental illness, 25, 87, 111, 155, 160, 206–207. see also Duration of untreated psychosis (DUP)

US Bureau of the Census, 213n115

US Department of Justice, 226n122, 226n123

US Food and Drug Administration (USDA), 184

US Medical Center for Federal Prisoners, Springfield, Missouri, 112, 207

Utøya (island), 131, 140

V

VA (Veterans Administration), 222

Valdez, Linda, 122

Vanity Fair, 192

Verbigeration, 113–114

Veterans. see also Routh, Eddie Ray
    avoidant reactions by mentally ill, 11
    fear-based responses by, 157–158
    incarcerated, 226
    at risk for suicidal mass murder, 190

suidical bent in, 16
traumatic brain injury in, 241
Veterans Administration (VA), 222
Video games, 2, 60
as addictive, 179, 183
Breivik, Anders and, 89, 174, 181
Cho Seung-Hui and, 174, 182
early intervention and, 256–257
graphics of gore in, 182
Holmes, James, 44, 82–83, 89, 174
as incitement speech, 257–258
interactive digital, 177–178
Lanza, Adam and, 57, 60, 65–66, 89, 174
linked to violent behavior, 184–185
neuromuscular pattern of firing and, 181
as outlet for aggression, 178
real *vs.* digital world distinction and, 161, 180
regulation of, 184
reward mechanism with, 178–179
suicide as reward in, 182–183
television commercial for, 173–174
Vieth, Peter, 120n82
Vietnam veterans, 11
Violence. *see also* Suicidal mass murders
autism spectrum disorder and, 169
against emergency medical service staff, 237, 239–240
guidelines for identifying potential, 247–257
mental illness and, 156, 186–188, 187–188
prevalence of media, 175–177
of rape victim, 249
relationship with abuse, 50
video games linked to, 184–185
Violence Against Women Act, 177
Violent media, 175–177. *see also* Video games
American Medical Association on negative influence of, 185
Breivik, Anders and, 65–66, 135
causes of suicidal mass murders and, 31, 34
impact of, 44, 53
Lanza, Adam and, 47–48, 49–50, 65
Virginia Tech, 224
Virginia Tech Massacre (2007), 2, 223. *see also* Cho, Seung-Hui
governor's report on, 27
psychiatric emergencies and, 13
verdict from trial of, 120, 121
Virginia Tech panel, 27

W

Wagner, Dennis, 126n83, 128n86
The Waltons (television series), 194
Warren, Matthew, 203–204
Warren, Rick, 203
Watertown, Massachusetts, 2, 6, 141, 242, 257
Weapons
access to, 17–18
ammunition clips, 242–243

Holmes, James and, 71, 92–93, 97, 98

Lanza, Adam's access and exposure to, 48, 51–52, 61

Routh's access to, 151

untreated mental illness and, 206–207

Weed, L.L., 219n120

Weinberger, Daniel, 39, 42, 44

Weisman, Jonathan, 1n1

Westberg, Edward E., 219n119

Western Connecticut State University, 56

Westview High School, San Diego, California, 82, 83

Whitman, Charles, 7, 9, 12, 19, 32

Winter, Jana, 80, 98, 99, 100n69

World of Warcraft (computer game), 47–48, 82

Wright, David, 112n79

Y

Yale University Child Development Center, 63

YouTube videos, 110, 133